It's Great to be Alive… Because He Lives

by
William E. Jamerson
as told to
Jean Willard

Edited by Joan Pleso

*God blessed this child of His in a marvelous way
and he grew up to become a soldier, a missionary, a pastor,
and an inspired children/youth minister.*

TEACH Services, Inc.
P U B L I S H I N G
www.TEACHServices.com

World rights reserved. This book or any portion thereof may not be copied or reproduced in any form or manner whatever, except as provided by law, without the written permission of the publisher, except by a reviewer who may quote brief passages in a review.

This book was written to provide truthful information in regard to the subject matter covered. The author assumes full responsibility for the accuracy of all facts and quotations as cited in this book. The opinions expressed in this book are the author's personal views and interpretation of the Bible, Spirit of Prophecy, and/or contemporary authors and do not necessarily reflect those of TEACH Services, Inc.

This book is sold with the understanding that the publisher is not engaged in giving spiritual, legal, medical, or other professional advice. If authoritative advice is needed, the reader should seek the counsel of a competent professional.

Copyright © 2012 TEACH Services, Inc.
ISBN-13: 978-1-57258-735-9 (Paperback)
ISBN-13: 978-1-57258-736-6(Hardback)
ISBN-13: 978-1-57258-737-3 (ePub)
ISBN-13: 978-1-57258-755-7 (Kindle)
Library of Congress Control Number: 2011943517

All scripture quotations, unless otherwise indicated, are taken from the Holy Bible, New International Version®, NIV®. Copyright ©1973, 1978, 1984 by Biblica, Inc.™ Used by permission of Zondervan. All rights reserved worldwide.

All scripture quotations marked KJV are taken from the King James Version Bible.

Published by

TEACH Services, Inc.
P U B L I S H I N G
www.TEACHServices.com

Dedication

I dedicate this book to Jesus Christ, my Lord and Savior, who loved me and gave His life to save me from my sins.

My dear mother, Ivy Pearl Doty Jamerson, read many inspiring and exciting books to me about men and women who dedicated their lives to "Go into the world and teach the good news of salvation." Remembering those wonderful stories a few years later helped me make the decision to faithfully follow Jesus' instructions.

I also dedicate this book to my sweet wife, June. She has stayed by my side through thick and thin for these sixty-five years. She was a great help remembering places and dates in chronological order.

The dedication of this book would not be complete without including my three sons—Gary, Dennis, and Kevin—who love me unconditionally. I did not spend as much time with them during their growing up years as I should have. For that I am truly sorry.

—William E. Jamerson

Acknowledgements

I never learned to use a typewriter or the computer, so this book might never have been written had it not been for Jean Willard, my companion in child evangelism. One day, after showing her clippings and pictures of my World War II experiences and my ten years of missionary life, I said, "I wish these stories could be put on the computer." Jean said, "I have a computer and I can do that." Since then I thought, *Poor Ray (Jean's husband) has put up with her spending hours and hours and days and days of reading, editing my written material, and writing page after page of my life's story until it has become this book. Poor Ray!* Many thanks, Ray! My hat goes off to you for being such an unselfish and patient husband.

I also want to thank the proofreaders—Joe and Mary Pleso, Fran Quattlebaum, and Betty Ponder. My appreciation goes to Carolyn Anderson for editing and suggesting a better word here and there to improve the quality of my story. Rick Pleso's expertise in the areas of graphic arts, design layout, and scanning and placing photos was extremely helpful. Joan Pleso aided in finding a publisher and preparing my story for publication. Many, many thanks! My hat goes off to each of you. Without your help this material would never have progressed this far.

I especially want to thank my precious wife, June. She has refreshed my memory so many times as I have recalled events, names, and dates. She has also been a wonderful help in editing the material Jean sent to us over the last few months. This reminds me that, "all things work together for good to them that love God" (Rom. 8:28). Finally, I want to thank Him for His many blessings and for the marvelous way He has guided us in putting this book together. To Him be all the glory, honor, and praise. Amen!

Table of Contents

Foreword ix

Chapter 1   California, Here We Come! 11

Chapter 2   Decisions 15

Chapter 3   Billy's Buddy 17

Chapter 4   High School Days 19

Chapter 5   Who Will Win the Battle? 21

Chapter 6   Greetings! 23

Chapter 7   The Parked Jeep 25

Chapter 8   Wally Squires 27

Chapter 9   Granted 29

Chapter 10 World War II—Battle of the Bulge in Europe 31

Chapter 11 We've Got to Stop the Germans 34

Chapter 12 Strange Noise 36

Chapter 13 Enough! 38

Chapter 14 Home, Sweet Home 40

Chapter 15 Michigan 42

Chapter 16 The Sign 44

Chapter 17 Howell Mountain 46

Chapter 18 Rescued 48

Chapter 19 Surprised 51

Chapter 20 Reaching Out 53

Chapter 21 Invited 55

Chapter 22 God Prepares the Way 58

Chapter 23 Bolivia	61
Chapter 24 The Campbell's Soup Box Clinic	64
Chapter 25 San Pablo	66
Chapter 26 Another Trek on the Altiplano	70
Chapter 27 Island of the Bells	73
Chapter 28 Revolution	77
Chapter 29 Time for a Vacation	81
Chapter 30 Amasias Justiniano	84
Chapter 31 Guaynay—"Bible Readings for the Home"	88
Chapter 32 God to the Rescue	92
Chapter 33 The Mines of Bolivia	94
Chapter 34 Two Villages in One Night	97
Chapter 35 *Supi Cola*	101
Chapter 36 Villa Esperanza	104
Chapter 37 Rolling Clinic Comes Alive	107
Chapter 38 Quime	109
Chapter 39 Let's Eat Like the Locals	111
Chapter 40 One-Year Furlough	114
Chapter 41 Floating Islands	116
Chapter 42 Let's Go Fishing	119
Chapter 43 Nevati, Peru	122
Chapter 44 Another River Trip	125
Chapter 45 The Jamersons' Three Musketeers	128
Chapter 46 Three Churches	133
Chapter 47 Orangewood Academy Student Missionaries	135
Chapter 48 Student Missionaries Minister	139

Chapter 49 *Clinica Vista Hermosa*	141
Chapter 50 A Typical Day for Student Missionaries	143
Chapter 51 Missing People	146
Chapter 52 Youth on the Beach	150
Chapter 53 Platte Valley Academy Miracle	153
Chapter 54 Nebraska	156
Chapter 55 What's Next?	159
Chapter 56 Warned	162
Chapter 57 How God Worked	164
Chapter 58 Who Needs Friends?	166
Chapter 59 God Works in Strange Ways	169
Chapter 60 Paradise	173
Chapter 61 Mike Thomas	175
Chapter 62 Retired—Retread	178
Chapter 63 Trade Winds Blow	181
Chapter 64 Can't Stop Now	184
Chapter 65 Treasured Memories	187
Chapter 66 More Treasured Memories	189
Chapter 67 God Worked Behind The Scene Again	193
Chapter 68 The Smiling Wheelchair Lady	196
Chapter 69 Dangerous Ground! Beware!	198
Chapter 70 Miracles Still Happen	200
Chapter 71 Looking Back and Looking Forward	204
Chapter 72 60th Alumni Reunion	206
Chapter 73 Sowing the Seeds of Truth	208
Chapter 74 Who Directs Your Life?	210

Foreword

The biography of William Edward Jamerson was written to point out what God can do for even the most humble. Bill grew up during the Great Depression. That was a tough time, and he began to feel he was among the poorest of the poor. He was also a slow learner, which led to very low self-esteem and an inferiority complex. Many times he was ready to give up on himself, but God never gave up on him. Bill's mother, Ivy Pearl Doty Jamerson, a loving Christian woman, did not give up on him either. She did all she could to "Train up *her* child in the way he should go," and she prayed "without ceasing" and trusted God to do what she could not. Bill hopes that after reading this book other mothers will be inspired to pray for their children and to trust God.

Bill's life was spared after an unforeseen experience with a Jeep while in training for overseas duty in World War II. He soon began to learn that God can and does make changes in people He loves if they are willing to be changed. "In all your ways acknowledge him and he will make your paths straight" (Prov. 3:6). Bill was willing. This text soon became his favorite. He praises God daily for preserving his life through the horror of the Battle of the Bulge in World War II and for making his paths straight through the following years.

This book is written with the hope that it will impress readers as to the joys of serving Jesus. May you be inspired to become missionaries and go into the world to share the wonderful gospel story of Jesus' extraordinary love. Do this, and you, too, will soon discover that there is no greater joy than sharing this good news.

May God richly bless each and every reader. Amen!

Chapter 1

California, Here We Come!

"Where you go I will go." Ruth 1:16

Once upon a time... This is the story of a boy, a soldier, a missionary, a pastor, and a man who loves leading young people to the Lord, even in retirement. His amazing adventures began on Ground Hog Day, February 2, 1924. This talented man was named after his father, William Edward Jamerson. He was a junior; however, he was not called Junior, but Billy.

William Edward Jamerson Sr. married Ivy Pearl Doty and had six children: Paul Maxwell (called Max for short), Virginia, Carmon (who passed away shortly after birth), Wanda, Bonnie, and Billy. They lived in a beautiful home on a hill in Niles, Michigan, when Billy was born. The address was 311 Cass Street.

Billy, at age 4 with his first ball

Billy's father was a carpenter who built custom homes. He was not very religious, but he was easy to get along with until he drank alcoholic beverages with his friends on weekends. His mother was very religious as Grandmother Doty had raised her in a traditional Seventh-day Adventist home and had taught her how to be a good wife, mother, and homemaker. She was also one of the Sabbath School leaders at the Niles Seventh-day Adventist Church and faithfully took her children to Sabbath school and church. The church met in a room above the firehouse or in their home.

Billy came as a big surprise to Mother. She was expecting a baby girl and had planned on naming her Mary Alice after her mother. The three girls were surprised as well, but were very happy that the new member of their family was a boy. Max was even happier, for now he had a brother. Billy was a strong, healthy baby and squealed with delight when one of his siblings rolled a ball to him. It wasn't long before a ball became his favorite toy.

Billy was still quite young when someone gave him his very own baseball glove. After that he was hooked on baseball. The Chicago Cubs became his favorite team, and he listened to every game on the family radio. Billy really loved baseball and played all positions. As he grew older, he usually played only outfield.

However, baseball was not the only ball game Billy loved. Over the years basketball became very important to him as well. He played center in that game.

Nevada City High School Yellow Jackets (Billy is #55)

As he grew bigger and stronger, the challenge of football became another passion. He played end, fullback, or halfback in that sport.

As Billy continued to grow, his dreams grew too, until he could visualize himself coaching these three sports at a major college. Yes, Billy loved sports! In fact, he loved sports so much that it was difficult for him to concentrate on schoolwork. So difficult, in fact, that he failed the third grade three times. Recess and physical education were always his favorite periods, but in time he began to keep up with his studies.

Father's drinking and the Great Depression caused the family to lose their beautiful home on Cass Street. However, father was able to buy a lot down the hill where he made cement blocks with the help of his homemade mold. He built a small new home for his family with these blocks.

The depression years were very hard on the Jamerson family, as they were for many folks. Food was very scarce. The children learned to gather mushrooms and wild greens, such as poke, lambs quarter, and dandelions. This enabled them to supplement their diet of beans, potatoes, and rice. Besides the shortage of food, new clothes were out of the question. Everyone had to wear hand-me-downs or something Mother bought at rummage sales. This really embarrassed Billy, and he began to develop an inferiority complex.

Winters were especially difficult for father because he had to work in the cold, even when the temperature dropped below zero. The children did not like walking to school in zero-degree weather either, but they were delighted when it snowed so they could use the toboggan father had made for them. Oh, what great fun they had sliding to the bottom of the Cass Street hill past their home. However, they hated walking to school when the snow was deep.

Billy was about twelve years old when his father decided he was tired of the severe Michigan cold and shoveling snow. He thought, *Maybe we should move to sunny California where it's warm. Besides that, I think maybe California will have better opportunities for work.* Father decided to take Max with him, and soon the two of them were headed for California to check out the opportunities. When they returned home, father immediately put a "For Sale" sign in front of their home. It didn't take long for the house to sell. When Uncle Herbert, father's brother, learned they were serious about moving to California, he got excited and decided he would go with them.

By this time only three members of the Jamerson family were living at home. Max had married Gert Jesswine; Virginia had married Russell Potter; Wanda had married John Vogelsang; and Bonnie had married Bob Shurte. When they all heard about the move to California, they decided they would move, too. However, it took them longer to get ready so they drove out later.

As soon as the Jamerson family packed their things, John and Wanda purchased a black Jordan with a straight-8 engine, and what a car it was! In just a few days they were ready to say goodbye to Michigan's cold miserable days.

John got behind the wheel of the Jordan. Then Father, Mother, and Billy climbed in followed by Wanda, Herb, and Guy, their son. That's when they discovered there was no room for Billy's dog, Sooner, a little curly-haired brown-and-white poodle that Father had given Billy. Father immediately found a box and fastened it on the running board of the car, and Sooner rode safely in it all the way to California. Everyone, including Sooner, was happy to be saying goodbye to the cold and snowy Michigan weather and heading for sunny California. However, they were sad to be leaving their many friends.

Traveling was slow and, as there was no money for tourist courts (motels), the best they could do each night was to park the car along the side of the road and sleep on the ground. When they awoke one morning, they had a big surprise. While they were sleeping, someone had quietly left a whole box of cantaloupe beside their car. What a treat that was to start their day! It was like finding water in the middle of a very dry desert. Everyone said, "Thank you, Jesus!"

After everyone was full of cantaloupe, they jumped in the Jordan and continued their journey. They had only traveled about ten miles when Billy looked in Sooner's box and discovered that the dog was not there. He was shocked and cried out, "Sooner's gone! My dog is gone!" John immediately turned the car around. Before long Billy saw Sooner running as fast as his little legs could carry him to the family he loved so much. Billy wiped away his tears then and said, "Thank you, Jesus, for giving my dog back to me."

The next day John saw a little lake in a town's community park, so he parked his car so they could all go for a nice little walk. When Billy and Guy saw the lake, they decided it was a good time for them to go fishing, and they caught a few. Billy still wonders what the park director would have done to them if he had caught them fishing.

They traveled on and finally came upon the Mississippi River. Uncle Herb, who was really tight with his money, finally parted with some of it and paid the toll, but it took a lot of pressure and coaxing before he did. As they crossed over the river, everyone laughed about the situation, including Uncle Herb.

A few days later the family reached a small town in Nevada. Everyone had been cold all day. John and Father knew they really needed to find some kind of shelter for an even colder night. But with little money, what could they do?

John drove slowly through the town but couldn't find anything. As he approached the outskirts of the next little town, Father suddenly pointed to some big billboards alongside the road and told John to pull behind them and park the car. It served as a perfect place to spend the night.

John built a nice fire, and soon everyone had gathered around it to warm themselves. As they were getting comfortable, they heard sirens in the distance. As the sounds grew louder, they all looked at each other and wondered what was happening. Then, much to everyone's surprise, a fire truck stopped on the road right beside them.

Firemen jumped out of the fire truck, and one of them asked, "What do you people think you are doing?" Father explained that they were just getting warm and planned to spend the night there. But the fireman insisted that they douse the fire at once and hit the road. What a sad moment that was. They had to pack up again and hope to find another safe place where they could spend the night sleeping on the cold ground.

When the family arrived in Reno, all were awestruck by the "biggest little city in the world," but they did not stop to sightsee. Soon they were awestruck again by the beauty of the great Sierra Nevada mountain range. No one had ever seen such mountains, and they were amazed at their beauty and majesty!

John's Jordan had served them quite well on their journey, but as the road grew steeper, the radiator began to overheat. Soon the instrument on the dashboard showed the engine was at the highest reading. John was very concerned, so he stopped the car to let it cool down. He got out of the car, loosened the radiator cap, and hot water spewed all over his hand. He was hopping around with his badly burned hand when a car drove past. The people stopped their car and asked if they could help. Fortunately, they had cold water to pour over John's hand and enough to put in the radiator. Everyone thanked them and God for the help provided. Soon the family was able to continue their journey.

Finally, they saw a sign that said "CALIFORNIA." Everyone cheered. When Billy looked at that sign, he thought, *What does the future hold for me? I surely wish I knew!* Little did he know then how, what, or where God's plans for him would lead.

Chapter 2

Decisions

*"Commit thy way unto the LORD; trust also in him;
and he shall bring it to pass." Psalm 37:5, KJV*

The Jamersons were thankful when the faithful black Jordan carried them safely over the highest elevation of the Sierra Nevadas. Soon they were enjoying the ride down the western slopes of the mountain. As they descended, John pulled into a parking area where they could look out over the valley below. Everyone was so excited. The beautiful golden state of California stretched for miles before them! Each wondered what lay ahead. But all too soon it was time to pile in the car again and hit the road.

Upon arriving in El Cerrito near Oakland, Father rented a room for the night, so they all had a shower and a very good night's rest. The next morning Father and John left the family, hoping to find employment. They both found work, and fortunately, they received their full pay at the end of each day. This sustained the family very well for a while, but it was not long before Father decided to move the family to Walnut Creek. Not long after that move, he moved the family again, this time to Martinez where they lived for the next few years.

Upon getting settled in their new town, Mother found a church to attend. She impressed Billy with the importance of spiritual values in his life. She always encouraged him to be faithful to God and to stand firm no matter what. She often told Billy to pattern his life after his brother-in-law Russell, because he was a good Christian man, had high standards, did not drink alcoholic beverages or smoke cigars or cigarettes, and he took good care of his body.

Father never took an active part in this spiritual training. However, Father did not object when Mother and Billy went to prayer meeting on Wednesday night at the little Martinez Seventh-day Adventist Church. People would often pray such long prayers at those nightly meetings that Billy would sometimes lie on the floor and fall asleep.

And Father did not mind when the two of them went to Sabbath School and church services on Sabbath either. Billy especially enjoyed the returning missionaries when they visited their church. Sometimes they even wore clothing from the mission field. And the stories they told of their experiences were always exciting and thrilling to Billy. He marveled at the miracles they reported. Sometimes Billy would dream of wading through the swamps of Africa or floating down a jungle stream in the tropical lands of South America. The missionaries' testimonies led Billy to make his decision to follow Jesus, and he was baptized into the Martinez Seventh-day Adventist Church just before his thirteenth birthday. But never once did it enter his mind that he would become a real missionary.

Billy faithfully attended Alhambra High School in Martinez. He especially enjoyed palling around with his good friends Sherrill Fry and Clell and Clair Patterson. However, there were times when he wished he could attend a Christian school and have a Christian teacher who would help and encourage him. When he mentioned this to his father, he found out in no uncertain terms that there was no money for such a luxury.

As time went on, Billy's studies became even more boring to him. The more he thought about the "old book stuff" the more he thought, *This is not for me.* Finally, Billy told his folks he intended to quit school. Father told him he had no choice in the matter, because the state required children to stay in school until they were eighteen years old, and he was only fifteen at the time. Billy was disappointed but not too badly since his real interests were sports. The next day he was back to his usual routine.

Chapter 3

Billy's Buddy

"I will never leave you, nor forsake you." Joshua 1:5

One of Billy's household responsibilities was to care for Sooner's daily needs. He was a very special member of the family, and even though he was not a housedog, he had his own glass dishes for food and water. He did not have a cozy little doghouse, but being a smart outside dog, he always found a comfortable place to sleep. Sometimes he slept in the shed. Most of the time he slept outside, depending on the weather. Billy enjoyed caring for Sooner, for he loved his little dog. Sooner loved him and followed him everywhere!

One morning Billy awoke to the sound of the doorbell ringing. But Sooner was not barking. Sooner always barked when the doorbell rang, so Billy knew something was dreadfully wrong. He jumped out of bed, dressed as fast as he could, and hurried to find his mother. "Have you seen Sooner?" he asked. Mother shook her head no. Then she suggested that maybe he had been shut up in the shed by mistake. Billy rushed out the back door and down the old weather-beaten steps as fast as he could. Before he got to the shed, however, he ran straight into the clothesline that stretched across the backyard, knocking him to the ground. Fortunately, only his pride was hurt when he picked himself up.

The heavy old door to the shed was shut and hard to open, so Billy braced himself against the wall and pulled as hard as he could. When it opened, he called for Sooner, but Sooner did not jump with joy as he usually did. Then Billy saw his best pal lying on the cold, hard, wooden floor. He knelt down beside Sooner and saw that he was alive but very sick. As he stroked his head, he told him he loved him and that he just had to get well. Then Billy heard Mother call him, "Billy, it's time for school." He left Sooner and ran back to the house. Breathlessly, he told his mother that Sooner was sick and asked if he could please stay home and take care of him. Mother was very sympathetic but insisted that he go to school. So, with a heavy heart Billy left his best pal in the shed and went to school.

Billy did not remember a thing his teachers said that day. All he could think of was Sooner. Poor little thing, sick and lying alone in the shed. At last school ended, and Billy hurried home. "How's Sooner?" he asked when he burst through the door. Mother stopped what she was doing, shrugged her shoulders, and said, "Oh son, I don't know, I have just been too busy to go out there and look."

Billy rushed out the door and down the steps. This time he was careful not to run into Mother's clothesline. Much to his relief, the heavy old door was still standing open. He hurried to Sooner and knelt down beside him. He could tell that Sooner was still very sick. As he rubbed his head and felt his nose and paws, he thought, *What can I do for Sooner?* Then he thought, *I know. He's probably hungry.* He hurried back to the house to find something special for Sooner. When he looked in the refrigerator and saw some leftover stew, he thought, *Yes, I'll leave out the vegetables and just give him some of the meat and potatoes. He will love that!*

Billy filled Sooner's glass bowl and carefully carried it back to the shed. He just knew Sooner would feel better once his tummy was full of his favorite foods. When he placed the bowl full of food in front of Sooner's nose, the dog gave one little wag of his tail, but that was it. Billy thought, *Maybe he's thirsty.* He hurried back to the house and filled his glass bowl with cool water. But Sooner did not even wag his tail once when Billy carefully placed the water in front of him. Poor Sooner. Billy did not know what else he could do for Sooner. He just sat there stroking him and talking softly to him until Mother insisted that he come back in the house and go to bed. With a heavy heart, Billy left his best pal and went to bed.

Billy did not sleep well that night. As soon as he awoke the next morning, he quickly dressed and rushed out to the shed. Would Sooner be better? When he saw that Sooner had not moved, had not eaten, and had not drunk any water, he knew Sooner was in trouble. What was Billy to do? He had already used all of his medical knowledge. There was nothing more he could do for him. Sadly, Billy had to leave him in the shed alone again, and off he went for another dreary day of school.

As soon as school ended that afternoon, Billy rushed home again and out to the shed. There he found that Sooner, his loving and faithful pal, was no longer alive. With tears streaming down his cheeks, Billy rushed to the house and told the family that Sooner was gone. Fortunately, his brother-in-law John was there. He took charge right away and found a box in which to lay Sooner. After carefully placing the curly-haired dog in his coffin, John carried him to his Model A Ford and placed the box on the back seat. Billy sat beside Sooner as John drove through the woods looking for a special place to bury Sooner. When he found a nice place, John parked the car, and the two of them quietly dug a grave. With tears streaming down his cheeks, Billy said goodbye to Sooner as he was laid to rest.

****

Billy still gets a lump in his throat when he thinks of his loving and faithful Sooner. He takes comfort in the thought that when he gets to heaven, maybe God will give Sooner back to him, or maybe He will give him another special dog to be his buddy.

Chapter 4

High School Days

"Study to shew thyself approved unto God" 2 Timothy 2:15, KJV

Billy's father made good money building nice houses, but he was an alcoholic and sometimes he spent more money on alcohol than he brought home, so the family was always very poor. Growing up in this environment and wearing hand-me-down clothes, or clothes from a rummage sale, increased Billy's inferiority complex. This inspired him to do his very best at everything he tried so he could "show them."

When school began the next fall, Billy's self-esteem was at zero. Although he had grown tall during the summer months, he had also broken out with pimples. This made him feel even worse about himself. Fortunately, the students at Alhambra High School did not notice the pimples because they were too busy noticing how tall he had grown. They urged him to join the basketball and football teams. Billy's low self-esteem began to change. Now he was looking at honor and glory for himself. He did not know what to think of it at first, but then he loved it.

Satan knew this was his moment to make Billy lose all thoughts of spiritual values and any thoughts he had of the mission field. At first Billy found the Sabbath could be observed with little trouble, but because he was such a good player, greater pressures were put on him to play in the Sabbath games, too. Then, unexpectedly, Father decided to move the family again and suddenly Billy's problem was solved. What a relief.

The new home Father built for the family was on Sugar Loaf Mountain, located just a few miles from Nevada City, California. It was a long walk to school for Billy, but he did not mind because there was an irrigation ditch right behind the family's new home. It was there that Billy loved to fish for trout. Most of the fish he caught were only six to eight inches long, but sometimes he would catch a ten-incher, which was really exciting.

Billy was beginning to feel grown up when he enrolled at Nevada City High School. He thought the time had come for him to be called "Bill" instead of Billy. He would always be "Billy" to his family, and to this day not one member of the family has ever called him plain Bill, but to the rest of the world, he was now Bill.

Bill chose easy classes such as shop and choir so his credits would be high enough for him to play ball. He signed up for Spanish, but it wasn't long before the teacher dropped him from the class because he couldn't keep up. Years later Bill wished he had studied harder. As you will see later, he had to speak Spanish.

Because he wasn't studying hard, he spent time playing hard, and Sundays were his day to sleep in. But on Sunday morning December 7, 1941, he woke up early for some reason. He got dressed and headed out of his room to find the rest of his family only to discover them all gathered around the radio. But they were not talking or laughing.

As he listened to the radio, he heard the news that the Japanese had bombed Pearl Harbor. Bombed Pearl Harbor! Bill was so angry he shouted, "Why those dirty, sneaking Japs! They can't get away with this! I'll join the army, and we'll show them." He wasn't the only one who felt that way. Many Americans had the same feelings. Patriotism had never been stronger. But Bill would have to wait awhile before he could join the army.

Chapter 5

Who Will Win the Battle?

"A student is not above his teacher." Matthew 10:24

Even though Bill felt grown up and wanted to defend his country, he was still just a schoolboy. He would have to let the adults take care of the war for the present time. His mind was soon focused on ball games again. Much to his surprise, at six-feet tall and 145 pounds, Bill made the varsity team in basketball, football, and baseball in the first season of his sophomore year at his new school. He was quite proud of himself.

Satan knew this and lost no time taking control of the situation again. One day one of his teachers requested something of him, but he replied, "You're too cocky for your pants." The teacher wasted no time in making sure Bill found out who the cocky one was, for he had to sit out three basketball games while his teammates played without him. That was a hard lesson, but Bill never talked back to a teacher again.

Satan didn't stop there. Soon the students and the coaches were all urging Bill to play in the Saturday games. They would say things such as, "What's so wrong with playing basketball on Saturday? It's only a game." Bill loved the Sabbath and earnestly wanted to keep it holy, but he had come to love sports so much and the way people made him feel so important that he began thinking that someday he could be a great baseball, basketball, and football coach. Thoughts of being a missionary had slipped from his mind.

The day finally came when Bill's Christian training and his principles were put to the test. His classmates said, "Next Saturday is our big football game, Bill. You are the star. We need you. All the guys and girls will be watching you. You just have to play."

Bill was torn between his desire to follow Jesus and keep the Sabbath day holy and his love of feeling important. As he was contemplating the situation, his buddy took his arm and said, "Come on, Bill. I'll take you home." The two boys got in his dark blue Model A Ford and drove to Bill's home. His buddy took over the conversation as he drove. "Bill, you must be there tomorrow. This game is the biggest one of the season and you just cannot let the school down. Come on. I'll come by and pick you up about 1:30 tomorrow."

What was Bill to say? His conscience said no again and again, but he loved sports so much and desperately wanted to play in the game. He thought of his mother. What would she think of him if he played? Could he disappoint her?

The next day was Sabbath, and Mother and Bill went to church. But all through the services Bill was not thinking about God; he was thinking about the game. He was quiet on the way home and felt like he had fishhooks in his stomach. About 1:00 he told his mother he was going for a walk. When she said OK, Bill took off. A few minutes later he saw his buddy in the blue Model A Ford coupe. Bill changed into his blue and gold football uniform and was ready for the big game. He did not feel right and knew he was not following Jesus. But when he and the team walked onto the field and the crowd cheered, all the miserable feelings left him. Satan had won the battle.

Minutes before the game ended, the score was zero-zero. The visiting team was on their eighteen yard line, and it was the fourth down. They decided to kick. The fullback was ready, and the ball was snapped. Bill rushed with all his might, and with outstretched hands he blocked the kick in the end zone and caught the ball. What a catch.

This play turned the game around and brought Nevada City High School a seven to zero win. The game was won, but Bill had lost. All the congratulations, back poundings, and everything else had increased his self-esteem and his self-pride. How sad. Bill had allowed sports to rule his life. He had gained the whole world and now his soul was possibly lost. The Bible tells us that King Nebuchadnezzar let pride get in his way, too, but God showed mercy to him and humbled him. Would God have mercy on Bill and take away his pride?

****

Bill still wonders, *If I had been in an Adventist school when I was young and so impressionable, would things have been different? Would my love for sports have decreased and the missionary spirit increased?*

It could have made a big difference.

Chapter 6

Greetings!

"For what is a man profited, if he shall gain the whole world, and lose his own soul?" Matthew 16:26, KJV

Bill was eighteen years old and halfway through his senior year in high school when he received a letter from Uncle Sam that read, "Greetings! Welcome to the service of the United States of America." Bill was shocked at first and so was his coach when he heard the news. "This can't happen!" he said. "I am the star of our team; they can't take me in the middle of the school year!"

Somehow Bill's coach got a deferment for him so he could stay in school and finish the basketball season. The rest of the school year was really exciting. The students treated him as if he was a hero, and he loved it. Bill was also excited about being drafted into the armed forces to fight the Japanese or the Germans—he didn't care which. But his mother cared. She was already brokenhearted over the downward path her son was taking and dreaded having him leave for the service. Would the army be his spiritual destruction? Would the spirit of missions die forever?

Oh, the tears of his mother as her prayers were steadily offered up for her precious son to stand true to the spiritual values she had taught him. Mother was so worried that she finally went to see John Hartman, the elder of her church, who knew that Bill was not living a Christian life. After they had prayer together, John promised he would talk to Bill and do all he could for him.

John Hartman soon visited with Bill and did his best to encourage him to follow the right path, but it was too late. Bill had already surrendered his life to the world. Sadly, John Hartman said, "Well, Bill, here are a few tracts, at least take them with you." Bill didn't want to hurt John's feelings so he took the tracts but his feelings for religion were gone. Would his mother's prayers be answered in time? Could Bill's desire to be a missionary ever be rekindled? Only time would tell.

Soon Bill found himself in the army's reception center at Camp Monterey, waiting for orders from headquarters. It was January 13, 1943, and he learned he was just another number: 39407317. No longer was he the big heroic ballplayer of Nevada City High School. No playing around. When those sergeants and corporals shouted orders, Bill had to jump NOW!

Bill had no inkling that two years later, on January 19, 1945, he would be called out of the ranks and awarded a Bronze Star medal, "For meritorious service in connection with military operations against an enemy of the United States in France and Luxembourg." Nor did he feel like a hero on April 22, 1945, when he was awarded another Bronze Star medal, "For heroic achievement in connection with military operations against an enemy of the United States in Germany." This military operation was later called the "Battle of the Bulge." Both medals were given "by command of Major General Paul." (Paul was the only name the Major General wrote on those awards.) Bill is humble about those medals he received, but he is also very proud that he did his best to preserve the freedom of the country he loves so much.

Those days were yet to come, but for Bill the great day came when he and the other recruits were standing in line waiting for their orders again. Numbers began to be called out and soon the sergeant commanded, "You men pack your bags and get ready to move."

As Bill looked at all the things he had to pack, he did not know what to pack first. Then he saw the ugly package of tracts. As he put them in the bottom of his duffle bag, he thought, *I'll never need these, so it's out of sight and out of mind.* He finished packing the rest of his things on top of them, and that's how the tracts went with him in spite of himself.

Soon it was time for the soldiers to board the transportation that would take them to their new camp. There they discovered they had not been taken to New York as some had expected but to Camp Haan near Riverside, California. Much to Bill's surprise, he learned that his group had been selected to form an anti-aircraft unit. He thought, *Oh, this is great! I'll be able to fight. Fight like the rest of the soldiers. I'll show those Krauts.*

When the officer sent Bill to Battery C of the 390th Battalion, which was to be his new home, he could hardly wait to show off his training. Drilling was a cinch; army life was great. Nights brought "passes" and plenty of fun following the world. However, some things did not appeal to Bill, such as drinking and smoking. These things were not good for an athlete. He thought the rest of the world's pleasures were OK, so he joined in every chance he had. However, none of these fun times really fully satisfied his soul. They only occupied time and never gave him a good feeling.

At last the six weeks passed, and the men were to be rated. Bill earnestly wanted to know his rating, which he soon learned was corporal. This was wonderful! He was on his way to the top. The good news was immediately sent to Mother and Dad. After that Bill worked harder than ever to earn a higher rank. He used all his strength to attain it, and in just six weeks he made sergeant. To Bill, this was success. However, while he was gaining the whole world, his spiritual life was sinking lower and lower. To Bill's mother, he had sold out and the devil was blessing him. His brokenhearted mother earnestly prayed, "Oh God, save him! Please save him!" Would God delay in answering her plea to save her precious lost son?

Chapter 7

The Parked Jeep

"Turn to me and be saved." Isaiah 45:22

Bill was really proud of himself. He had full responsibility of two half-tracks, or gunning units, and two crews of eight men each, making a total of sixteen men. The half-tracks were really killing machines. Each half-track had two wheels in front and tracks in the back, which is the reason they are called half-tracks. One half-track had a turret with four 50-caliber machine guns mounted on top, and each could shoot 600 rounds a minute. The other half-track also had a turret with two 50-caliber guns and one 37mm antitank gun. All the 50-caliber guns could be aimed at the sky to bring down an incoming airplane, but the 37mm antitank gun was the only one that could destroy an approaching tank. To protect ground troops, Bill's outfit practiced long hours shooting at the target sleeves pulled by airplanes.

The day came when orders were given for the 390th Battalion to go on a real practice mission of war. The two-week mission was at Camp Edwards near Barstow, California, where they would sweat it out in preparation for battles in Europe or Asia. Their training was essential, for these young men were soon to be called to active duty.

Bill was given a compass reading where his unit was to camp. When they reached this special area, they had to work like madmen to get the two half-tracks dug in, then guard the area all night so the other outfit did not capture them. Little did the men know what would happen. Little did Bill know what the outcome of this mission would be for him. All he wanted was success.

Sleep? No one had any to speak of, for they were on alert at all times. One of the men was so tired while walking on his evening guard duty that he dozed off and fell flat on his face. Now that truly was a rude awakening.

Finally, the night was over. At least now they could breathe easy and relax a little while on alert, even though they knew there was one more tough night ahead of them. Bill had no clue at the time that this night was going to be the most important one in his life. Something was going to happen that would influence his whole career.

As darkness set in that evening, all remained on high alert to every sound: the bark of a lonely coyote, flying owls, the movement of a tired companion. Then, all of a sudden the phone call came. When they heard the secret word, they knew they had their marching orders, which were: move their position to another place. But how? It was very dark, and all the men were so tired. But they had to move AT ONCE.

Quickly the convoy was formed, and they began to move out over the dry, cold desert floor to the new place where they were to camp. All that could be seen were the hills silhouetted in the far distance and dark vehicles on the move. About 1:00 in the morning the column suddenly stopped. It seemed as if they were going to stay for a while. What a break; a rest stop. Bill told his buddy to take over for a few minutes because he couldn't stay awake a moment longer and to let him know if and when they were to move again.

Bill had only been asleep a short time when he was rudely awakened. Something heavy was on his chest. "Hey!" he shouted. "Get this thing off of me!" It was a Jeep! As the driver backed the Jeep up, Bill prayed, "Oh God, save me and I will serve You the rest of my life." He was humbled at last. Even though he felt all right when he stood up, he was told to wait for the medic to come and check him.

That night was Bill's "Damascus Road" experience, for there on the desert sands, the Lord heard his plea for help. The years of wandering were ended. The "prodigal son" had returned. The fires of service were ignited once again. With the freshness of that early morning, Bill experienced the wonderfully clean feeling of sins forgiven. Once again, peace filled his heart. It was an experience Bill has never forgotten.

But what was Bill to do? Here he was a sergeant, a competent soldier. He was not classified as a conscientious objector. What could he do now? The army doesn't let you quit, but if he tried, would he be court-martialed? Bill had no idea what he should do. While he sat on the front of the half-track, he prayed again and asked God for help. How would God solve his problem?

Chapter 8

Wally Squires

"In all thy ways acknowledge him, and he shall direct thy paths."
Proverbs 3:6, KJV

As Bill was waiting for the medic to come and examine him that morning, he was also pondering his problem. Then he remembered a Bible verse he had known in days gone by: "In all thy ways acknowledge him, and he shall direct thy paths" (Prov. 3:6, KJV). Bill felt in his heart he had acknowledged God, and he decided then and there that he would just have to wait patiently for Him to direct his path.

The medic, Sergeant Walter Squires, arrived to examine Bill. Bill didn't know it then, but Walter was a Seventh-day Adventist, and he was going to play a major role in helping Bill.

After examining Bill, the sergeant informed him that he would have to go to the Camp Edwards Hospital for a thorough examination. They needed to be sure he was all right after having a Jeep park on his chest. If he had suffered no injuries then he could report back to Battery C.

A few hours later Bill checked in at the army hospital where, even though he felt all right, he had to submit to a complete examination. After hearing his story, the doctors examined him very thoroughly. A few days later they all agreed that he had suffered no injuries whatsoever. No broken bones, no punctures, and not even any bruised skin. A miracle! Praise be to God for His wonderful watch care.

While in the hospital, Bill learned that two of the young orderlies in his ward were Seventh-day Adventists. He told them all about how he had once been an Adventist but had let worldly pleasures influence him. He had lost his spiritual vision and forgotten the church and his Savior. He told them about the Jeep parking on his chest, how he had called out to God to save him, and of his promise to serve Him and follow Him all the way for all eternity. Bill's confession led to long serious talks with these young men, and they earnestly encouraged him to take his stand for Christ. Their fellowship together also strengthened him for his future.

Bill was thrilled when these two young Adventist men invited him to go to church in Barstow with them on Sabbath morning. He told them he would do his best to get a pass. He really wanted to go to church with his new buddies but did not know how his situation was going to turn out or what was going to happen to him. But one thing he knew for sure: he wanted God's way alone to rule his life.

After earnest prayer for the guidance of the Holy Spirit, Bill got in a Jeep. As he bounced along the rough desert road, he wondered, *How can I best approach the officers and men? I must tell them I can no longer run the two gun units, nor can I carry a gun anymore. What will they say?*

When Bill arrived at the 390th Battalion area, the Jeep came to a stop in front of Lieutenant Solomon and the rest of the officers. His mind raced on, *How can I tell them my plans? Will they cooperate?* A short time after hanging around the area Bill finally approached one of the officers he had confidence in and liked very much and told him his story. He said, "Sir, I cannot go on like this. I cannot kill, so will you please help me?"

To Bill's great relief, the officer told him that he had known some young Adventist men in the Hawaiian islands and had liked them very much and had great confidence in them as soldiers. The officer promised he would plead his case.

A few days later Bill was called in before the captain and this officer. He went in and saluted them, gave his name, and told his story, adding that he was ready to answer any questions in a truthful way. They began to talk to him about what the army was and about what he was doing. Bill explained his stand and one of the officers said, "I think this can be worked out, but this will cost you your stripes. That means a reduced salary. You will be a private again."

The thought ran through Bill's mind, *That means I'll lose $78 a month.* But he did not care. All he wanted was to be right with God at all times. His experience with the Jeep parked on his chest had taught him how quickly life could be snuffed out. He wanted the assurance that he was ready for eternal life. As he looked the officer in the eyes, he replied, "It is all right with me. I don't mind losing the money or the stripes as long as I am right with God."

"Fine, soldier," the captain said, "we'll see what we can do for you. Go back to your men, and we will let you know when we have something for you." Bill hurried to his pup tent and began searching for the package of tracts he had buried in the bottom of his duffle bag. As soon as he had the package in his hand, he opened it and spread them on his bedroll. There they were, all the tracts he had so despised. And there was his Bible. Bill sat down at once and began to read and study. After that, Bill spent many hours in his pup tent praying and pleading that God would direct his path.

Chapter 9

Granted

"Is any among you afflicted? let him pray." James 5:13, KJV

The morning finally came when Bill was called out of the ranks. He fell out and went forward. The officer said, "The colonel will talk with you now, Bill." Trembling and praying, Bill struck off over the desert sands to the main office. There he saw the elderly colonel waiting for him. At last he got up the nerve to go up and salute him and tell him his name.

The colonel already knew Bill's situation, so he asked, "Sergeant, do you know what this means?"

Bill replied, "Yes, sir. I believe I understand."

"It means you are a private again with no stripes."

"Yes, sir. I know, sir."

"Then pack your bags and be sure you get those stripes off before you report to the medical unit."

What a relief. Bill smiled and said, "Yes, sir. Thank you, sir."

As soon as his duffle bag was packed, he marched over to the medical unit of the 390th Battalion. As he approached the unit, he saw Captain Lombardi, the doctor in charge, and hoped he was a good man. Bill reported to him, and the captain told him to see a young man by the name of Walter Squires. Bill would be living with his outfit.

Joy filled Bill's heart as he renewed his acquaintance with Wally, as his friends called him. This seemed like another miracle to Bill. Just think, among sixteen medical men, a good Christian Adventist. To Bill, at this time in his life, Wally was his "Jonathan," and he was "David."

Friday morning Wally said, "Bill, if we are going to get our passes tonight, we must work hard today to prepare for inspection tomorrow." They worked hard all day, and just before the Sabbath hour arrived, they approached the sergeant to request their passes. The sergeant turned and checked with the captain who said, "They are good workers, let them go."

What a Sabbath. One that Bill will always remember. Joy and peace filled his heart as he sang the familiar hymns again. It was so wonderful. God had guided his life thus far, and with his new friend, he knew a great life was ahead of him.

Still, there were concerns for the rough days ahead. Outfits were being sent out for overseas duty almost every day, and all the men knew the same orders could come to them at any time. Would Bill be able to make it through the war? Would his missionary desires ever be fulfilled? Only the Lord knew.

****

Bill and Wally on top of the Empire State Building in New York City

Years later Bill went to visit Wally one Sabbath. He was told that Wally was at barber school. Bill went there and found Wally busy in the first chair. "Wally, what are you doing here on Sabbath?" Wally did not say anything, but when he finished the haircut, he laid down his tools and left with Bill.

The good news is that Bill convinced Wally to go to Pacific Union College and get his degree in education. After graduating, Wally taught at the San Gabriel Academy and Glendale Academy. Eventually he became a chaplain at the Glendale Seventh-day Adventist Hospital. Wally died much later of a heart attack and was buried at Forest Lawn Cemetery in Glendale, California.

Wally Squires was a good Christian man and a lifesaver to Bill. Bill treasures the days they shared together. He and June still miss Wally. Bill thanks God for giving him such a dear and special friend.

Chapter 10

World War II—Battle of the Bulge in Europe

"A thousand may fall at your side, ten thousand at your right hand, but it will not come near you." Psalm 91:7

The day arrived when Bill's outfit was called up and they boarded a train that carried them all the way across the United States to an army camp near Boston, Massachusetts. They stayed there for a while, but none of the soldiers received passes because it was feared some would go AWOL. It was just as well, for during that time the men were given all their shots. Bill said later he felt like a pincushion by the time he was given his last one.

On June 21, 1944, the 390th Battalion was ready to board the Aquitania. This ship was the second largest ship in the world at that time. As Bill stood on the dock, weighed down with full field pack, he gazed at that large ship and thought, *"A thousand may fall at your side..."* And he wondered if he would be one of them. He looked around and knew that all of the other men were thinking the same thing, for that is the curse of war. But where were they going?

Bill was not afraid, for he was tired of being a stateside soldier. He was anxious to get going and do his part in serving his country. The orders

Bill is wearing his full field pack, ready to go to Europe

were soon given, and the men began to board the ship. It did not take them long to find their quarters and their bunks, and wouldn't you know, Bill's bunk was the one on top.

Bill was seasick by the time the ship reached open waters. He was so sick at times that he could hardly get out of his bunk to relieve himself and crawl back up onto his upper bunk. Some of the men who were not seasick spent their time gambling on the floor beside their bunks.

When Bill was not too seasick, he prayed and studied his Bible. He always thanked God that He had watched over him while he was "in the world." He also praised Him for bringing him back into His fold, for now he knew that he could face the future, even if it meant his life.

Eight days later, June 29, the Aquitania arrived in the port city of Glasgow, Scotland, which is located in the land of the midnight sun. At times the sun does not set there until midnight, so wooden shutters had been attached to the windows of the barracks to close off the light. The men were very thankful for those shutters after unloading their gear and equipment because they were ready for a good night's rest. A week or so later the men were ordered to board a small English train that took them near London, England, where they stayed for about one month.

On July 14, 1944, just forty-five days after D-Day (the first French invasion), the 390th Battalion got its orders to sail for France. At this time the Germans were fighting hard to hold those French shores so the men knew they had to go. As they crossed the English Channel, the weather suddenly turned very warm. The only thing the men knew for sure then was that it was going to be hot when they landed and that some would lose their lives. The Germans did not want more troops in France, but the 390th Battalion landed safely at Utah Beach, and the men were relieved that they had not come under enemy fire and no one had lost their life.

The men dug their foxholes and pitched their tents over them. Lowell Jentoft was Bill's foxhole companion. He was a dentist's son who always looked forward to mail call each day, hoping for a letter from his girlfriend in Duluth, Minnesota. He talked about her every night as they lay in their sleeping bags. And every night they were interrupted by the sound of approaching bombers as shells burst all around them. Bill prayed that the bombs would not fall on them. Some did land nearby but not on them, and Bill always thanked God that nothing serious happened to them on this strange beachhead. Surely God was watching over them.

The Germans were watching also. One day an airplane suddenly appeared flying very low over Bill and Lowell's foxhole. They knew the pilot meant to strafe the American troops, but the plane was hit before the pilot could fire a shot. The men all cheered as they watched the plane flying away with smoke streaming from its rear.

A few days later it began to rain, and it rained for days. The Germans were retreating over a large portion of France; the men traveled day after day in the rain but were barely able to catch up with the Germans. Some of the men never had a chance to dry their clothes or their boots. Many soon developed trench foot, which caused serious problems. This very painful condition can cause permanent nerve damage. Trench foot causes the foot to look red and shiny. Sometimes they feel wooden, itchy, or tingly. If they develop blisters and ulcers, then gangrene can develop. It was very important for these men to be treated early. Bill was very busy treating each one the best he could, but some had to be sent back to the medical aid station for further treatment.

By now, the men were all questioning, "Where are the Germans going?" The answer came. They were retreating to the Siegfried Line. Here the Germans could bunker down in a strongly fortified fort near the French Maginot Line. The men knew trying to advance and overthrow the Germans would be rough, and the question for Bill was, which of the medics would go with the infantry?

Every man was on alert because it was rumored that they were to go soon. Bill was weary of waiting and eager to see some action. One day he was so anxious that he asked his superior officer if it were possible for him to go. (He was to regret this later.) The officer replied that he would ask and he did. Then the never-to-be-forgotten day came when the men were chosen to stop the spearhead by the Germans in the Battle of the Bulge, and General George C. Patton's third army was ready.

Bill's name was called to go as the medic, and fear filled his heart. He suddenly realized the seriousness of the task and the dangers involved. His dream of being a missionary might never be fulfilled now. Yet, here was his chance to serve his country. He had to go; he was ready.

Snow was on the ground when Bill's outfit began to move. It was very cold traveling in those cold iron half-tracks all night. Early the next morning Bill was riding in a Jeep when he came upon American soldiers lying dead on the ground. He praised them in his heart for giving their all for their country. Now it was time for others to take over. But the question loomed in his mind, *Who's going to come out alive?*

Left to Right: Wally Squires, Bill Jamerson, The Captain

Chapter 11

We've Got to Stop the Germans

"The angel of the Lord encamps around those who fear him, and he delivers them." Psalm 34:7

The column, of which Bill's Jeep was a part, consisted of about six tanks, two tank destroyers, eight half-tracks, and one company of infantry. As far as Bill knew, his helmet was the only one that bore the medical insignia, the red cross on the white background, on all four sides.

The column came to a valley with the mountains just ahead of them. They were pushing forward but the column was slowing; some resistance must have broken loose. The lieutenant asked Bill to scout it out. Suddenly it seemed to him as if the powers of heaven had broken loose. The German's had spotted their column. Shells, screaming like banshees, rained down on the valley and burst all around the column in a demoralizing barrage. These shells were rightly named the "Screaming Meemies." Bill dove under a Jeep while other men hid wherever they could, each hoping for protection from those horrible deadly shells.

Orders were soon given to advance, and Bill noticed that everything seemed to be very orderly. While the men pushed along, Bill rode in the Jeep with the driver, an infantry soldier. Suddenly, right before them, they saw a German with something in his hand. Bill asked the driver, "What is it?"

"It's a hand grenade!" he yelled.

At that moment Bill was impressed to shout, "Over there!" as he pointed to an area away from them. The German soldier turned and threw his grenade where Bill pointed before surrendering.

Later, Bill saw a German soldier coming down a hill with his hands over his head, calling out, "Kamarad! Kamarad!"

An American soldier nearby shouted, "I'll blast him and that will be the end of him."

Bill shouted back, "No, no, no! Let's not kill him! He's a prisoner of war! Send him back to the rear." The soldier obeyed Bill, and that German was also taken prisoner.

Occasionally, Bill's tank force was fortunate enough to stop and rest for a while, and those moments of rest were always appreciated. The men would sit down beside a half-track while Bill read some of the psalms to them. The men especially enjoyed the twenty-third Psalm. Bill always encouraged them to have faith and trust in God and he assured them that God would be near them.

Bill recalls the day their armored column was moving forward when they came upon a pocket of German infantrymen waving white flags, wanting to surrender. One of the tank drivers who saw what was happening decided that, with the tank and the infantrymen riding on it, they would investigate, so they moved forward. Suddenly there was a loud roar when they reached the plateau. The watching men scattered, but sadly they soon realized that their tank had been hit and blown out of commission and that some of the men had been killed.

The soldiers then saw that there were enemy foxholes dug all over the hillside to the right, and they knew they were filled with Germans trying to ambush them. What should the men do? Hastily they readied their machine guns and began riddling the hillside. The Germans soon realized they were no match for the Americans.

The tank force decided to move on, hoping no more tanks or lives would be lost. As they raced across the field after the Germans, they expected to be stopped by more antitank guns at any moment, but the enemy was on the run. What a feeling. Yes, the Germans were running, but would they be waiting for them ahead, waiting to attack the column again? If so, there would be a bloody battle and who would survive?

When night came, the men were fully exhausted. They needed sleep, so they went into the woods nearby and posted a guard. But before Bill could lay down and get some sleep, he decided to go among the men and see if he could cheer them up a bit. He spoke with many of them, but soon all was quiet for the night. Each man had a good quiet night's rest with no disturbance. But what would the morning hold for them?

Chapter 12

Strange Noise

*"Look up, and lift up your heads;
for your redemption draweth nigh." Luke 21:28, KJV*

Bill remembers well those days. He had his stripes back, and his pay was now $78 a month. He also remembers the K-ration food he and the other soldiers were given. They only provided about 800-1,200 calories, far less than required for highly active men, but they were also given candy bars to give them more energy. That helped but K-rations got old in a hurry. However, there were times during the lull in fighting when the men had freshly cooked meals, and these were greatly appreciated.

Bill recalls one Sabbath morning when he and the other men were able to eat their K-rations in peace and quiet. That was wonderful. But soon it was time for them to pull out. When they reached the top of another hill, they looked down into a lovely picturesque German village nestled between the hills in the valley. They knew German soldiers were there just waiting for them, so the tank commander gave orders to fire upon the village. Instantly, shells were fired and hurled toward the silent village. Unknown at the time was that the Germans had turned the village into a fortress and were determined to defend it at all cost.

The men felt the earth shake when the German big guns riddled the hill they were on. Bill jumped in the foxhole he had just dug, but he was not able to stay there long. He heard screams and knew that some of his men had been hit. Shrapnel was whistling all around him but safety was forgotten as he crawled across the field on his belly as fast as he could to help each wounded man. He worked like a madman, dressing wounds and evacuating some to the aid station.

The Germans had the Americans pinned down. Their barrage just kept going on and on, but thoughts of surrender never entered the soldiers' minds. Bill looked around and saw that men on all sides of him were praying. When he heard a Catholic soldier

Bill with Nazi Banner

near him reciting his rosary, he knelt down and prayed also, rededicating his life to God and praying once again, "Oh Lord, make me a missionary, and my life is Yours forever."

Suddenly Bill heard a strange noise coming from the sky, so he looked up. He did not see anything at first, but he heard a noise, *b-r-r-r, b-r-r-r, b-r-r-r*. A small airplane finally came in to view, circling above his head. When he realized it was an American Piper Cub, Bill thanked God, for he felt as if the Lord had sent an angel. He watched the plane circle. When the pilot saw that the men were pinned down and needed help, he dipped his wings and flew off to get the help they needed.

Soon the men heard, *Swish! Swish!* They all wondered what that sound was, but it did not take long for their question to be answered. The pilot had spotted the large German guns that had pinned them down and he radioed for help. American artillery had come to their aid. At last the men could get up.

The captain shouted, "Let's go get them, men. We can take the village now." The column moved forward. Except for an occasional sniper shooting at an American, the men marched down the hill without much difficulty. But this was not serious fighting now. As the men slowed down, the captain shouted, "Men, see that bridge? If it is bombed or destroyed, we will be stuck, so let's go." The column began to move again, but this time it was not as easy because the whole flat field had been dug up. The Germans had no intentions of letting the Americans move forward.

Shells began whistling all around the men. Bill lay flat in a half-track, hoping to stay where he might be safer. Suddenly a voice rang over the radio, "Medic! Medic! Report to half-track quickly! Very quickly!"

Bill jumped out of his half-track and ran up the road as fast as he could and was soon at the side of a wounded gunner. As Bill looked at the wounded soldier, he saw that a shell seemed to have gone through the man's face, and he had swallowed his tongue. What could Bill do? His friend Wally had given him the only medical training he had ever had, but treatment for a swallowed tongue had never been mentioned. Bill did all he could to release the man's tongue but it was not enough. Sadness filled Bill's heart, and tears streamed down his cheeks as the man died in his arms, another horrible tragedy of war.

Chapter 13

Enough!

"Well done, good and faithful servant!" Matthew 25:21

It did not take long before the Americans were in the quaint German village. Bill got out of the half-track and went to a nearby building. He stood in the doorway talking to some fellow soldiers for a few minutes before they entered the building. Suddenly a German mortar shell landed in the doorway where Bill had been standing only a few moments ago. Everyone ran to the basement where they discovered some of the villagers hiding. They were there hoping to save themselves with the American soldiers. It was not long before an American soldier came looking for a medic.

When he saw Bill, he yelled, "Come quickly." Bill ran up the stairs where he found his buddy of the night before, a sergeant, lying motionless on the floor. As Bill examined the wounded man, he saw that one of his legs was nearly severed while the other leg was badly injured. He quickly placed a tourniquet on the severed leg. Bill did all he could to save the sergeant's other leg before sending him back to the aid station. Unfortunately, the next day he learned that the sergeant had lost so much blood that he had died during the night.

After the war Bill received a letter from the sergeant's parents asking him to tell them all about their son's death. Bill answered their letter. As tenderly as he could, he explained what had happened.

Bill will never forget that night. The German shells just kept coming, but the Americans were not leaving. They had come to stay. All night Bill prayed again and again, "Please, Lord, save us." He said later that he had a strong impression that God heard his prayers. He felt sure that God was directing his life and would find a place for him to work in His mission field.

Medics don't stay on the front lines very long because it is too hard on them emotionally. So it was that one day Bill's commanding officer came to him and said, "Bill, you have done a great job, but you need to go behind the lines now and rest for a while. Another medic will relieve you."

Bill was very happy to hear that and replied, "Thank you, sir! I have done the best I could." When Bill reached the safety of the medical aid station, he once again thanked the Lord for His watch care and blessings.

A short time later the Americans moved into Austria and on to Czechoslovakia.

Suddenly it was V-E Day! Bill and everyone else jumped with joy when they heard the good news. Oh, how they rejoiced! The war was over! Hallelujah! At last they could go home! Home sweet home! How sweet the sound!

Again, Bill felt confident that God was directing his path, but where would He lead him? Would he really become a missionary? Bill vowed again to do all he could to keep his promise to God and serve Him the rest of his life.

Chapter 14

Home, Sweet Home

"Behold, I stand at the door, and knock..." Revelation 3:20, KJV

Yes, the war was over. Bill and his outfit were sent to Munich, Germany, where they were housed in nurses' quarters while waiting to return home. Finally the great day came when Bill was told that he could leave Europe. Bill could hardly wait. He and others boarded a large victory ship in Antwerp, Belgium, and the ship set sail for New York on September 28, 1945. But they were not even out of sight of land when he was seasick again. Oh, so seasick. But each day was bringing him closer to home. Home, sweet home!

After many days at sea, he saw her—the Statue of Liberty, standing in the rain and holding the torch of liberty! The very torch of liberty for which they had all been fighting. Rain, mixed with tears, streamed down Bill's cheeks. How happy and proud he was to be an American. All seasickness was gone now; he was so very proud of his country.

Soon the men realized the ship was swinging to the starboard side. What was happening? They saw a small boat filled with American women who had come out to welcome the men home. The women sang songs to express their happiness, and joy and gratitude filled Bill's heart.

The ship docked on October 6, 1945. As soon as the men got off the ship, the women invited them to go with them to a cafeteria where they could eat all the steak, hamburgers, French fries, sodas, or whatever they could possibly want to eat or drink. But Bill was not interested in food. What he wanted more than anything else in the world at that moment was cold fresh milk. And how wonderful that cold fresh milk tasted after months and months of drinking only warm powdered milk. He thought he would never get enough of that delicious cold milk, and he thanked God that he was among those who had come home alive. But the best was yet to come.

What more did Bill want? He wanted to see his mother, father, sisters, and brother. Then he wanted to choose a companion for life. This was very important to Bill. He was already an "old man" of twenty-two years, but he knew he would have to be patient and wait for the Lord to lead.

A few days later, October 15, 1945, Bill experienced one of the most wonderful experiences of his life. It was discharge time at Camp Beale in Marysville, California.

Bill waited impatiently for his name to be called so he could receive his discharge papers. When he heard his name called, he jumped up. At that moment, he discovered that his first cousin, Richard Pitman, had been seated right in front of him. Richard was surprised, and he jumped up, too. Both men laughed and hugged each other. What a wonderful surprise for both of them.

With discharge papers in his hand, Bill said goodbye to his cousin and headed for home. What a thrill it was when he went up the hill to his home on the outskirts of Nevada City, California. Never had that brown house looked more beautiful. He rushed up to the door and knocked. His mother answered the door, and what a surprise she had. "Billy! Billy!" she cried, "You're home!" Tears of joy rolled down the cheeks of his loving mother.

Dad came to the door then and said, "My boy! You're here! What a great day! You're home at last." He opened his arms wide and hugged Billy close. The following days were never to be forgotten, but soon Bill knew it was time he found a job. But where? What did God want him to do?

Bill waited for the Lord's guidance, and one day a man came up to his front door and knocked. When Bill opened the door, the man said, "Hello. I am Elmer Brackett, and I want to show you what I am doing." Bill's curiosity was instantly aroused, so he invited Elmer to come in the house. A few minutes later Elmer was showing Bill some books. "These are Christian books, and they must be in the homes of people because they will win souls for the Lord. God can use you, and it is something you can easily do."

Bill thought about it for a moment, and then said, "OK, I'll give it a try."

"I felt sure God wanted to use you in this work," Elmer said.

"Please, will you show me how to do this work?" Bill replied.

Bill soon became deeply engrossed in his new work as a literature evangelist. What a thrill it was to witness to the many different families. It was hard work, but he loved it because he knew God was guiding his path.

However, Bill still felt the need for a life companion. When would he have that privilege? Where would he find her? God knew how much he wanted a life partner who would go with him to the mission field. But Bill wondered, *Why hasn't God opened the way for me?*

Chapter 15

Michigan

"The way of the righteous is made plain." Proverbs 15:19, KJV

Bill did not realize it, but God was working very hard behind the scene. He impressed Bill's sister Virginia, and her husband, Russell Potter, to move from Michigan to California. They talked it over, and by March 1945 both of their hardware stores had sold. Then God inspired Virginia to write to Bill and ask him to come to Michigan and drive their extra car to California for them.

Bill was curious when he received her letter and wondered why she was writing to him. As he read the letter, he knew instantly that God was leading him. He had been writing to two girls over the last year. Both lived in Michigan, and both were attending Emmanuel Missionary College, now called Andrews University. Amazing.

It was not long before Bill was en route to Michigan. Sometimes he hitchhiked, and at other times he rode a Greyhound bus. When he arrived in Bronson, Michigan, Virginia and Russell welcomed him with open arms and handed him the keys to their second car, a two-toned green and cream Chevy. Joy instantly filled Bill's heart.

The next day Virginia said, "There is no need for you to sit around here all day. Why don't you go over to Emmanuel Missionary College and see June Hosler for a while? I am sure she would be glad to see you."

Bill jumped at the chance, but he nonchalantly said, "OK, I might as well." As he got in the car, he thought, *I can check on June today and see if she could be the girl that fits my ideal of a life's companion. Then I'll check out Betty, but I sure wish I knew which one is the right one.*

June's parents, Chancy and Myrtle Stiles Hosler, had been very close friends of Bill's parents when they lived in Michigan. When the two families would get together, Bill and June, who was three years younger than he was, would sometimes play together. So their friendship went back a number of years.

Since Bill had surrendered his life to God, he knew that whomever he chose had to be willing to go where God called him. He was concerned when he arrived at the college. Bill's niece Joyce met him and took him to the girls' dormitory. Even though Bill had known June a long time and had been writing to her for a couple of years, he was really nervous as he walked up the stairs to the front door of the girls' dormitory.

He thought about her letters to him and how much he enjoyed them. He had not seen her for a number of years and wondered what she would be like now. Bill noticed a young lady coming down the stairs. She was tall, blonde, and beautiful. When he realized it was June, he thought, *Wow! She is much prettier than her photo.*

June did not hesitate and came right over to Bill and Joyce. They chatted for a few minutes, and then Joyce said she was sorry to leave them but she had to get back. Bill was happy about that, for now he could be alone with June and they could talk. They talked as they sat in the students' special private room, and then they took a stroll along the St. Joe River.

One of the things Bill asked June was how she felt about the Spirit of Prophecy writings. This was very important to him, for he was a Seventh-day Adventist with plans to be a missionary, and he firmly believed Ellen G. White had been inspired by God to write the numerous books, articles, and testimonies that the church published.

When he heard her favorable comments, he felt quite sure she was a real Christian girl, and from that moment on, he never again thought about checking out Betty. But how would he know if June was the one God wanted him to have? Would she fit in his future plans?

That night Bill prayed and talked to God about June. He told Him about how much he wanted to be a missionary and of his plans to find a life companion. He told God of his need for a good wife who would be a real helpmate to him in every way, willing to go any place in the world with him; one who could take it when things got tough in the mission field.

Then he asked God for a sign. "Lord, you know there is a song I like very much, but I can never remember it. If June is the right girl for the future you have planned for me, please bring that song continually to my memory." Then he waited and waited. But he still could not remember the name of that song or the words. Would God give him the sign he requested?

Chapter 16

The Sign

"Therefore, the Lord himself shall give you a sign." Isaiah 7:14, KJV

Bill and June enjoyed each other's company over the following weeks. But all during this time Bill was waiting and hoping the name of that special song would pop into his mind so he would know that God had answered his prayer.

Bill was still waiting for a sign from God when school was almost ended. Only a short time remained. When was God going to answer his prayer, or was he going to return to California alone? Suddenly the words to "Oh, Sweet Mystery of Life, At Last I Found You" popped into his mind. Again and again he heard those words, and Bill shouted, "Yes. That's the song. That's the song." He was thrilled that June was the girl God had chosen to be his wife, for he loved her dearly. Yes, God had finally answered his prayer. Amen to that.

Bill then realized he would have to ask "the" question. He also knew it was not going to be easy. That evening Bill took June for a ride in his car, and when he found the courage to ask the question, he parked the car. Turning toward her, he said, "June, will you marry me?"

June had not expected Bill to propose so quickly, so she quietly said, "Bill, let me think about it until tomorrow, and then I will tell you. OK?"

Bill did not sleep well that night. He kept waking up and thinking, *Will she say yes? What if she says no? Then what shall I do?* All through the day those questions kept popping into his mind until he could hardly wait for their date that night. As soon as he saw June that evening, he felt in his heart that her answer was going to be yes. And when she smiled and said the magic words, "Yes, I will be so very, very happy to be your wife," great joy filled Bill's heart!

But when Bill asked June's mother for permission for them to marry, she said, "No." She wanted June to get her degree in nursing. June's dad was a friend of Bill's dad, so he was silent and did not say yes or no.

June loved Bill and was determined to marry him in spite of her mother's response. When she learned that her friend was getting married, too, she asked Bill, "Why don't we have a double wedding at Emmanuel Missionary College?" When June's mother heard about their plans, she told them that if they insisted on getting married they had to do it in Beloit, Wisconsin.

Bill had already purchased a marriage license in Michigan, so he quickly purchased another one in Wisconsin. He could hardly wait for their wedding date. While June and her mother were busy planning the wedding and looking for just the right wedding gown, he got busy and painted and decorated the inside of the little Beloit Seventh-day Adventist Church. He remembers that he even bought a pair of Johnson shoes so he would look "spiffy" at their wedding.

Bill and His Bride

The great day finally arrived, and Bill's heart began to beat faster as he watched his lovely bride walk down the aisle wearing her beautiful white wedding gown. June's heart was beating fast, too. Soon she was looking into the eyes of her handsome groom, smiling her sweet smile and saying "I do." Bill and his lovely bride were married on a beautiful spring day, May 25, 1946.

Bill was not aware at that time that the flame for the mission field was already burning as brightly in June's heart as it was in his heart.

After the wedding, the bride and groom loaded the car with their belongings and started their honeymoon trip to California. Bill was really looking forward to settling down and getting back into colporteur work. He felt that kind of work was acceptable for a while, and he enjoyed going door to door selling books, but it was not exactly what he had imagined God had planned for him. He was really anxious for God to open the door for them to go to the mission field.

Bill was glad to be home again. His parents were happy, too. They gave June such a warm welcome that she felt as if she had come home as well. Bill enthusiastically went about going door to door, and he sold many books. He often gave Bible studies too, which he really enjoyed.

Bill was also an enthusiastic leader in his church. As the members began telling him he should be a minister, he began thinking, *Maybe they are right.* Perhaps he should start thinking seriously about becoming a minister. But he quickly put that thought out of his mind when he remembered his school days. He had better just be content selling books and being active in the church. But was this the end of the path on which God had been leading Bill?

Chapter 17

Howell Mountain

"I am the good shepherd, and know my sheep, and am known of mine ... and they shall hear my voice." John 10:14-16, KJV

Bill was leading out in the Missionary Volunteer programs at the Grass Valley church when two elderly ladies, Mrs. Rodrick and blind Mrs. Stearns, invited June and him to a social event. During the evening Mrs. Rodrick said to Bill, "Young man, you must not be satisfied with what you are doing. God has a greater work for you to do." Mrs. Stearns added, "Yes, Bill, you must go to college and prepare to be a minister. God has given you a fine voice, and it must be used for Him."

This gave Bill a lot to think about, and he talked it over with June. He was not earning much money, and neither of their families had money with which to help them. Where could they get college funds? Bill knew that the G.I. Bill would help some, but would it be enough for them to make it?

The thought of being a minister kept rolling around in Bill's mind. It would not go away. Other thoughts came into his mind as well, such as: *You, a minister? You are a carpenter's son. You barely got through high school. You don't even use good English, let alone perfect English. You don't have the brain power for college. All you know is baseball, basketball, and football, so forget college.* Yes, you guessed it. Satan was working hard to discourage Bill to forget about pursuing the ministry.

But God had plans for Bill. Once again, Mrs. Rodrick and Mrs. Stearns were His instruments. They encouraged him again, "You must be a minister, Bill. Make plans now to go to college this year, and do not delay. We are sure God has a place for you in His vineyard." Bill argued with them, but they insisted again and again that he must go to college.

Bill and June asked each other, "What shall we do?" At last Bill said, "Well, let's visit Pacific Union College, and I will try to enroll. What do we have to lose?" When Bill's dad heard their plans he told Bill he would not last there six months. But his dad didn't know what God had planned for Bill.

Soon Bill's light blue 1937 Hudson Terraplane was packed, and they were driving to St. Helena and then up Howell Mountain to Pacific Union College. Bill parked their car, and as he stood before Irwin Hall, he began to feel like a fish out of water. But here they were. He prayed, "Lord, You must have a place for me here, for You have directed me here. Please do what You think best for me."

Bill and June knew the G.I. Bill was going to help with their finances, but they would have to depend on God to provide the rest. That is exactly what they did, and soon they were directed to a trailer home in Veteran Heights, where they unpacked their car and settled in. But Bill knew that God had led him up Howell Mountain, and this was where He planned for him to be.

****

Much later, Bill became mayor of Veteran Heights. Who knew? God often works in mysterious ways.

Chapter 18

Rescued

"Let not your heart be troubled." John 14:1, KJV

That first quarter in college was one Bill will never forget because Satan was hard at work doing his best to discourage him. He was almost successful when one of Bill's teachers told him he should give up the ministerial classes and take industrial arts instead. Bill was a little discouraged at this suggestion, but he was still convinced that God had called him and was leading him, so he refused to take the teacher's advice.

Bill's college classes were really difficult for him, and oh, how he did study—term papers and outside reading, thousands of pages and questions. He spent hours working on them. Sometimes he spent all night, but with June's help, he would finally finish them. At the close of the quarter, he breathed a big sigh of relief and thought, *Well, that's done, but I am pretty sure I failed those final exams, so I might as well quit.*

That attitude changed when he stopped at the post office and learned that he had earned straight C's. He could hardly believe it. He said to himself, *Not too bad, eh? All C's! Now I will prove to my dad that he was wrong when he said I would never make it past six months.*

A few days later Bill received a statement from the college saying that he owed $150 and needed to make arrangements for payment. What was he going to do? He was slowly walking away from the post office with the bill in his hand when his friend Art Morgan approached. "Why so glum?" he asked. When Bill told him about what he owed, Art said, "Well, don't be so downhearted. You can work for me."

Art and Bill had a lot in common. Art had wanted to work in the mission field, too, but he was now a contractor. He not only gave Bill a job but he taught him how to build houses. He also encouraged Bill and fanned the flame in his heart to be a missionary. Art was pretty good about paying him, even though it was not always on time. (One time he paid him with a white turkey instead of cash, and Bill remembers that the turkey was quite tasty). Art was a great friend to Bill, and Bill still feels it was Art's kindness and caring that made it possible for him to stay in college.

College became a real struggle for Bill his second year. That was the year he learned there was going to be a new addition to his family. They were very excited about the news, but it caused Bill a lot of concern, for he knew there would be added expenses. He thought, *Going to school is hard enough, but now a child is coming. How will we manage? Should I drop out of school for at least a year?*

But they did not need to worry, for God was their Guide and Provider. This time He sent Dr. Homer Wolfsen and his wife, Grace, to their home. Bill had known him in Germany, so it was a very pleasant surprise visit for him. They had a very nice evening, and after dinner Homer said, "June, did you know it is easier for women between the ages of eighteen and twenty-five to give birth?" June said she was glad to know that for she was in that age range and believed she was pregnant.

Homer smiled and said, "I would like very much to be the physician who delivers your baby, but that would mean you would have to come to my office in Oakland from time to time before your delivery. Think it over; then let me know." June told him she would do that.

Bill and June talked it over, and the next week June went to Oakland for her first checkup. Homer was very glad to see her. After examining her, he said she should deliver her baby around May 19. June had her own idea and thought it would be closer to May 23.

Everything went very well for June over the next few months. But on May 19 she was awakened early with contractions. She shook Bill awake and said, "I think maybe it's time you take me to the hospital." Bill quickly jumped out of bed and got dressed. While June was dressing, he put the bag she had filled with the things she and the baby would need in the car. A few minutes later they were on their way to the hospital in Oakland.

But their baby had a mind of his own and decided he did not want to be born on May 19. He would rather wait so he could celebrate his parents' second wedding anniversary with them. At 3:50 on the afternoon of May 25 he made his appearance. His proud parents were delighted with their beautiful eight-pound, eight-ounce baby boy. They promptly named him Gary Edward Jamerson. What a wonderful anniversary present for both parents.

As June was busy getting ready to leave the hospital two days later, Homer came in and informed her that he and Grace were taking her and baby Gary to their home for ten days to two weeks. June had not expected such a kind offer and said, "Oh, that is too much of a burden on Grace as she has enough to do with your six-month-old adopted daughter."

After explaining that a lady came every other day to do the household chores and her being with them would not be a burden on anyone, Bill and June gladly accepted their kindness. This was a blessing that made it possible for Bill to continue his studies while June rested and recovered from childbirth. They both thanked God.

Bill could hardly wait to see his precious wife and son again, and as he drove down Howell Mountain, he began singing, "With Jesus in the family, happy, happy home."

June was happy to see Bill, too, as she was anxious to get home again. As she gathered up her belongings, Bill mentioned to Homer that they had not received his statement. Homer smiled and said, "That's because there isn't one."

Bill and June were surprised and very appreciative but it was very difficult for them to accept such a kind and generous gift. They said it was far too much but no amount of coaxing would change Homer's mind.

They were in for another blessing a year later when Homer learned Bill was having a problem with his appendix. He immediately called Bill on the phone and said, "Bill, I want you to come to Oakland, and I will remove your appendix." Bill quickly accepted his offer, not realizing at the time that Homer's heart of gold would once again refuse to be paid for his services. To this day, when Bill thinks of Homer, he is again reminded of the text that says, "There is a friend who sticks closer than a brother" (Prov. 18:24).

****

Over the years Bill and June have praised God many times and thanked Him for friends like Homer and Grace. They feel their thoughtfulness and kindnesses are recorded in God's book of remembrance in heaven, and one day soon they will receive their rich reward for being so thoughtful and gracious.

Are you inspired now to be more thoughtful, kind, and generous? Jesus is hoping you are.

Chapter 19

Surprised

"Ask and it will be given to you." Matthew 7:7

Bill and June have thanked God many times for watching over them and guiding their way and for giving them their beautiful, healthy baby boy. Gary was their pride and joy. His hair was blonde and curly and many times people would come up and ask if they could touch it. Gary was a good baby, too. He slept through the night and even slept through the worship hour at church.

But money was really scarce, and Bill felt he just had to find a better paying job. He soon found one and was hired as a psychiatric technician at the Napa State Hospital for the mentally ill. His hours were from 3:00 p.m. to 11:00 p.m.

One Friday night Bill and a short skinny aid went to give medications to a tall African-American man. As soon as Bill unlocked the door, this tall handcuffed and anklecuffed African-American man jumped him. The aid fled right away and called for help. Before help arrived, Bill had managed to get loose and lock the door. Later another team came, and this time they managed to give the man his medication and lock him in a cell reserved for mentally-ill patients who were violent.

This incident was just one of many that increased Bill's desire to keep the Sabbath day holy. One day he felt the time was right to tell the hospital administrator he was resigning so he could observe the Sabbath. Much to his surprise they told him he could not only have Sabbath off but that he could keep his job, too. Once again Bill praised God for working things out for him. What a great God!

Later, Bill's hours were changed to 11:00 p.m. to 7:00 a.m. This was really hard on him, for as soon as he got off work in the morning, he had to rush to his 7:30 a.m. class. There were times when he could hardly keep his eyes open during class. However, there were times when he was able to study a little at work and catch a wink or two of sleep. But he was always tired and always concerned about his grades. Would they be high enough to pass?

Two of Bill's friends, Nick Poulos and Wayne Hill, did not have to work to pay for their education, so Bill thought they would get straight A's for sure. But when Bill received his grades, he couldn't believe his eyes. A big A! He thought, *This cannot be right! I am sure I did not earn this.* He told Professor Hardin about the mistake with his grade three times, and each time the professor promised he would correct it, but to this day it has never been changed. God was still in control! To this day, Bill insists he desperately needed that big A.

Satan had not given up on Bill, and over the years there were times when he thought he should change his program. His biggest temptation came when Percy Christensen, the president of Pacific Union College, said, "Bill, we have been watching you and would like to offer you a scholarship to go to Oregon State to be a physical education professor."

Bill's heart skipped a beat. Imagine—a professor in sports. The long ago desire of his heart! You can be sure that the devil was there tempting Bill to accept the offer. Bill did think about it for a moment, but he took a deep breath, looked President Christensen in the eyes, and said, "Thank you very much, sir, but I feel strongly that God has called me to the ministry." Satan was disappointed, but not God and the angels! They were thrilled with his victory!

The devil did not give up trying to discourage Bill though. One day Professor Raymond Cottrell, one of Bill's teachers, called him into his office for a counseling appointment and said, "Bill, I think you should change your program. It is my impression you are not the type of person to be a minister."

Bill was shocked to hear this, but he calmly said, "Sir, that may be so, but I feel this is where God is leading me." With that he turned and left the office. Another victory!

****

Interestingly, after Bill had served in Bolivia for five years, this same professor approached him and asked if he would be willing to tell the mission story at the Takoma Park Seventh-day Adventist Church in Washington, D.C. This greatly pleased Bill and gave him a lot of satisfaction as he stood before the congregation in his devil-dancing costume.

May we all remember that God sees each man's future and where he comes from, and He does marvelous things through those who are fully surrendered to Him.

Many years later Bill performed the funeral for Raymond's brother, Ken Cottrell, in Paradise, California. God works in strange ways!

Chapter 20

Reaching Out

"Go into all the world and preach the good news." Mark 16:15

During Bill's senior year, he had to present oral examinations before eight professors. He prayed that God would be in control. To this day he doesn't know how he answered them, but the Lord led him in his responses, and he praised God for that blessing.

It was during this senior year that Bill was inspired to start what he called a Branch Sabbath School. There was an auditorium in the area near Fairfield, California, called Shipyard Acres. The police chief gave Bill permission to hold the meetings there, and the chief's wife and two daughters regularly attended.

Fairfield Califoria – Branch Sabbath School – 1949

The name Branch Sabbath School was shortly changed to Story Hour. The program was so successful that Bill started another one and then another. Soon there were seven Story Hours functioning in nearby towns with an average attendance of about 255 children, and four more Story Hours were in the planning stage. Amazing!

God then inspired Bill to invite theology students to come to a meeting at Irwin Hall and learn the methods being used for this work. Many students responded, and all were excited to learn of other ways to reach children and their parents.

Some of the college students began taking an active part in visiting the parents of the children attending the Story Hour. One student, Fred Elkins, went to the home of a blind lady and read Bible stories to her. Bill remembers that ten or fifteen years later her daughter called and asked him if he had been the leader of those Fairfield meetings. When Bill said yes, she told him she and her mother had both been baptized and were now Seventh-day Adventists. Again, Bill praised God for those two ladies and for the Story Hour's ministry!

Another miracle that came out of those meetings was that one of the daughters of the police chief attended Pacific Union College and married Bob Cowan, one of the ministerial students. The good news is that her life and many others were changed because of those Story Hours.

Graduation day came at last, and thirty theology students graduated. None was happier than Bill! He had been working forty hours a week and studying fifteen or more hours. He thanked God for June's help and patience. Now he was looking forward to other projects that would win more souls for the Lord.

All thirty students knew that only about ten of the best would be called. Bill feared he would not be on that list because he was an average student. His confidence continued to remain strong though, for he knew in his heart that God had a place for him somewhere in the mission field.

Betty Bailey, one of Bill's friends, happened to be riding to work with him one day when the conversation turned to the mission field. As they talked, she mentioned that her father, Dr. Stump, was the educational secretary of the South American Division. Bill did not believe her at first, but then she said, "I hear you want to go to a mission field, and if that's true, you really ought to go see him."

Bill believed her then, and his heart jumped with joy. "Oh, I would love to!" he said. "This is the dream June and I have had since we were children. Will you really introduce us to him?"

"I will be happy to," Betty replied. "Come over one evening next week."

Bill was elated and could hardly wait as the days slowly passed. At last the time came when he and June went to meet Dr. Stump. What an evening it was! Dr. Stump told them about the work in South America and saw right away that they were very enthusiastic about going to the mission field. At last he said, "I will be happy to talk with some of the men from our division and ask them to talk with you."

Bill replied, "Oh thank you, Dr. Stump, we will be ready and waiting for the call."

Bill and June were elated when they went home that night. But later Bill thought, *Will he forget? It is highly possible for a busy man like Dr. Stump to forget about a young couple and their zeal for the mission field. Maybe we should pray about this.* And they did pray.

Chapter 21

Invited

"Come to me, all you who are weary and burdened, and I will give you rest." Matthew 11:28

God was in control, and soon Bill and June received word that Elder L. H. Olson, the president of the Inca Union of Seventh-day Adventists in South America, wanted to see them. (Elder Olson later became secretary of the South American Division in Uruguay.)

Bill and June were thrilled. The dream of their life was about to materialize! The hours lingered until it was time for them to go to Graf Hall at Pacific Union College. Elder Olson was waiting for them when they arrived, and he graciously invited them to come in and be seated. Bill began the conversation by telling him that since childhood the desire of their hearts had been to be missionaries. Elder Olson was happy to hear that. After telling them a few things about the Inca Union in South America, he then turned to June and asked if she could stand isolation and a humid climate. She quickly said, "No, I prefer not to live in a humid climate."

Bill's heart sank! *Now we're out!* he thought.

Elder Olson understood how June felt though. "Well, that is OK as I have two calls. One is for a couple to go into the jungles of Peru to live in isolation in a place called Nevati. The other is for a supervisor of Indian missions in Bolivia. Your home would be La Paz, Bolivia. I think this is the best place for the two of you."

What a relief. Bill was elated. "Oh, that sounds great. Can you get us there?" he asked.

Elder Olson replied, "I will do my best. Just be patient."

Bill and June thanked Elder Olson and said goodnight. By now both were feeling as if they were on cloud nine again. They knew in their hearts that if God was leading them He would see that they got this post. They had never been happier.

It was at this time that Pacific Union College began to receive calls from local fields for young intern ministers. Would Bill get one? Satan surely did not want that to happen, and he went to work again trying to discourage Bill. Soon Bill began thinking, *I don't stand a chance. My grades were sufficient to graduate, but no more, so I doubt they will call me*. However, God was still working in Bill's life, and He knew that Bill needed some experience.

Bill's heart sank when he learned that only seven of the thirty ministerial students received calls. *My chances of getting a call now are pretty slim, but I am still going to put my trust in God and do my best to wait patiently for His call.*

He was cheered up a little later when Nick Poulous and his wife called to invite them to go to Oakland to a party their folks were having for the members of the Grand Avenue Seventh-day Adventist Church. They gladly accepted the invitation and enjoyed the evening very much. Little did they realize God had arranged for them to attend that party. It was truly a divine appointment.

A few days after the party June's next-door neighbor, Sophie, who had become her best friend, knocked on her door and said she had a phone call for her and to hurry. June quickly followed her and answered the phone. She could hardly believe her ears when she was told that the Northern California Conference was offering Bill a job as an intern at the Grand Avenue Seventh-day Adventist Church in Oakland. June was thrilled and so excited! She thanked the pastor on the phone, and Sophie, and quickly called Bill at Dr. Merle Godfrey's home where he and Art Morgan were putting shingles on the roof of the home.

Bill was surprised when Mrs. Godfrey called up to him and said he had a call from June. He was concerned then and wondered what was wrong. When he answered the phone, June said, "Bill, guess what? Elder Ernest Branson, the pastor of the Grand Avenue Church in Oakland, just called. He noticed your enthusiasm and interaction with people at the party and wants you to work with him. He has already arranged everything with the conference president."

Bill could hardly believe his ears. Instantly the thought came to him, *In all thy ways acknowledge Him, and He will direct your path.* He praised God!

This was Bill's first call, and he was thrilled at the thought of being the associate pastor of the Grand Avenue Seventh-day Adventist Church, which was next to a beautiful little lake in Oakland. However, he was not so thrilled when he heard his duty was to lead the music for the future evangelistic meetings. Bill thought, *Me, lead music! Music was my most difficult course in college!*

God surely moves in strange ways, for Ernest Branson was soon called to be the president of the Greater New York Conference, and Elder Ben Mattison was called to replace him as pastor of the Grand Avenue church in Oakland. He cancelled the evangelistic meetings right away, and much to Bill's relief, he did not have to lead music after all.

A little later the Northern California Conference asked Bill to be the regional missionary volunteer leader for the East Bay area. He was well qualified for this position, and it was one he enjoyed very much. God surely does have a way of working things out once we surrender our will to Him.

God was not only working in Bill's life but he was also working in his father's life. Bill's father had finally quit drinking and decided to follow Jesus and become a Seventh-day Adventist. He was baptized June 12, 1947, by Pastor D. G. Sather at the Roseville Seventh-day Adventist Church.

Let's all praise God every day for His patience as He works out His will in our lives.

Chapter 22

God Prepares the Way

"Let them give thanks to the LORD for his unfailing love and his wonderful deeds for men." Psalm 107:21

Elder Olson had not forgotten Bill and June and their desire to serve in the mission field. He had recommended them to the South American Division, and six months later Bill and June received a letter from Elder Olson with a solid invitation to go to La Paz, Bolivia, and work with the leaders of the Indian Mission Stations. Bill and June had never been happier.

Elder Carl Becker was president of the Northern California Conference at that time. When Bill received a phone call from Carl asking him to come to his office, he looked forward to seeing him again. Bill had enjoyed many picnics together and great ball games—Carl was a great athlete. Carl was glad to see Bill, too, and said, "Young man, since your call is for Bolivia, I will release you from your ministry at the Grand Avenue Church, but for any other place than South America I would say no." He said that because he had once received a call to go there but had been unable to accept it at that time. Now he urged Bill to accept the call.

But he did not have to urge Bill and June to go at all, for they had been hoping and praying for just such a call. They had not expected it to come quite so soon, but grinning from ear to ear, they told Carl they would be very happy to be missionaries in Bolivia.

Bill and June had enjoyed working at the Grand Avenue church for six months and felt bad about leaving. But they were also very excited about finally going to the mission field.

The letter Bill and June received from South America instructed them to sell most of their furniture and bring only the bare necessities with them. The letter also recommended that they sell their car and buy a Jeep. They read that letter many times during the following days.

While June packed their clothing and kitchen items, Bill was busy selling everything he could with the exception of their bed, stove, and refrigerator. He even sold their automatic washing machine. June was sad about selling it. Later they had to buy a wringer-style washing machine, which made extra work for her.

Soon everything Bill and June were taking to Bolivia was packed in wooden containers ready to be placed on the ship they would board. By the time they were ready to leave only one problem remained, which was that their almost-new Studebaker car had not been sold. Then, just hours before Bill, June, and almost three-year-old Gary were to board the ship that would take them on their journey to La Paz, Bolivia, Bill sold their Studebaker for $1,450. What a relief! But now there was no time to shop for a Jeep. Why hadn't God answered Bill's prayer? Time would tell; maybe God had other plans.

It was a day filled with mixed emotions when Bill, June, and little Gary stood on the dock in the San Francisco harbor and said goodbye to the friends who had come to wish them bon voyage. It was especially sad when they began singing "God Be With You Till We Meet Again" as the little Jamerson family boarded the ship that would take them to the mission field.

They did not know what to expect, but they were excited. And once on board the Grace Line's SS Santa Juana, they quickly got settled in their room. Just before noon the ship's whistle blew and the sound of the engines grew louder. On April 27, 1951, the ship slowly left the dock and moved them out to sea. The happy couple were on their way to the mission field at last. Great peace filled their hearts for they knew the Lord would be with them wherever they went.

Bill, June and Gary boarding the "SS Santa Juana"

Bill strolled around the ship the next day, and much to his surprise, he noticed a little red Jeep with four-wheel drive. Was it their Jeep? He didn't know, but he wistfully hoped that someone had kindly provided it for him.

Bill was sadly disappointed a few days later when the ship docked at Buenaventura, Colombia, as he watched that little red Jeep being taken off the ship. *That's too bad!* he thought, *That would have been a great Jeep for me!*

While in that port, Captain Lindholm, their ship's captain, decided to take the Jamerson family and some of the other passengers on a nine-hour fishing trip at sea. He managed to get a barge from the Grace Line Shipping Company, and soon they cast off.

Of course, Bill got seasick right away. But he loves to fish, so he laid on his stomach and fished from the back end of the barge the whole time they were at sea. He was thrilled when he caught a big red snapper and even prouder when the ship's cook prepared it for dinner that evening.

June did not do so well on that fishing trip. She had not noticed how high the waves were when they were on board the big ship. The waves were huge and she was very afraid at times that the big waves would swallow them up. Besides that, those heavy waves caused her to fall when the steward brought her lunch. Fortunately, only her dignity was injured, so her happy spirit returned when she and Bill were on board the SS Santa Juana again.

The next exciting event on board the SS Santa Juana occurred on May 25 when Bill and June celebrated their fifth wedding anniversary and little Gary's third birthday. The ship's baker created a beautiful, delicious cake for them, which they shared with the twelve other passengers and the ship's officers. It was a fun and festive day enjoyed by all!

After traveling for thirty days, the ship arrived safely in Arica, Chile. There was no dock where they could tie up, but several small boats came out to take their boxed belongings back to the concrete landing on shore. As the little boats bobbed up and down, June thought, *Well, there goes everything we own into the ocean.* Then she wondered how in the world the three of them would get to that concrete landing. Just then a small metal basket swung out from the landing to the ship and the little Jamerson family were told to climb in. A few moments later they were safely on shore and thanking God for His blessings once again.

Chapter 23

Bolivia

"And my God will meet all your needs according to his glorious riches in Christ Jesus." Philippians 4:19

There was no one to meet the Jamerson family when they arrived on shore, but they were happy to get their "land legs" back after being on the ship for a month. As they stood there wondering what to do next, a gentleman came up to them. He spoke some English and explained that he would take them to a hotel where they could eat lunch and rest until the train departed for La Paz at 6:00 that evening.

The Jamersons were very happy that the South American Adventist Division had arranged this for them, so they accepted the ride and enjoyed a delicious meal, which included soup. They learned at that time that soup was a very important part of South American meals.

Bill, June, and little Gary were very excited that evening as they boarded the train that would take them to La Paz, Bolivia. At exactly 6:00 p.m. the engineer blew his whistle and the train began to move.

They were quite comfortable after June arranged their belongings in their little stateroom. They rode the train all night and had a good night's rest. The next day the train took them higher and higher. They thoroughly enjoyed seeing the beauty of the majestic Andes mountains as well as the beauty of several glaciers and three other special and magnificent mountains.

The train kept going up, up, and up all night and all day to higher and higher elevations. The next morning when June stood up to get dressed, she quickly sat down again. She was so dizzy she felt like a top spinning. She thought, *Oh, this must have been the change in elevation.* After that she was very careful when she stood up.

Later that morning the train stopped at the station overlooking La Paz, the city where the little Jamerson family would make their home for the next five years. It was at this train station that Delmar Holbrook and Sérgio Bendrell, Seventh-day Adventist missionaries, boarded the train. Bill was unaware that they had been looking forward to their arrival, but what a joy it was to him when they found them.

They barely had time to find a seat when the train commenced going down the short distance to La Paz, which has the highest elevation of any capital city in the world. Before they knew it, Bill and June were gathering their belongings and carrying them to a taxi.

The missionaries took the Jamerson family to a nice restaurant for lunch. They were all laughing and talking at the same time but that changed a moment later when little Gary suddenly vomited. What a mess and how embarrassing not being able to explain to the proprietor what might have caused it. Little Gary's parents wished with all their heart they could speak Spanish. Fortunately, the missionaries came to their rescue and explained to the proprietor that the "gringos" had just arrived from the United States by ship to Arica, Chile, and evidently little Gary had not yet adapted to the change in altitude. The proprietor understood, smiled, and graciously accepted their apology.

Little Gary was quickly cleaned up, and soon they were enjoying their first lunch in Bolivia. When they finished eating, Delmar took them to a hotel and promised to come back the next morning to take Bill to see a building that housed several garages.

Bill was excited when Delmar arrived the next morning and drove Bill to one of the garages. When he unlocked one of the garage gates, Bill's eyes nearly popped out of his head. There was a little red Jeep with four-wheel drive. Even more to Bill's amazement, he was able to purchase the little red Jeep for his own use with the money he had received from the sale of his Studebaker. Had he purchased a Jeep in the United States, it would have cost him more than $3,000. Instantly, Philippians 4:19 flashed in Bill's mind, *"My God will meet all your needs according to his glorious riches in Christ Jesus."* Once again Bill praised God for providing for their needs.

A couple of days later the Jamerson family traveled to Cochabamba where the mission's headquarters were located. After that visit Bill and June knew it was time for them to get down to business and learn to speak Spanish. Bill deeply regretted that he had not studied more when he had taken Spanish in high school. He dropped out of class after his teacher said he would never make it. And now, here he was in Bolivia needing to communicate in Spanish. Who knew. Had Bill's teacher known, she would most likely have had more patience with Bill. That was behind them, so Bill and June quickly put forth their best effort into learning the language. June was far better at learning Spanish than Bill was—she is still more fluent now.

One thing that surprised Bill and June about the bleak plateaus of the Andes surrounding La Paz was that there were only a few eucalyptus trees now and then. But they were not surprised at seeing the Indian ladies in their brightly colored skirt, blouses, and shawls. All the ladies had black, brown, or gray derby hats perched on their heads and long black braids hanging down their backs. Some had young babies wrapped in their shawls and slung over their shoulders and back and tied in the front.

June recalls that some of the ladies sold empañadas. These delicacies were made of dough, rolled out and cut in small circles filled with cheese, meat, or vegetables with raisins. Chili spices were added to a sauce for the meat and vegetable fillings. A small amount of filling was then placed on the dough which was folded over and sealed. A dab of the sauce was then brushed on top and they were baked or fried. They were delicious.

Bill and June learned many things about their new home in the first few weeks of arriving. They knew that Bolivia was known worldwide as the land of llamas. They also knew about the alpacas and their beautiful fur which is harvested to make sweaters and rugs. Vicuñas also have beautiful fur, but they are not domesticated so you rarely see anything made from their fur. They did not know much about the birds in Bolivia, only that there were many condors. They learned that most of the 350,000 Aymara Indians living in Bolivia were sun worshipers. Bill knew then that his work was surely cut out for him.

He had not given much thought about the Indians living in the tropical Amazon basin of Bolivia, but it would not take long before he learned about them firsthand. He also learned about the wild life there: the ant bear, jaguar, puma, sloth, tapir, many species of monkeys, possum, skunks, rattlesnakes, boa constrictors, alligators, and lizards.

The jungles were also home to some of the world's most beautiful birds, such as macaws, parrots, and hummingbirds. Yes, Bill's work was cut out for him, and he praised God that he was there to help bring those precious souls the good news of salvation.

Chapter 24

The Campbell's Soup Box Clinic

"A cheerful heart is good medicine." Proverbs 17:22

Bill was excited about beginning his work among the Aymara Indians in their mission field. The day finally arrived when he was ready for his first six-week trip in the mission field. He was eager to find out if there was a need for medical work among the Indians, and he hoped that his medical experience during World War II could be of some help.

Bill vividly remembered the day he had talked to the mission president, Edmund Clifford, and how excited Elder Clifford had grown when he learned that Bill had served as a medic in the war. He had been so excited that he immediately called the treasurer, J. Perez. After talking it over, they decided to lend 5,000 Bolivianos to this worthwhile cause. In those days that amounted to about $25. It was not much to Americans, but it was enough for the rolling clinic of Bolivia to be born.

Bill's medical chest at that time consisted of a small Campbell's soup cardboard box, which he filled with standard medicines and equipment he had used in Europe during the war. He was confident this would cover all his needs. Elder Clifford had some dental forceps in the office and gave them to Bill. Bill added the forceps to his medical chest.

Bill's little red Jeep was soon loaded, and after hugging and kissing his family, he waved goodbye and set off on his first adventure with the rolling clinic. That first trip was one never to be forgotten, for he soon found there were many kinds of sickness among the Indians. Many suffered from malnutrition, tuberculosis, and eye disorders that often led to blindness. His treatments ranged from putting a little argyrol in the eyes to opening and cleaning ulcers. What surprised him the most was to see so many decayed and rotten teeth.

Bill's little red Jeep and Aymara Indian patient

Up to this point, his only experience in dentistry had been on board the ship that had brought them to Bolivia. The purser had been in a lot of pain and asked Bill to pull his abscessed tooth. Bill had hesitated a moment, but had then took his forceps and pulled the tooth, never dreaming that he would be pulling many more teeth in the near future.

Bill learned a lot more about teeth on this six-week trip. It was not uncommon to find at least four or five teeth in one mouth that were rotten to the gum line and usually an extra tooth was protruding out the front of the mouth. These all called for extractions, and in about four hours in one of the villages he had stopped at Bill pulled twenty-two teeth. As this work was new to him, it was quite a job. Bill was exhausted when he returned home after his first trip.

****

Bill was thrilled when his soup box clinic grew to include two boxes. Later it became a three-soup-box clinic, and then the three boxes were replaced with a large metal box containing two medical trays. Each was always installed on the back end of the little red Jeep, and Bill was very thankful for a better-equipped clinic to take on future trips.

Of all the Indians who came to Bill with their physical problems during his years in Bolivia's mission field, he encountered many who had been treated by witch doctors prior to visiting him. He did all he could for each one of them, but sadly there were some whom he had to turn away, because they required the skill of a professional doctor.

Chapter 25

San Pablo

*"Seek the Lord while he may be found;
call on him while he is near." Isaiah 55:6*

Ed Clifford, president of the Bolivian Mission in South America, decided he should see what this new missionary, William E. Jamerson, was made of, so the day came when he and Bill left La Paz to go down to Chulumani. The altitude drop between the two locations was 7,000 feet. How would this affect Bill? And the dangerous dirt roads! Could he handle it?

After leaving La Paz, they saw a few vicuñas, llamas, alpacas, and sheep. Some were in the distance, but some were closer to the dusty and bumpy unpaved road, and Bill was thrilled. He really enjoyed seeing those magnificent animals.

The first part of their trip wasn't so bad, but as they traveled farther, the road began to curve and wind like a snake down the mountain. Eventually they had to gear-down the Jeep. Then came the worst part of their trip when the road became very narrow. Sometimes they had to back up until they found a place wide enough for the oncoming vehicles to pass. This was not as bad as looking down and seeing a drop of 500 or more feet straight down to the river below. Now that was scary!

Bill had been warned about the treacherous mountain dirt road, but it had not really prepared him for the sheer size of the granite walls that seemed to reach up to heaven or drop down hundreds and hundreds of feet to the river below. But what really amazed him was how the local people had carved the narrow winding road out of the sides of the sheer walls, including tunnels with openings for windows. Bill was amazed and marveled at the magnificent sight, but he prayed that God would send His angels to keep them from going over the side.

After about six hours of traveling, they arrived at the Seventh-day Adventist hospital in Chulumani. Dr. Elmer Bottsford and his wife, Grace, gave Bill and Ed a very warm welcome. They were very grateful for a clean place to stay and good healthy food to eat. What a joy it was to be with fellow North American missionaries and to speak English with them.

But this was only the first lap of their trip. What was ahead was a trip Bill would never forget. After spending a few days in Chulumani, it was time to continue their journey. They got up early and drove to a place where they were to meet some Indian men with mules who were to take them farther into more jungles. The men and mules finally arrived, and after their equipment had been loaded, Bill chose to ride the white mule. This was the first time he had ridden a mule or a horse any distance, so this was a new experience for him.

It wasn't long before Bill was rubbing his neck and back. As he got off the mule, he said, "This is not a pleasant ride!" He walked awhile before riding the mule again, and this was the way it was for three days. Whether riding or walking, it seemed to Bill the greenery of the jungle went on forever. They did see an Indian hut occasionally, and once in a while a lizard would run in front of them or a colorful bird would be startled and fly away. Everyone was amazed to see so many wild turkeys moving in the trees. It was truly an amazing sight!

One day as they were approaching another Indian hut, Bill saw a papaya tree. Hanging from one of its branches were large beautiful yellow papayas. Bill loves papaya, so he picked one. While he was eating the papaya, the Indian man living in the hut came out to greet them. He was friendly, and Ed talked to him awhile.

Bill noticed something that caught his interest, so he asked, "What are those?"

The Indian replied, "Tiger teeth. I kill tigers sometimes."

Bolivian Indian Hut

Bill thought, *Tigers don't live here! They must be puma or jaguar teeth. But tiger, puma, or jaguar teeth, what's the difference? We have no guns!* Then he remembered the angels of heaven were with them, and this gave him comfort.

On the last day of their journey before reaching San Pablo something happened that Bill never forgot, for it was not a pleasant experience. Somehow Bill got separated from the others and was left all by himself in the jungle. It was getting dark by then, and now he had no guide. The thought of tigers crept into his mind, and he was afraid. *What's going to happen next? I don't know the way! What should I do?* His mind raced. Then he closed his eyes and prayed to God, asking for His protection and for Him to direct his way.

The dark of night had quickly closed in while Bill was praying. When he opened his eyes again and saw how dark it was, he was still a little fearful, but a moment later

God impressed him to grab the rope around the mule's neck and walk beside him. What a blessing that was, for Bill realized then that the mule knew the way. He never let go of that rope, and side-by-side they confidently walked along the trail in the dark. So it is with Jesus. He will never let go of us even when life becomes hard and difficult.

At last Bill heard Indians shouting, and soon he could see the little lights they were carrying in their hands. They had found him. Bill thanked his heavenly Father for hearing his prayer as the Indians led him into the village of San Pablo.

Early the next morning Bill wondered if he should teach Bible truths to the Indians first or tend to their medical needs. Both were badly needed, but he decided to set up his clinic first. A few Indians gathered around him and watched everything he did. As soon as his equipment was set up, he asked if anyone would like to have a tooth pulled. Bill's words were clear, but the Indians laughed. He kept repeating what he had asked, but each time they laughed louder.

When Ed heard the Indians laughing, he came over to Bill and told him they were laughing because he was saying, "abre la vaca," meaning, "open the cow." He told Bill to change the "va" to a "bo," and say "abre la boca." When he did this, the Indians understood and stopped laughing. Soon Bill was pulling teeth.

In addition to pulling teeth, Bill and Ed got involved in helping the natives fix their rice machine. Several years ago missionaries had brought a rice machine to the Indians. Using mules, they had hauled it in piece-by-piece. After being reassembled, it had become very important because it could do all the hard work of hulling the rice. The Indians had previously done this by beating the grain with sticks. Now, after years of hard use, the rice machine no longer worked.

Ed asked to see it when he learned it was broken. He quickly looked it over, then set to work. Soon, with a little ingenuity and much mechanical aptitude, he had their precious rice machine in good working order again. And oh how happy the Indians were. Ed and Bill were just as happy as they were that he had been able to repair it.

After several more days of treating the Indians' physical problems, sharing their faith, and repairing the rice machine, it was time for Bill and Ed to get back on their mules and start toward home.

On their way home, Bill thought about their trip. *So, this is the mission field. My dreams have come true, and I love it even if there are hard days. The feeling of serving others is everything I had dreamed. Thank you, Jesus, for giving me this opportunity.*

Ed was also thinking. *This is one missionary I don't have to worry about. He certainly passed the test with flying colors.*

****

Bill doesn't remember how many teeth he pulled on that trip, but he thinks he pulled about 500 during the five years he spent in the mission field of Bolivia. He remembers the most teeth he ever pulled in one day was sixty-four. That's a lot of teeth.

Pulling teeth was not the only new thing Bill had experienced on that trip. The dangerous roads had been quite the experience. Later, Bill took June and little Gary with him on a trip along the same road, and as he was driving around one of the curves, he suddenly had to stop. The mountain had come down across the road, and a big truck with its load of freight was stuck in the middle of the avalanche.

The Indians riding on top of the freight were jumping off as quickly as they could. Just as they reached the side of the road, the mountain began sliding again, and it did not stop until the truck had been pushed over the side and dropped down to the river. The Indian women were so frightened they were shouting, *Madre, Mia! Madre Mia!* (My mother!) What a scary time that was for the Jamerson family, as it was for everyone.

Chapter 26

Another Trek on the Altiplano

"How beautiful ... are the feet of those who bring good news, who proclaim peace, who bring good tidings, who proclaim salvation." Isaiah 52:7

Once again Ed Clifford, president of the Bolivian Mission in South America, decided to go with Bill on another trek through the barren 250 miles of the Altiplano. About 350,000 Indians were living there above the city of La Paz, and those poor Indians desperately needed medical attention. Ed was hoping that news of Bill's little red Jeep and his soup box medical clinic had been reaching some of them.

Shortly after they left La Paz, they noticed an Indian in the distance. He was running toward them. Bill and Ed wondered what this was all about. When the Indian came closer, they could tell by the expression of pain on his face that something was terribly wrong. Then the breathless man began telling them his problem and begging for their help. Bill could not understand a word, but Ed was able to tell Bill that the man had a broken collarbone.

In a professional voice, Bill said, "You say you have a broken collarbone? Let me see." The man hesitated a moment, then slowly began to take off his shirt. When his shoulder was exposed, Bill was shocked. "What is that?"

The man explained that a witch doctor had placed a fat lizard with an incision in its abdomen over the man's broken collarbone to "heal" it. Bill knew then that all he had heard about Indian superstitions had been true.

There was nothing Bill could do for the Indian's broken bone, but he told him to catch a ride on the next truck that came by on its way to La Paz and go to the hospital where the staff would take care of him. Ed conveyed Bill's message to the Indian. He smiled weakly, nodded his head, and sat down beside the dusty road to wait for a passing truck.

As Bill waved goodbye, he pressed his foot on the gas pedal, and they were on their way. When they saw a truck coming toward them, he and Ed thanked God and prayed that the Indian would catch his ride and soon be getting proper treatment in a hospital.

Bill was saddened that he was unable to do more for that Indian, and his sadness lingered for a while as they continued their journey. Both Bill and Ed wondered, *Did that Indian get on that truck and go to La Paz?* But Bill's thoughts soon turned to other things he had experienced in the mission field.

Bill set up his clinic on the back of the little red Jeep in the next village, and the Indians gathered around him. One of them complained of a bad toothache. When Bill asked him to open his mouth, he saw immediately that the problem tooth was a wisdom tooth. He said, "This needs to come out. Do you want me to pull it?" The man nodded his head, and Bill gave him an injection of Novocain. A few minutes later Bill took his dental forceps and began to extract the tooth. But the tooth would not budge. He tried repeatedly, but to no avail. He finally told the poor man that he could not extract it. He would have to go to La Paz and see a dentist. The man said, "Oh, it's alright, I'll just go home and put some lizard oil on it, and it will heal up fine."

Bill never failed to be amazed at the superstitious sun-worshiping Indians' use of the witch doctor's recommendation to put lizard oil on their rotten teeth. He never saw the Indian again and doubts that he followed his instructions. Truly, the region needed more missionaries to bring the Indians the good news of Jesus and to meet their physical needs.

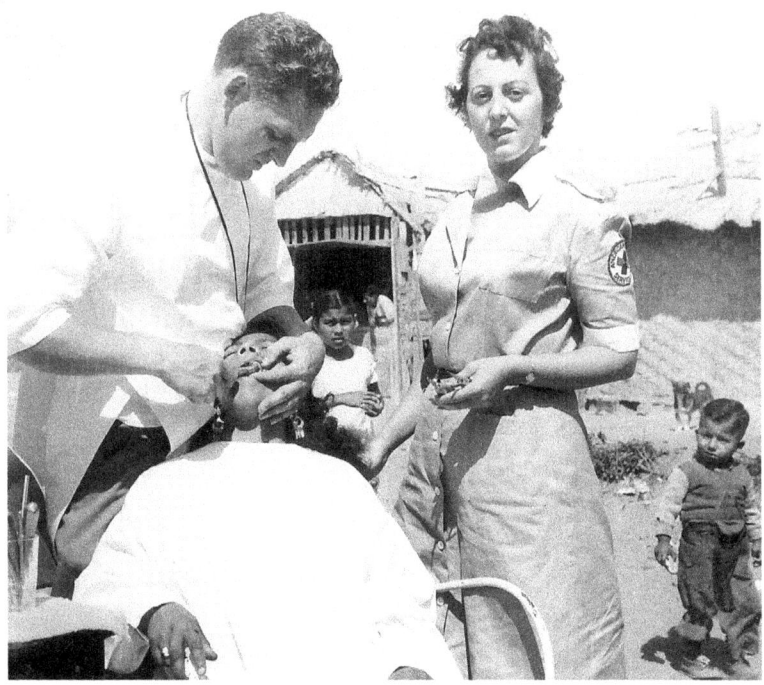

Bill, assisted by his sister (Bonnie) pulling teeth

Pulling rotten teeth was a major problem among the Indians. By the end of that day Bill had pulled about twenty teeth as well as treated others for different needs, and he was getting very tired. Just as he was putting his tools away, Ed came running up with a little two-year-old boy in his arms. As he placed him in Bill's arms, Bill could see he was barely breathing and that he was very weak. He prayed that God would save him, and as the little boy's breathing became stronger, Bill thanked God for hearing and answering his prayer.

Bill asked to be taken to the little boy's home where he could be given more treatment. They took him to a typical Indian hut: a room about eight by ten feet with one bed and a table. The child was placed on the table, and the mother was asked to bring rags for fomentation treatments. While the mother tore up some of her clothing for the rags needed, Bill gave the little boy an injection of penicillin and began the fomentation treatment. Many prayers were offered on behalf of the little boy. About 1:30 in the morning, he was resting well and had taken in a little food for the first time in several days. There was a lot of rejoicing as Bill and Ed left the family and their sleeping son to climb into their own sleeping bags. Just before drifting off to sleep both men thanked God for calling them to be missionaries in Bolivia.

This little boy had pneumonia and his life was saved

****

When Bill returned to the village several years later, this same mother came up to him. She was holding her son's hand and said, "*Señor*, this is my son. You saved his life a few years ago, and I just want to thank you again for all that you did for him that night."

What a thrill it was for Bill to see that this toddler had grown into a big, healthy boy! He silently prayed, *Thank you, Lord, for using me in this special way.*

Sadly things didn't always have a happy ending for the Indians living on those high plains. Many times Bill would see a small procession of Indians moving along the road. As his little red Jeep would draw closer, he would see a small casket being carried and knew it contained a child. This was a common occurrence for Indian families. They know there is little chance of a newborn baby living, so they rarely shed a tear over its death.

These processions always made Bill sad. He knew that if he had not treated the two-year-old little boy's pneumonia when he did he would have been in a coffin, too. Once again he thanked God he had been used to save the boy's life.

Chapter 27

Island of the Bells

"Baptizing them in the name of the Father and of the Son and of the Holy Spirit." Matthew 28:19

Lake Titicaca, at 12,500 feet, is the highest navigable lake in the world. Its color constantly changes from deep green to brilliant blue to dull gray. This giant lake is 3,821 square miles of pure water. The lake is usually peaceful in the mornings, but the gentle waters are often whipped to a frenzy by fierce winds in the afternoons.

The land around the lake is desert-like with water holes now and then. Llamas and other four-footed animals can be seen roaming there, as well as shepherds tending their flocks. The Indians living in this ancient Inca land live in adobe huts. It is very cold at this altitude, and there are not many trees. Animal dung is used for firewood in their clay stoves for warmth or for cooking.

****

Bill's trip to Lake Titicaca was the result of the Indians living on the Island of the Bells asking for a missionary to come and minister to them. Bill was very happy to answer their call. He could see the Island of the Bells in the distance when he arrived at a little village on the shores of the lake. As he attempted to make arrangements to go to the island, a policeman stopped him and said, "You can't go to that island. It's in Peru." Bill thought for a moment, then said, "Well, if I cannot go there, is it all right if I set up my clinic here and treat the sick or pull some teeth?" The policeman gave him permission. As soon as the clinic was set up, people gathered around him hoping he could help them. Bill treated them all. When he was finished, the policeman gave him permission to go to the Island of the Bells.

A couple of Indians soon agreed to take him there in their little boat. Bill wondered what it would be like to visit the island. What kind of people lived

Bill climbing an olive tree at Lake Titicaca

there? What kind of wild animals would be there? These thoughts ran through his mind when an Indian man suddenly picked him up and carried him on his back to the little boat.

Bill was really surprised at this, but he was equally surprised that the authorities would permit such a little boat as this one to sail upon the sometimes dangerous and windy waters of Lake Titicaca. A moment later the Indians placed their long poles into the crystal clear depths of the shimmering waters of this Bolivian lake high in the Andes mountains. Slowly they began to move through the bulrushes to the open lake. Bill thought, *Oh well, the calling is there, and I must answer the challenge even if it is treacherous.*

After riding along for some time over the beautiful blue water, the two Indian men were hungry and began to eat tulle stems. Bill had not eaten for several hours either, and he was hungry, too. The cool crispness of the air seemed to intensify his hunger. He decided he would also try the tulle stems. He found them edible, but not very satisfying.

Bill thought a lot about the beautiful lake as they glided along. In most places he knew the water was about 300 feet deep, but in other places the bottom had never been found. He also knew that a storm could blow up at any moment on this highest navigable lake in the world. This gave him a very insignificant feeling, for he was not being guided by the most skilled boatmen, and their craft was not the strongest.

The wind did come up, and soon they were speeding over the choppy waves to the Island of the Bells. About four hours later, due to the favorable winds, they were within a stone's throw of their destination. This was Bill's first visit, and he was full of questions.

As they drew near the island, a large group of Indian men appeared on the shore. The two Indians accompanying Bill recognized one of them as the chief, who seemed a little apprehensive. When the boat nosed onto the sandy beach, about twenty-five Indians ran toward them, and Bill called out, "*Missioneros! Missioneros!*" (Missionaries! Missionaries!) The Indians had no idea that this strange boat approaching their island carried ambassadors for God, but now a great beam of sunshine came upon their faces, and they began singing a hymn. Bill was thrilled with their warm welcome.

They led him along a narrow trail dotted here and there with humble huts made of adobe blocks stacked one upon another. The roofs of these huts were made of straw, laid on about a foot deep, to keep out the rain. They had no flooring and, unless the owner was well off financially, there were no windows, just a little opening for a door.

When they reached the hut Bill would be calling "home" for awhile, he was shown his bed, which was made of adobe blocks about two feet high. Bill had his bedroll with him, and a woman came in and handed him some sheepskins. Bill wasted no time getting out his can of DDT and spraying them. The woman soon returned and gave Bill some blankets. Bill was taking no chances and quickly sprayed them too, hoping that would take care of all the "cooties" if there were any.

Later, when two Indians came to Bill and asked him to please come and take care of their wounded friend, Bill told them to bring their friend to him. Soon they returned carrying him in a blanket and laid him on the ground for Bill to examine. Bill learned then that the man had been hunting, but his gun had accidentally gone off, shooting him in the leg.

What was Bill to do? He did not have the kind of equipment needed for wounds like this, but he felt he had to do something. A moment later he took a razor blade from his razor to open the wound. Looking around, he saw that one of the Indian women in the crowd had a needle holding her shawl together. When he asked if he could use it, she smiled and gave it to him. Then he noticed another Indian woman spinning wool nearby and asked her if he could have some of her thread. She, too, smiled and willingly gave him some.

Bill built a fire and sterilized his equipment. When that was completed, he told the Indians that he needed to ask God to help him care for the injured man. The Indians understood and gathered in a circle around Bill while he prayed. After prayer Bill proceeded to remove seven or eight bullets. He then made a paste of some of the sulfa tablets he had brought with him, laid the paste in the wound, and bandaged the man's leg. He also gave him an injection of penicillin.

The next day Bill told Bible stories to the Indians. When he asked if there was anyone who would like to be baptized, an entire family stood up: a husband, his wife, and a fifteen-year-old son. Bill thought to himself, *What a good little family group.* When Bill asked the father and mother rather difficult doctrinal questions, they replied in the Indian dialect, "Ask our son; he will tell you."

Juan had gone to school in one of the 150 Adventist schools in Bolivia, and he responded in good, clear Spanish. Bill soon realized that this family was prepared for baptism and Juan, the son, was the most prepared of the three. Then came a moment of sadness, which Bill could never understand. The father said, "We are ready for baptism, but you cannot baptize Juan. He is too young."

"Too young?" Bill questioned. "He knows the doctrines by heart. He can repeat the entire law and has answered everything for you folks."

"Well," his father said, "we want him to wait." Juan, with tears in his eyes, knew he would have to wait to be baptized.

Bill asked Juan's parents the last question, "Where did you learn the message?"

Their answer surprised Bill. "Last year we went to the Peruvian mainland and studied there nearly every week with an Adventist teacher." Yes, they had crossed the lake many times in their little boat learning the words of truth, and the pastor had blessed them and given them entrance into God's church family.

It was a great thrill for Bill to see the members of the little church on the Island of the Bells gather along the shore of sparkling blue Lake Titicaca and sing the baptismal hymns. But Juan was not happy, for he had wanted so much to be baptized, too. Bill asked Juan's father again to let Juan be baptized, but he gave the same answer. The parents had made their decision, and Juan had to wait.

To Bill, Lake Titicaca was one of the most beautiful lakes he had ever seen, and he was very excited about the baptisms that took place that day. They were the first that had taken place there in more than five years. The Indians rejoiced, also. The four-feet deep waters of the lake were so clear that day that Bill could actually count the toes of the newly baptized Indians. It was a day to remember.

When the time came to board the boat again and head for home, Juan clung to Bill's hand and pleaded, "Please, please return next year and baptize me." Bill promised he would do his best. Then he waved another goodbye as the little boat moved away from the Island of the Bells.

Bill did not forget Juan, but Juan had to wait more than a year to be baptized because of the bloody revolution in La Paz. This event forced Juan and his family to move away from their straw-roofed adobe hut. Juan faithfully attended the Indian church in the capital city of La Paz, and he became a frequent visitor to Bill's office. The happy day came when Bill baptized him. However, they were both sad that his baptism had not been celebrated in the beautiful sapphire waters of Lake Titicaca.

****

One of the most interesting things Bill saw while on the Island of the Bells was the wooden lock on his door. It and the wooden key had both been made by hand, and it really locked and unlocked. He brought one home with him and enjoyed showing it off many times when he spoke of his experiences at camp meetings and other places.

Bill cherishes the memories of serving the Master in the highlands of Bolivia. Seeing precious souls find Jesus, each in their own special way, glorified God, and Bill rejoiced.

He also cherished the times he was able to treat the people's physical ailments. And based on their appreciation and requests for additional treatment, it was clear that Bill was conducting an important work. In fact, years later Bill received word from the man he had operated on at Lake Titicaca that he wanted Bill to come back and take out another bullet. Sadly, Bill was never able to return, but he hoped that another young missionary had been able to get there and remove the bullet.

Chapter 28

Revolution

"You will hear of wars and rumors of wars." Matthew 24:6

June was pregnant and Bill had come home to spend the Easter celebration with her and little Gary. On the Wednesday prior to Good Friday in 1952, he got up bright and early to take his good friend, Carlos (Sérgio) Bendrell to the *El Alto* station to catch the train back to his home in Cochabamba, Bolivia. While he was gone, June was busy with her daily chores while talking with her good friend, Rebecca Goldhammer, a Chilean nurse. She worked at the Seventh-day Adventist hospital in Chulumani and stayed with them when she came up to La Paz to buy supplies for the hospital.

When Bill returned home, he had a puzzled look on his face. June asked, "What's wrong?"

He shrugged his shoulders and said he was not sure but something seemed to be out of the ordinary in the downtown section of La Paz. The streets were deserted, and there were no street sweepers with their little short brooms cleaning the debris from the main thoroughfares. He told her about seeing a couple of men with black armbands around the upper part of their arms. They had stopped a taxi cab and quickly taken possession of it.

Bill was impressed that he should not leave home that day. A short time later they were shocked to hear the sound of machine gun fire. The sound seemed to be coming from the direction of a nearby residential area. At the sound of more and more guns being fired, they all wondered, *What is happening?*

It was not long before they heard machine guns being fired again. This time the shells seemed to be flying over the church next door and their home. Little Gary was frightened and began crying. June and Bill did their best to comfort him, and so did Rebecca. Kneeling down, they prayed that God would send angels to protect them. Soon Gary's tears stopped streaming down his rosy cheeks. God had answered their prayer.

Rebecca was a jewel of a friend to Bill and June. She was always so cheerful and helpful around the house and with little Gary when she visited them. Her grandparents and mother were American, so she had grown up speaking English. Sadly her grandmother had died in the 1906 San Francisco earthquake and fire. Her

June is wearing a Bolivian outfit

grandfather and mother survived. Later, her grandfather's job with the American government took them to South America. While living in Chile, Rebecca's mother had met and married a Brazilian German, and from this union Rebecca had been born. With this background Rebecca was fluent in English and Spanish, and was very helpful in correcting Bill and June's Spanish.

Thursday afternoon they again heard the sound of more guns being fired. When they began hearing the ambulance sirens carrying the wounded to the clinics, they realized there must be a revolution. It was getting dark when they discovered there was no electricity. There were no lights, no possibility of using the electric stove, and the refrigerator could not function. If the electricity was not restored, they would lose their frozen food. To make matters worse, their water had been shut off. Fortunately, they kept boiled water on hand for drinking, so they did have some water. Rebecca suggested they turn on the faucet in the bathtub just in case the water came on again during the night.

Little Gary and Bill were beginning to get hungry. Bill got out their little primus, a little round stove that had a receptacle that could be filled with *ron*, a type of fuel. Bill used the attached pump to pump up the pressure, then he lit it with a match, and soon they had light and a good flame for June to do a little cooking. June was a very good cook and soon had a delicious meal prepared for them.

They all went to bed early that night, but sleep was fragmented as the noise of the machine guns was constant. Sometime during the night Bill heard the sound of running water. He jumped up quickly and put the plug in the tub. The next morning they praised God for His promise, "His bread will be supplied, and water will not fail him" (Isaiah 33:16).

The fighting continued the next day, so it was impossible to go outside or run errands. From time to time during the day, they could hear tiles falling from the roof of the church next door and ambulance sirens screeching their sad mission.

Suddenly they heard something! Someone was at their gate! Who was it? Bill went to investigate and found that it was one of their church members, nineteen-year-old José. He had been sitting on the curb outside of his house when a bullet struck him on the left side of his nose and exited by his right eye. The clinics were full, so he decided to come to Bill and June for help. He came to the right place, for Rebecca was there and tenderly treated José's wounds the best she could before putting him to bed.

Friday morning the machine gun noise seemed to be subsiding. By noon they heard that the revolution had ended, and they thanked God for that. When all was quiet, Rebecca suggested to Bill that they go to the nearby clinic to see how the wounded were being treated. Bill thought that was a good idea, so he picked up the key to the lock on the huge wrought iron gate at the entrance to their property. They said goodbye and left June to care for little Gary alone.

When they reached the clinic, they saw many wounded men and heard their moans and groans. Rebecca asked the clinic personnel why they were not giving them medication for their pain. When they did not give her an answer, she went looking for the right medication and was soon administering the needed help to the wounded men.

It was only a short time after Bill and Rebecca had left when June heard someone rattling their big iron gate with great force. When she looked out and saw four officers neatly dressed in khaki with swords at their sides, she was instantly filled with fear. June's mind raced furiously. *What shall I do?"* she thought. Finally, she decided to go to the gate.

The officers stopped rattling the gate when they saw her coming toward them. June very calmly asked what they wanted. One of the officers said, "We want to search your house as we have been told there is a colonel from the opposite side of the conflict hiding in there."

June shook her head as she said, "No, *señors*, there is no one hiding in our house."

They did not believe her and insisted she open the gate so they could search the house. June told them she did not have the key to unlock the gate and that they would have to climb over the big iron gate if they were going to search the house. Much to June's surprise, the four officers began climbing over the iron gate. She thought they would tear their clothes on the pointed iron spikes, but they did not. As soon as they entered the house, they began searching behind the sofa and chairs, under the dining room table, the kitchen area, every closet, and every room. When they saw the unmade bed where José had been, June explained that he had just been taken to the clinic.

The officers were ready to leave just as Bill and Rebecca returned. As Bill unlocked the gate, one of the officers asked him to unlock the church too, so they could search the church tower. Bill quietly opened the church door. The officers looked around but decided not to search the tower because climbing it would be difficult. Everyone breathed a sigh of relief as they watched the officers leave with their swords rattling by their sides. Praise God! The revolution was over, and they were safely in their home again. It had turned out to be a very good Good Friday after all.

They learned later that the nine-story building only a block away was not an apartment building but a building that housed the offices of the minister of defense for the Bolivian government. The army and police force were at odds with each other and had decided to fight it out. No one knows to this day who won the war. It seems that in Bolivia fighting like that is the way they demonstrate their anger. Sadly, 3,000 men were wounded and 1,000 died in the conflict during the three days of fighting.

Bill, June, Rebecca, and Gary were very thankful that the revolution was over. Water was flowing again, and the electricity had been restored. After dinner that night, they once again knelt down and thanked God for His angels that had so lovingly protected them through this restless time.

Not long after that, Bill and June had something else for which to be very thankful. On July 15, 1952, they became the proud parents of their second child: a bouncing seven-pound, six-ounce baby boy whom they named Dennis Keith. What a blessed addition he was to the family!

Chapter 29

Time for a Vacation

"Praise the name of the LORD, for he commanded and they were created He set them in place for ever and ever." Psalm 148:5, 6

The Jamerson family had been in Bolivia for a little more than a year, and now that the local revolution was over and peace reigned, they began looking forward to their first six-week vacation in the mission field. They wanted to go where they could be warm on the seashore, away from the cold like they experienced at the 12,000-feet elevation of La Paz, Bolivia.

After being told that the mission owned a three-story red building in the center of a small seaside city, they decided that was the place for their vacation. They quickly packed their bags, boarded the train in La Paz, and were on the way. When they reached Guaqui on the shore of Lake Titicaca, they boarded a steamer that carried them across the beautiful blue lake to Puno, Peru. They saw many beautiful sights on their trip, and they praised their Creator for this blessing.

Gary and Dennis crossing Lake Titicaca

After crossing the lake, they boarded another train for a full day trip to Arequipa. It was a nice comfortable trip, but there was not much to see on the way except a few llamas being herded by Indian families. The Indians were dressed in their colorful native costumes. Occasionally a vicuña ran gracefully across the plateau.

Just before the train entered the city of Arequipa, they saw the beautiful snowcapped Misti volcano—what a sight. It was so beautiful against the blue of the sky. They looked forward to spending a few days in this beautiful city so they could adjust to the lower altitude. Now they were here and hoped the snowcapped volcano would remain quiet and calm.

After a week of resting and seeing the sights, they boarded the train for the last part of their journey to the sleepy little seaport city of Mollendo where they could bask on the beach and swim in the ocean. Oh how good it was to be out of the cold and the high altitude of La Paz.

They had no problem finding the three-story red building next to the town's plaza.

June, Dennis & Gary with Misti in the background

Bill took out the key and unlocked the main door. The building had no elevator, so they had no choice but to carry their belongings up to the third floor. After opening the door and stepping inside, the first thing Bill saw was a large opening in the wall facing the ocean. He dropped the luggage and said, "Wow! Look at that view!"

Just then he heard June say, "Oh no." Turning away from the view, Bill saw tears in her eyes. June's mother had taught her that cleanliness is next to godliness, and this vacation motel was far from what she had expected. Pigeon droppings were on the floor, the furniture, and the bed! Everything was a mess. Bill put his arms around her to comfort her and said, "Please don't cry, honey. I will go to the store and get some disinfectant. I will clean everything up until it's all spotless. OK?"

When he returned with the cleaning supplies, June and little Gary pitched in to help. It took a lot of hard work for them to mop the floors and clean the furniture. June found clean linens in a cupboard. After making the bed, they all stood back and thanked God for helping them get the place in a livable condition.

Just then four-year-old Gary asked, "Where is the bathroom?" Bill had not thought of that, so he went in search of that special room. He finally found it on the second floor. It was well equipped with a large drum and a bucket to dip out the brown water to pour into the toilet. What an interesting experience for this American missionary family. One they would never forget.

They were hot and tired after cleaning their penthouse, but it was a beautiful day, so they changed into their swimsuits, went downstairs, and walked to the ocean. Not many people were there, but a Peruvian man came over and greeted them. Then he said, "Young fella', you need to learn to swim." With that said, he picked up Gary and threw him into the water. Quicker than lightning Bill jumped in and pulled Gary to safety. That day Gary began his daily swimming lessons, and what fun he had.

Bill loved to go fishing, so he went out a couple of times to try his luck. But it seemed the fish did not like his technique, so he quit. Sitting before the large opening in their penthouse apartment wall was so restful and peaceful that he and June spent a lot of time just looking at the ocean.

One morning as Bill was looking out the large opening in the wall, he noticed that a ship had come into the harbor. He thought it was the SS Santa Juana, the same ship that had brought them to the mission field a year ago. Bill asked June to take a look to see if it really was and when she did, she said, "Yes, it is the SS Santa Juana! Let's go see if we can get on board and see Captain Lindholm."

When they arrived at the pier, they saw a small boat going back and forth from the ship. Bill did not hesitate to ask if he and his family could be taken out there to see their friend, the captain. Before they knew it they were on their way to the ship. After coming aboard, they met Captain Lindholm. What a greeting they received, and what a great visit they had with him. He told them of his travels around South America and how they could always find Coca-Cola, Singer sewing machines, and Seventh-day Adventist churches—what a unique combination. But the part about Adventist churches was very good news to Bill. It was also great to see the old crew was still aboard. It was great fun visiting with them.

When it was time to say goodbye, the captain reached for a large box filled with grapes and other fresh fruits and handed it to Bill. Bill was elated! They had really missed these familiar fruits during their year in Bolivia, and they were very thankful. Bill asked, "Is it possible for us to get these fruits off the ship?"

The captain replied, "No problem, I'll take care of it." And he did. His Peruvian workers were quickly given cigarettes, and after that there was no problem of any kind.

When the Jamerson family returned to their red-mansion-penthouse-apartment that day with their treasure of fresh fruits, it was like Christmas. What a treat. Oh, how good it was to taste those old familiar fruits. When they arrived back at their vacation home they had another surprise. Other missionary families had moved into the other apartments—one family from Argentina, and one from Peru. What great fun they had together after getting acquainted. Swimming, table games, and picnics. It was all so good.

Bill and June looked forward to going to the plaza in the evenings. Sometimes they would hear a radio playing "God Bless America," which always made them a little homesick.

All too soon their vacation was over, and they were on their way back to cold La Paz. It had been a wonderful vacation. As they remembered why they had come to South America, they felt blessed and thanked God for the beautiful world He had created and for the opportunity He had given them to win souls for Him.

****

Over the course of their ministry in Bolivia, Captain Lindholm brought them boxes of items they needed and were unable to purchase locally. They treasured these items similar to the things June's parents always sent. What a friend Captain Lindholm was to them. Bill and June were always so appreciative of his thoughtfulness.

Chapter 30

Amasias Justiniano

"You have been faithful with a few things; I will put you in charge of many things." Matthew 25:21

Jose Amasias Justiniano. This name means nothing to most people, but to Seventh-day Adventists in South America, he is regarded as a great man who started with nothing and succeeded in doing great things for the glory of God.

He was born and raised in the oriental part of the tropical Amazon region of Bolivia, which borders the country of Brazil. Portuguese was frequently spoken there, so Amasias learned to speak that language fluently. This was a great help to him later when he became a colporteur selling books. His mother, Corina Cuellar, and father, Marcelino Justiniano, often called their beloved son, "Pepito." Amasias' father raised and sold cattle and untamed horses.

One day in the early 1950s, Amasias' mother wrote a letter to a lady asking her to repay the money she was owed. Then she asked Amasias to take the letter to her. This lady lived some distance away and suffered from leprosy. Amasias was an obedient fourteen-year-old son and bravely mounted the horse his father prepared for him.

Amasias' horse gently trotted along the road over the barren plains of Bolivia and, two hours later he arrived at the lady's home. Amasias quickly dismounted and knocked at the door. A moment later he politely presented his mother's letter to the lady. After reading the letter, the lady handed Amasias the money she owed. He thanked her and quickly wrapped the money in several banana leaves in order not to touch it more than necessary. Then he mounted his horse, waved goodbye, and turned for home.

The horse and rider were about halfway home when the horse became frightened by a nearby puma and began running at full speed. Suddenly, the animal stepped into a hole and fell, which sent Amasias sprawling. He lay unconscious for a short time. Fortunately, a traveler who was passing by stopped and administered first aid to Amasias' badly injured leg. Then he helped him mount his uninjured horse, which had been quietly eating nearby.

Amasias' parents could see that their son was in a lot of pain as soon as he arrived home, so they quickly helped him into bed. Amasias' mother began to do everything she could to make him comfortable while his father took care of the horse.

Several days passed but the pain in Amasias' leg did not go away. They took him to the local hospital in Magdalena. The hospital had no X-ray machine and could not accurately diagnose his problem. However, they treated him for various conditions, one of which was for a snake bite which they thought could be the reason his leg was so swollen that he could not walk.

Some time later a missionary by the name of Mr. Walter arrived. When he looked at Amasias' leg, he recognized that it was infected. As he made a small incision and drained the wound, he told Amasias' parents to take him to *el Hospital de Guayarmerin de los Adventistas*, where the doctor in charge, Dr. Elmer Bottsford, would be able to treat his leg. Amasias' father believed Mr. Walter and immediately sold four cows to pay for Amasias' plane ticket there and money for his expenses.

There was no one waiting for Amasias when he arrived at Guayarmerin, and there were no taxis in those days to take him to the hospital. Unknown by anyone, God was already working in a special way for Amasias, for He alone could see the future of this young man.

Nearby was a man with a two-wheeled cart. Amasias explained to him that he could not walk and needed to go to the hospital. He asked the man if he would take him there. The man agreed and helped him onto his two-wheeled cart. What a strange sight it was to see a patient, seated in a two-wheeled cart, arriving at the hospital. Amasias did not mind though, he was just thankful to be there.

After being admitted, Ana Marker, the director of nurses, and another nurse named Bernita, soon helped Amasias settle in his room. Ana's husband was the chaplain of the hospital. When he visited Amasias, he told him not to worry because he would talk to the treasurer of the hospital and Dr. Bottsford, the medical director, and everything would be handled.

The next day the treasurer of the hospital and Pastor Marker told Dr. Bottsford about the young patient's badly injured leg. Dr. Bottsford immediately went to see Amasias. After examining the wounded leg, the doctor told him it was very fortunate that he had come to his hospital because they had just purchased a new X-ray machine, and a patient, like him, was needed to test the machine's capabilities. Amasias was very happy to hear that news.

After looking at the X-rays the next day, Dr. Bottsford told him he had very serious osteomyelitis, inflammation of the bone or bone marrow, but that he would operate on his leg anyway. In fact, the doctor performed two surgeries on his leg. Thanks to his skills and God, Amasias did not lose his leg.

Amasias worked two years in the hospital to pay for his surgeries and his living expenses. During this time he studied and learned all he could about nursing from Dr. Bottsford. The most beautiful part of this time spent with the doctor was that he learned to know and love Jesus as his personal Savior.

Amasias was now eighteen years of age. He was a humble, dedicated, sensible, responsible young man and had a great deal of mercy for the patients. Dr. Bottsford saw the potential in him to be a future minister for God, like Timothy in the

New Testament. He told him about the Seventh-day Adventist college in Vinto, Cochabamba, Bolivia, where students studied to prepare themselves to become ministers. Then he said, "I am not rich, but if you would like to go there, I will pay your tuition and help you with your expenses until you can manage on your own." Amasias was thrilled and soon found himself in a plane on the way to Cochabamba.

He was a good student who studied and learned all he could, but he knew he would need to earn money for his future schooling. But what should he do? He prayed, and that summer God impressed him to go to La Paz to see Pastor Bill Jamerson, the director of the Indian Mission Stations. Bill was impressed with Amasias and took him on several of his mission trips, teaching him how to treat the Indians' physical illnesses, how to pull teeth, and how to communicate with them.

When they returned from their last mission trip together, Bill gave him permission to buy medical supplies on his account with the two pharmaceutical labs in La Paz. Amasias was so thankful and praised God for this blessing as he hurried out to buy his supplies. As soon as the medicines were packed in boxes and strapped on the back of his mule, he was on his way to the villages on the Altiplano ready to treat the sick or wounded.

Amasias charged the Indians for treatment and the medication. What was left after covering the cost of the medications belonged to him. This was how he could afford to pay for his ministerial training when he returned to the Vinto Seventh-day Adventist College.

He spent the next summer colporteuring in the mines of the southern part of Bolivia. He sold many books there and praised God that he could speak some Portuguese. This ability helped him earn two or three scholarships. The people at the college called him *patino* (silver) because he earned so much money.

Amasias and his friend, Edgar Cortez, who had also earned scholarships, traveled to La Paz for a month's vacation. The director of the colporteur work congratulated them on their scholarships. When they left La Paz, they traveled to Chulumani, Bolivia, a territory in the south where tropical flowers and delicious tropical fruits grow. There was also a government hospital operated by Seventh-day Adventists and administered by Drs. Del Emery and Elmer Bottsford.

One day Amasias and Edgar went to a place nearby called Choylia where they became acquainted with a mother and her lovely daughter, Lydia Escelia Cordero-Telleria. Amasias fell in love with Lydia, and eventually they were married.

Amasias finished his ministerial courses in Bolivia, and then decided to continue his studies at Union College, now a university, near Lima, Peru. By this time God had given him three children. This was a difficult financial time for Amasias and Lydia, but he was determined to finish his advanced ministerial course at Union College. Bill Koenig was the farm director of the college at that time. With his blessings, Amasias was able to work on the school's farm until he graduated. Bill always found him to be very reliable and trustworthy with whatever work he did.

Amasias diligently studied and finished his ministerial course. He then became an evangelist. He was an excellent evangelist and the Inca Union appointed him head evangelist for Peru, Bolivia, and Ecuador. Amasias was so successful in his ministry as an evangelist that the South American Division called this Bolivian young man to be the ministerial secretary for the entire South American Division.

So, because of a broken leg, a missionary doctor, a great love for Jesus, and a strong determination to work hard, Amasias was able to cover some of the Andes with medical work, go to school, and teach the good news of Jesus' love to all who would listen. God blessed Amasias and used his hunger to win souls for Him and bless South America.

****

After thirty-nine years of service to the church, Amasias passed away June 8, 1998. He is sleeping until that great day when the dead in Christ will be called from their graves, and he will see Jesus face to face and be with his family and the thousands he brought to know Christ. What a day of rejoicing that will be when we can all make friends with this great soul winner.

Amasias is survived by his wife and three children. Lydia lives in Loma Linda, California, near her daughter. One of the things that brings her joy these days is singing in the choir. Amasias' legacy lives on through his children: Anita is the wife of Randy Roberts, pastor of the Loma Linda University Church; Samuel is a cardiologist working in Mexico; and Mirtha works in San Jose, California, as a Spanish translator for large companies.

Chapter 31

Guaynay—"Bible Readings for the Home"

"Do not fear, for I am with you." Isaiah 41:10

"Bill, you must go to Guaynay. The South American Division sent a letter to Ed Clifford stating that there are people ready for baptism, and they are anxiously waiting for a Seventh-day Adventist missionary to visit them."

Bill wanted to go even though he had just returned by mule from a long trip into the jungle to visit and baptize people in San Pablo. That had been a three-day trip by mule each way. Now, another jungle trip! He wondered how June and Gary would accept this.

June was a great missionary's wife, and she agreed to the assignment right away, not realizing it was a very dangerous trip: jungle trails, mules crossing rivers, rafting down rivers, and plenty of walking. The day came when Bill had to say goodbye to his family in La Paz again and go off with his Indian worker in his little red Jeep.

After an hour of driving, they came to a tree lying across the road. They parked the Jeep, gathered all their equipment, and started walking. Walking was common to Bill from his military service, so he didn't mind continuing the trip on foot. They had only walked a short distance when they met a group of Indians. Bill was the only white man and thought that he would not be accepted, so he did not mingle with them. His Indian worker walked among them and hired a mule for the next leg of their trip.

As Bill laid in his sleeping bag that night, his heart suddenly began to beat faster when he thought he saw something. Unsure about the crowd around him, he prayed about it. When he awakened the next morning and found he had made it safely through the night, he said, "Thank you, Jesus, for always being near me."

The next day was another day of walking and following the mule, which was loaded with their belongings. They came to a river that had to be crossed. Bill had heard of piranhas, fish that swim in groups and can attack a person and, in a very short time, strip and eat a body, so he was very nervous. What should he do? They had to cross the river because seven souls were waiting to be baptized.

Bill led the way and slowly removed his clothing. He made a pack of them, put it on his head, and bravely started across the river, praying all the time that the angels of the Lord would encamp around them. Suddenly he felt something brush by his leg! He held his breath! Could it be a fish ready to devour him? But nothing happened. He let out his breath and thanked God for His protection.

They traveled many hours before arriving at the Indian village of Santa Fe. The Indians came out to visit. Bill realized they were Aymara Indians from their home in the highlands of Bolivia. He could hardly believe there were Seventh-day Adventists who had left the windy 13,000-feet plateaus to seek the warm weather of the tropics. What a wonderful experience.

Bill and the workers enjoyed passing the Sabbath with the Santa Fe church members and eating the good food they provided. But they couldn't stay long as there were seven souls waiting for his visit, and there was more jungle walking ahead.

A little later one of the Indians said, "You can walk two days, or we can make a raft and float down the river, but it will be dangerous in the rapids." Bill decided floating by raft on the river would be better than walking up and down through the hot jungles for the next two days. That wasn't anything to look forward to. He would take his chances with the river.

As Bill walked to the river, he saw what he called his "fifty-cent raft" made from small logs. "That's not for us!" Bill said. "It's too small and too narrow."

They said, "Pastor, we can take vines and tie on some more logs. That will work." And that's what they did! When it was finished, they put their things in rubber bags and got on board the raft. One Indian boy sat up front and the other one sat in the back to control the raft.

All was going well and the rapids were presenting no problems. But one of the boys shouted, "The worst one is ahead!" Suddenly they hit the rapid and the raft quickly spun around. Then Bill heard a cracking sound. The raft was breaking, but the boys were able to get it to shore. What would they do now?

They found more poles, tied them together, and were on their way again. Things were easy ahead, and they arrived at their destination. An Indian man was waiting on the shore for the missionaries to come. He led them to a home and gave them fresh, delicious food to eat.

Within a few hours Bill's feet began to hurt. *What is this all about?* he wondered. They were badly swollen, and he could barely walk. He soon realized that his feet had been exposed to too much sun on the raft and were severely sunburned!

For the next few days he could barely walk. Each night he would sit on a chair and preach the good news to the Indians. After teaching them each evening, Bill thought, *These people know the Bible so well. How did they get ready for baptism?* He finally asked them how they had learned of the Bible, and what a story they told.

One of the men answered, "A man came here many years ago and stayed for awhile. He showed our father a book called *Bible Readings for the Home*. My father bought the book. Many years passed and then he died. One day we decided to go through his things and found the book. We studied it, accepted all it taught us, and desired to be baptized. There was an address in the book, so we sent a letter, and now you are here to baptize us."

Bill baptized those precious souls in that beautiful river, and joy filled their hearts. Bill marveled at the way God had worked in the lives of these people, and he thought, *Yes, God can finish the work in His own way.*

As the days passed, Bill began to get homesick for his family. He prayed that God would let him go home soon. Bill told the new church members it was time for him to return to La Paz. They brought a mule and put a saddle on it, and Bill headed down the trail for the airport in Guaynay, a one-day journey. Riding on a mule is not as easy as it appears. After traveling a few miles, Bill began sliding off the saddle and over the head of the mule. The Indians said, "Sorry, pastor; we will fix it." A few more miles and Bill was sliding over the head of the mule and onto the ground again. "That's it," Bill said, "I will walk the rest of the way to the airport." And he did.

Not knowing where to go when he arrived in Guaynay, he approached a man who was part of a large group of people and said, "There are no roads here. How can we get to La Paz?"

The stranger replied, "We are all waiting to go to La Paz. The airplane is over there. It brought in passengers and supplies, but now we are waiting for the weather to clear again so we can leave." Then he added, "The airstrip is very small as you can see, and a few planes have crashed on takeoff. You can still see them by the side of the air strip."

Unexpectedly, Bill heard his name over a loudspeaker, "*Señor* Jamerson."

That is interesting, he thought. *Who could know my name in this jungle? Should I answer the call?* He decided to head to the office and see what was going on. Once he informed the workers in the office that he was *Señor* Jamerson, he was informed that he could get on the plane that the crowd of people were waiting for and fly to La Paz. *Is this for real?* he thought.

Then they shouted, "Get going!"

He followed their orders and quickly boarded the plane. As he sat down, he said, "Thank you, Jesus!" Bill then asked the pilot, "When are we leaving?"

The pilot replied, "When we can. It could be days or a few minutes. The Andes are covered with clouds, and it is impossible to leave right now as I see it."

Bill was so homesick that he asked the pilot, "Can we try leaving now? I want to get home and see my family."

The pilot thought for a moment and then replied, "OK, we'll try."

The people cheered as they boarded the plane, and as soon as they were buckled in their seats, the pilot took the plane as far down the runway as he could. The motors roared and a moment later they were off the ground. The pilot made many circles to gain altitude so they could climb over the Andes. The sky was still cloudy. Everyone was nervous, and the passengers prayed as they held on to their prayer books and beads. Bill was worried, too, but he prayed to his heavenly Father, "Oh God, please get us to La Paz."

Suddenly the clouds opened, and the plane soared through the clear sky. No sooner had it gained altitude when it began to go down. *What is happening?* Bill thought. But when he looked out the window, he saw the city of La Paz below them. The plane landed a few minutes later. The airline owner came out to welcome everyone and asked the pilot, "Are you going to return?"

He answered, "No, never! The weather is too terrible up there. I took the one and only opening in the heavy cloud cover and made it. But never again."

Bill thanked God he had made it safely home at last. He later learned that his friend, Charles Christensen, had purchased his ticket on that plane. He thought, *In all thy ways acknowledge Him and He will direct your path.* God's timing was always perfect!

Chapter 32

God to the Rescue

"Ask and it will be given to you." Matthew 7:7

Charles Christensen was a Seventh-day Adventist missionary who had hopes of establishing a school, church, and evangelism center in Oruro, Bolivia, a very large city at about 13,000-feet elevation. He later became president of the Bolivian Mission. Money was raised, and Charles soon found a great place to start his project in the center of the city. After purchasing the property, the government renters said they would vacate their offices the next day. But tomorrow never seems to come to some people, especially for government renters, so Charles wondered how he would ever get them to move.

A little while later he came to La Paz and asked Bill to accompany him to Oruro to help move the renters. They both knew it would be an almost impossible chore. But after much prayer they were impressed that all things were possible with God. He would come to their rescue. They must first do whatever they could do and faithfully put their trust in Him.

A few days later they were traveling across the Altiplano on the rough dirt roads. They frequently saw children wearing colorful woolen caps while they tended the family sheep. Occasionally they saw an Indian man and his wife with their llamas carrying fifty or more pounds of goods on their backs.

They also saw some beautiful and colorful llamas. Some were brown and white and others were black and white. Llamas are not very courteous creatures to strangers and frequently spit at people if disturbed. Bill and Charles had learned that lesson the hard way so they always gave them plenty of room and respect.

After a day of traveling the treeless and barren terrain of the Altiplano, they were happy to see the city of Oruro in the distance. The job ahead of Bill and Charles was not something they were eagerly anticipating, but they planned to do the best they could and wait for the Lord to do what they could not.

Early the next day Bill and Charles visited each regular renter. All were willing to move out for the sake of a new school in their city. Then Bill and Charles approached the government offices. They expected many excuses because they had occupied the offices for years. But the renters quietly explained that they were more than willing to move; however, they had much furniture and equipment with no place to move to and it could take a year or two before they could move.

Bill and Charles knew that there was an empty place just down the road that would suit the government offices just fine, but what could they do about it? Suddenly God impressed them to go to the Canadian Electric Company in town. Perhaps they would have a solution to their problem. So the two men went directly to their office and had a nice chat with the very friendly Canadians.

God was already working on their hearts. When they heard about the plans for a new school in their city, they said, "Sure. We will be happy to take our trucks, cranes, and any other necessary equipment. We can have them moved out and into their new offices in only one day." What good news! And what a blessing!

Bill and Charles were thrilled and quickly made arrangements for the new offices. They returned to the renters and gave them the good news about the electric company's willingness to move them to their new office in just one day at no cost to them. They readily agreed. The following day Bill and Charles were thrilled as they watched the big rigs and crane pull up in front of their building. What a joy it was to see that crane lowering the furniture and equipment down the outside of the building and moving it all into the truck. By the end of the day the renters were happily occupying their new offices. Bill and Charles thanked God for solving their problem so quickly and for helping them to faithfully trust in His promises.

With that problem settled, Bill gladly helped Charles with his plans for the new Seventh-day Adventist school before returning to La Paz. Soon the new school was ready to enroll students. All possible because of God's rich blessings.

Chapter 33

The Mines of Bolivia

"Freely you have received, freely give." Matthew 10:8

At that time Sérgio Bendrell, a Peruvian by birth, was in charge of all the publishing work at the Bolivian Seventh-day Adventist Mission. He lived in Cochabamba, Bolivia, but frequently came to La Paz. He always stayed with Bill and June when he came to La Paz, which was always a joy for them. He was such a delightful person and soon became Bill's best friend. His greatest talent was working with people. It seemed he always knew the right things to say so people felt very comfortable when they were in his company.

Sérgio never turned down the opportunity to be Bill's companion when he took his little red Jeep in the mission field. Sérgio accompanied Bill on his yearly trip to the mines of Bolivia. Most of the mines were owned by foreigners and mined for gold, tin, or other metals.

As Bill and Sérgio traveled, they saw very little vegetation on the Altiplano. Occasionally, they saw small Indian villages with adobe huts and roofs covered with straw. Trucks, loaded to the top with all kinds of goods, would pass them. These trucks never failed to have several Aymara Indians sitting on top of their loads. The women, dressed in very colorful skirts and shawls, sometimes had a baby in their arms or hanging on their back.

That seemed very dangerous to Bill. He was fully aware of what could happen when you hit one of the big holes in the Bolivian dirt roads. The Indians watched for these holes, and when they would see one, they would call out, "Watch it." To Americans, this sounded like "watchee," so they called all potholes "watchees."

Bill and Sérgio finally arrived at one of the mines in Bolivia. Though exhausted from their hard trip, they went directly to the main office. Sérgio, speaking in Spanish, informed the mine director that they were on their annual trip to the mine to collect money to aid in the operation of the Seventh-day Adventist Bolivian missions, including their educational and medical work. The mine director knew them from their yearly visits, and he welcomed them. He then gave his donation and said they could eat and sleep there at the mine's expense. Bill and Sérgio graciously thanked him and went to the rooms provided for them. That night they enjoyed a welcomed good night's rest.

The next morning Bill and Sérgio were up bright and early, ready to carry out their plans for the day. Most of the mine's foreign engineers spoke English, so Bill visited with them in their homes. At the end of their time together, he always asked for contributions to help the mission work in Bolivia, and he usually received checks from $25 to $100.

One family in particular was unforgettable. After telling them of their work in Bolivia and displaying pictures, they were preparing to say goodnight when the husband turned to his wife and said, "Wife, we have some tithe money saved. This is such a great work, let's donate it to this project." His wife happily agreed, and when she returned to the room, she placed $250 in Bill's hand. What a gift! God had surely touched their hearts in a special way.

Bill and Sérgio visited other families and always ended by asking them for contributions to help the mission work in Bolivia. They received funds every time but none ever equaled the generosity of that one special family.

God had impressed Sérgio with an idea a few years prior, and he said, "Bill, why don't we go down in the mines and see if each worker would be willing to donate one day's work to help educate the children?" Bill thought it was a great idea and requested permission to go down in the mines. God had already worked on the hearts of the officials, and they quickly cleared the way for Sérgio and Bill to enter the mines.

Bill and Sérgio were excited as they dressed in the clothing they were required to wear in the mine. They stopped at each level as they were let down under the surface of the earth while the boss at each level graciously allowed the workers to gather around them. As Bill showed the pictures, Sérgio spoke to them in Spanish. Many of them shouted out, *"Una Mita."* This meant that they were very happy to pledge the salary of one day's work so their country would have new schools for their children. What generous gifts these workers pledged.

Bill and Sérgio were so happy with the workers' generosity that they had not noticed it was getting hotter at each level. When they realized how hot they were and saw it was 115 degrees, they told the boss they were ready to be taken above ground. When they saw the blue Bolivian sky, they took a deep breath of fresh air and thanked God for His many blessings.

After leaving the mine area, they went to the main office. The treasurer had already been told of the men's pledges to donate one day's work for building schools in little villages. He was surprised so many had made this pledge, but he quickly gave Bill a check for the proper amount. God had truly touched many hearts and the two missionaries rejoiced in the Lord!

However there was one time when Satan stirred up some of the religious leaders and caused the treasurer to refuse to give Bill the check for the workers' gifts. How sad! But this time they had the gifts in their hands and were looking forward to giving them to the Bolivian Mission treasurer.

What a joy it had been to work for the Lord on this trip. Souls had been told about the Seventh-day Adventist mission ministry and funds were raised to continue the mission work. After being away from home so long, it was also a joy to be on their way home to join their families. As Bill and Sérgio waved goodbye to their friends, they thanked God for His many blessings and praised Him for His goodness. What a wonderful way to end their trip to the mines.

Chapter 34

Two Villages in One Night

"Pleasant words are a honeycomb, sweet to the soul and healing to the bones."
Proverbs 16:24

Bill was very happy to be heading home again after being away for several weeks. He knew he was missing a lot by not seeing much of Gary and Dennis. They were growing up, and he was always amazed at how tall they had grown while he was away. Gary and Dennis missed their daddy, too. When they would see the little red Jeep pull up in front of their house, June thought the whole neighborhood could hear their squeals of delight.

June was happy that Bill was home, also. After their warm family greetings, she prepared a good meal for Bill while he took a shower. After dinner it was time for family worship and then a good night's rest.

Bill slept soundly in his own bed that night. The next morning he was rudely awakened when Gary and Dennis jumped in bed with him. He didn't mind though, as it was fun laughing and roughhousing together while June prepared breakfast. Oh, how good it was to be home enjoying the companionship of his sweet wife and playing with their precious sons. It was all so good.

A few days later it was time for Bill to say goodbye to his family again. His deep hunger and thirst to minister to the Indians living out on the Bolivian Altiplano did not allow him to stay home very long at any one time. He just had to tell the Indians about Jesus and His love for them and to treat their physical problems the best he could.

Bill carefully checked his little red Jeep to assure it was in good shape for the trip. He replenished the supplies he knew he would need. Finally all was ready. He kissed his family goodbye one more time and got in the Jeep. June and the boys were sad to see him leave, but they bravely waved to him until the little red Jeep was out of sight.

Within a short time Bill was out on the cold, desert-like Altiplano headed for one of the seven mission stations. There was only a little brush here and there or a small tree that would catch his attention once in a while. An Indian child tending the family's flock of sheep always caught his attention. Indian parents often sent their ten- or twelve-year-old boys or girls to the desert to tend their sheep. These children could always be seen wearing their colorful *chula* (hat), which was always pulled down over their ears. These hats were made of tightly woven wool and were really nice and warm.

While driving Bill saw a four-horned ram among an Indian's sheepfold. He was surprised because he had never seen one like that. An unusual sight. He arrived at the mission station, and after warm greetings, the mission director said he would join him and be his guide. When Bill asked where they were going, the Indian director said, "We are going to a new place where there are a lot of Aymara Indians interested in learning about Jesus. Maybe a new church or school can be established there after you preach the gospel to them. They are already looking for something better than what they have.

It was very late in the afternoon and getting dark when the director pointed and said, "There! That's the Catholic church. See the steeple? That is where we are going."

Bill looked around and asked, "Where are the people?"

"You will soon see," he answered.

Just as Bill stopped the Jeep, they saw an Indian coming toward them. He was wearing a brown poncho over his shoulders to keep warm, and Bill called out to him, "What is that I hear?"

The Indian shouted back, "Church bells! The bells are ringing to call the Indians to come to the church." The director told Bill that sometimes many years went by before a Catholic priest showed up. He was very happy that he was bringing a good Seventh-day Adventist missionary to give them the good news of the gospel.

Another Indian soon appeared. He was wearing a brown poncho over his shoulders and carrying a white sheet. Bill was really glad to see that sheet. It was exactly what he needed on which to project his film. He got out of the Jeep and found a few nails. Before they knew it the sheet was nailed to the front door of the little Catholic church.

There was no electricity, but Bill set up his projector anyway. He pulled up the hood of the Jeep, hooked the projector to the battery, and it was ready to go. Still, there were no people. Suddenly little oil lamps were seen flickering in the dark from all directions. Soon thirty or forty Indians were sitting on the ground in front of the church.

Bill was thrilled to see them and put the filmstrip about heaven in the projector. As the film was being shown, he told them about our future home, that there would be no suffering, pain, sorrow, cold, or want, and that Jesus had promised heaven will be our home forever some day. These were truly "pleasant words, and sweet to the soul" to the Indians.

As Bill pointed to the beautiful picture of heaven, he asked, "Do you want to be in heaven?" Many raised their hands and answered, "Yes! Yes! Yes!" Bill was very happy to see that so many had raised their hands. He then invited all of them to give their hearts to Jesus. As Bill prayed, God worked in a special way that night and the

Holy Spirit touched their hearts greatly.

Many of the Indians hugged Bill and thanked him for his message that night. With the promise of God deep in their hearts, they began streaming across the fields toward their homes. Oh, how happy Bill was knowing that they would have a new home in heaven some day. He praised God and thanked Him from the bottom of his heart for the special way the Holy Spirit had touched the Indians' lives.

The last Indian was just leaving when the Indian director told Bill they must be on their way and visit one more village before calling it a night. Bill was surprised. Though he was tired and weary, he happily packed up his equipment. Soon they were on their way again, and he looked forward to telling the Indians in the next village the wonderful story of Jesus' love and sacrifice.

But it was getting late, and Bill was concerned. Would there be Indians waiting for them this late when they arrived? When he mentioned this to the director, he was assured that they would be waiting for them, and he was right. They were waiting for them.

These Indians had heard only a little bit about Jesus and had never seen a Seventh-day Adventist missionary. They were eagerly searching for a new life in Jesus. With warm greetings and many hugs, they showed Bill how happy they were that he was with them.

The Indians gathered around the side of an old building and sat on the ground. They watched intently as Bill set up his projector for the second time that night. He connected it to the battery and inserted the film on the topic of heaven. Soon the Indians were learning more about Jesus and what a great place heaven is, so different from earth with sickness, pain, death, grief, cold, windy homes, and the lack of food they experienced daily. The Holy Spirit was doing His work, and the Indians had no trouble understanding where they wanted to be in the future. After giving their hearts to Jesus that night during Bill's closing prayer, the Indians said, "You must come back tomorrow."

Bill was there bright and early the next day. He quickly set up his clinic on the back of the little red Jeep. Indians began gathering around him once again, watching intently as he pulled teeth and cared for the sick or injured.

Several hours later the director came by and said, "Come, Bill! The Indians have something they want to show you."

Bill could not imagine what was on their minds. They had not gone far when Bill noticed an Indian standing in front of a nice house. He asked, "What's up?" The director informed him that after last night's message the Indians had made the decision for Bill to make this house the permanent location for a Seventh-day Adventist church. Joy quickly flooded Bill's soul! Oh, what a thrill it was to be in the mission field and to preach about the second coming of Jesus and heaven.

An Indian hurried up to Bill as he was walking out of the new church. He handed him many articles they had studied from and said, "We no longer need these things, for we are all Seventh-day Adventists now. We plan to go to heaven with Jesus when He comes, so we can be with Him and enjoy heaven forever and ever."

As Bill took the items from the Indian, he thought, *Truly, the Holy Spirit has once again fulfilled His mission and many precious souls are now preparing to meet their Lord*. He praised God for these blessings.

Chapter 35

Supi Cola

"Trust in the LORD." Psalm 115:9

    In October 1954 Bill was preparing for a trip into a very remote area known as Arcopongo. This would be the first time in nearly ten years that an American missionary had been there to visit. He knew he could take his Jeep only part of the way, then he would have to change and use mules for the rest of the trip. This meant he could carry only a limited supply of medicines for the sake of the poor mules. As Bill thought about it, he wondered just what medications he should take that would enable him to be the biggest help to the Indians. He decided to give this burden to the Lord and let Him choose the right medications while he was packing.

    Moises Aquilar, the Quime mission director, decided to go with Bill. Both men knew that traveling through the rugged mountains of Bolivia could be very dangerous at times. Crossing the high rugged mountains was always very dangerous as you never knew when you would have to face a sudden snowstorm. Some storms were so severe that people had been found frozen to death.

    The trail to the Arcopongo area was an exceptionally dangerous trail. About five miles of it was called *Supi Cola* (the tail of the devil). The name implies how dangerous it could be. Fortunately Bill and Moises had put their trust in Jesus, and they had no problem whatsoever as they traveled the trails through the rugged mountains of Bolivia. Each praised God for watching over them.

    News spread quickly that missionaries would soon be arriving in the Arcopongo area. The Indians living there seldom saw a stranger who could help them. They hardly knew what to expect of the visiting missionaries, but there were a lot of smiles and laughter when Bill and Moises entered their village.

    It was not long before more Indians began streaming in from far and near. They watched in amazement as Bill set up his clinic. When his clinic was in order, Bill immediately began treating their wounds, eyes, or pulling their rotten teeth. Some of the Indians who had gathered around Bill had come just to see an American. Others begged him to give them an injection just to see how it felt, but most came seeking help for their physical problems.

    Some of the Indians Bill treated earlier in the day came back and gave him six chickens. Bill graciously accepted them, but he knew he could not carry six chickens with him in his little red Jeep. He decided to quietly give them to the poorest family he could find just before he and Moises left for home.

While Bill took care of his chickens, Moises stood up and opened his Bible. The Indians understood right away he was going to tell them about Jesus. They gathered in front of him and quietly sat on the ground, listening intently as he told them about God's love for them, Jesus' loving sacrifice, and their heavenly home. They loved what they heard, and at the end of his sermon, many gave their hearts to the Lord.

Some of the Indians in that village decided the best way to show how much they appreciated the missionaries' visit was to prepare a special meal for them. When the sun came up the next morning, they promptly began preparing the meal.

Bill and Moises awakened refreshed. Their plan for the day was to just take it easy and make sure their equipment would be ready for their trip home the next day. After breakfast they visited with some of the Indians. As they were leaving one family, an Indian man came up to Bill and said, "Pastor, I love God. I am a Seventh-day Adventist and I do not understand why my sheep are dying."

Bill thought for a moment. Maybe the sheep were dying because he was unfaithful paying his tithe. When he asked the Indian about this, he replied, "No, Pastor! When I get ten new lambs, I sell one and give my tithe to the mission. When I get twelve or fourteen new lambs, I do not know how to give tithe on them."

Bill suggested that he keep a record of the leftover lambs for that year. The next year when new lambs begin to appear he could pay tithe on the ten and save the other new lambs for the following year's count. The Indian smiled, nodded his head, and said, "Yes! Now I understand, and I will do what you say." Bill learned later that the Indian had no more problems with his sheep mysteriously dying.

That afternoon the two missionaries were led to a field and invited to sit down. Bill was hungry and looked around for the food, but there was none displayed. One of the Indians began to dig in the ground right in front of him. Bill looked at Moises and asked, "What do you think this is all about?"

Moises was not sure, but it soon became apparent when the Indian scraped away more soil and exposed steaming mutton and potatoes lying on hot rocks. Bill smiled and said, "Just think. A steam pressure-cooked dinner here in the wilderness!"

A moment later the Indian graciously handed Bill the head of the sheep he had just uncovered. Bill smiled as he accepted the sheep head, but he could hardly believe his eyes when he saw it still had wool on it. He felt there was no way he could eat any part of the sheep head, so he graciously gave it to Moises, who gladly accepted it and began eating the delicacies along with the steamed potatoes.

Bill praised God for the Indian's thoughtfulness and kindness while he enjoyed his portion of mutton and potatoes. In Bill's opinion, the best part of their visit to the Arcopongo area was seeing a lady who had a badly swollen arm. Her husband came to the clinic and asked Bill if he would go and see his wife. Bill asked, "How far is it?"

The man pointed and said, "It is very close, over there on the hill." Bill had experienced the way the Indians judged distances. To them, nothing seemed far away. Bill knew going there would mean at least a two-hour trip. He also knew he would not be able to go with him at that time. A moment later he gave him some medicine with instructions. He then told the Indian that he would try to go with him the next morning and see what he could do for her.

About eight o'clock the next morning an eight-year-old boy came to take Bill to see the sick woman. Moises did not think they would have time to go, so Bill told the boy he was sorry but he could not go. The boy was deeply disappointed.

As Bill traveled along the trail with Moises, his conscience would not leave him alone. He decided to take the supplies he thought he would need and walk back down the trail. After much walking at 10,000-feet elevation, Bill finally caught sight of a little adobe hut. How happy those poor people were to see him. When Bill looked at the woman, he was sure he had never seen such a pitiful case of swelling. Her arm was at least two or three times larger than normal, and her fingers were like sausages.

Bill needed more light, so he helped them take her outside the hut. This move pained her a great deal, but it could not be helped. Bill prepared her arm, cut a small incision and drained off about a pint of fluid. He covered the incision with a bandage and told the family he hoped he would be able to return the next year. They had prayer together, and before leaving he encouraged them to get better acquainted with Jesus.

As he walked back up the trail, he was very happy he had been able to relieve this poor woman's pain. He prayed that more souls would be won for the kingdom the following year.

Bill spent many hours laboring to ease the suffering of the Indians in Bolivia and save their souls. He was convinced that many lives were prolonged because of his clinic. He had relieved the pains of hundreds, nay, thousands, and had told the good news of Jesus to many more.

After Bill arrived home safe and sound, he and June knelt and prayed daily for those dear people.

****

The Lord needs more dedicated people like Bill, to say, "Here I am, Lord, send me." For truly, the harvest is ready, but the workers are few. Amen!

Chapter 36

Villa Esperanza

"Then have them make a sanctuary for me, and I will dwell among them."
Exodus 25:8

"Get up, friends," called Dr. Waldo Stiles early one morning. "This is the day we have waited for so long. We must be on our way to arrive in good time at the old Indian village of Villa Esperanza."

This village was two full days of travel by mule from La Paz, the capital of Bolivia at that time. It was only a small village of about fifty families. It was a place well-known and often visited by tired Adventist missionaries and doctors on their way to the Seventh-day Adventist hospital in Chulumani, which was another full day of travel away.

Of course, things had changed since the years when the early missionaries passed that way in the 1930s. The former beasts of burden had been replaced with Bill's little red Jeep clinic, so the Indians often called Jeeps "Yankee mules or burros" because they carried the missionaries on their rounds of visitation.

Bill had never heard of Villa Esperanza until Dr. Stiles had told him of the pioneers "hanging their hats" there while their tired mules rested, and they took nourishment. On this morning the doctor was anxious to get started early. His little son, John, was ready and waiting before any of the others. He wanted to see if any Adventists remained in this village.

The little red Jeep wound around the mountain on what has been called the worst road in the world. Some say that one has not seen South America until he/she has been to Chulumani. Others say, "Never again for me."

Everyone had strange feelings in their stomachs as they traveled those hundreds of narrow one-car curves and looked down 500 to 700 feet or more. Bill noticed a look of fear on the doctor's face as he was driving, so he invited him to drive. They exchanged places, and the doctor eagerly grabbed the wheel.

The many white crosses along the road reminded the drivers to be very careful. There was one very large white cross beside the road, which indicated the spot where a truck had fallen over the cliff and many people had been killed. Truly, a vivid reminder of the danger they were in.

In some places on that dangerous road, the rocks hung so low overhead that trucks had to move slowly so the people on top of the loaded vehicle would have time to duck in order not be dragged off. Sometimes the Jeep would stop short, and they would find themselves only inches from the bumper of a truck coming toward them. That meant backing up the mountain until they arrived at a place where the truck could pass. It is not surprising that the drivers were not too happy when they had to pass on the outer edge. Bill and Dr. Stiles wondered if perhaps the older missionaries had been safer with their four-footed mules.

At last they reached the village of Villa Esperanza. Dr. Stiles was excited and looked around for the old church. He soon saw that there was nothing standing but the walls. He began questioning the villagers and found an old blind brother. "Yes," he said, "I remember the days when our pastors came. It was thrilling. They would arrive so weary that they went right to bed. In the morning they would tell us wonderful Bible truths, and then they would all too soon continue on their way. How wonderful it would be to have them again."

Dr. Stiles said to him, "But, friend, are there no other Adventists here?"

"No," he replied. "They are all gone. Only the younger generation is here, but they drink alcohol and take part in the Catholic feasts."

Dr. Stiles was sad to hear that, but he and Bill were very glad when they saw the younger children coming to their meetings. It appeared they were becoming interested in the things of God. They were even happier when some of the boys took them to see an old abandoned Catholic church. It had a roof in very poor condition, but the boys insisted it could be remodeled and turned into a Seventh-day Adventist church.

The doctor said, "Bill, I have some money from a friend that can be used to build the roof." Then he gave him the responsibility of purchasing the materials and seeing that the work was completed.

Bill and the little red Jeep did not waste any time hurrying over those torturous roads to a sawmill where he purchased the needed materials. Bill opened the front window of the Jeep and loaded everything. To this day he cannot help but wonder how that little red "Yankee burro" ever carried the load. But it took the lumber and the galvanized tin up the hills and over the bumpy road without any trouble.

When Bill arrived at the church, he expected to find the young village men sharing their enthusiasm in seeing the old building reconditioned, but they only sat by quietly and unconcerned. They said, "The lumber is wet. We must let it dry first." Bill did not hesitate. He grabbed a two-by-four and headed for the church, hoping his actions would prove contagious. He soon discovered that only two small boys assisted him.

One of the young Indians located some tools and brought nails. When Bill began to cut rafters, the others realized that he meant business and a few came to help. Shortly after that nearly all the young men pitched in to work on the church. Bill's problem with those young men was that he had not understood the characteristics of the Indians and had failed to give them time to think through the matter.

After two days of hard work, the tin was put on the roof and nailed down firmly so it could not be easily torn off. Pleased with the progress, Bill gazed at the little church from up in the bell tower. At that moment some of the men came to report that they had used the last piece of material. Everyone was sad then, for only half of the roof was covered. Yet, it was better than the open air, and it did look like an Adventist church.

Bill and Dr. Stiles had to say goodbye to their new friends the next day and start for home. Their hearts carried a great burden for those people who longed to have God's church finished and the message of Jesus shining clearly in Villa Esperanzo. However, they had faith that God would not fail His people. And God did not fail them; the church was completed a year later, much to the joy of the villagers, Bill, and Dr. Stiles.

What a joy it was for Bill and Dr. Stiles to see the transforming power of the message in the hearts of the Indian people and to see the light of Jesus shining again in Villa Esperanza.

****

In the coming years, this village became a favorite stopover for many mules and Seventh-day Adventist pastors. Their true light changed the lives of the Indian people there as surely as it changed the unused church in that community into a Seventh-day Adventist house of worship. The transforming power of God's message truly caused great things to happen in the Bolivian mission fields.

Bill still prays for the great Inca Union. He is especially happy when the thirteenth-Sabbath mission offering for the quarter goes to projects there, for he knows that many more souls will hear the gospel of Jesus and be in the kingdom.

Chapter 37

Rolling Clinic Comes Alive

"With my mouth I will greatly extol the LORD." Psalm 109:30

God had new plans for Bill and the physical needs of the Indians. It was at this time that the Bolivian mission voted to purchase a new white suburban SUV. This vehicle would be converted into a mobile clinic that would serve to carry the medications needed and provide a clean place for Bill to carry on his work.

Then came the staggering question—how could clinical vehicles be brought into the country? They had no official permission to import such vehicles and, if they did, the duty on them would cost close to 100 percent of the purchase price. As was Bill's habit, he took the problem to the Lord and asked Him to perform the miracle needed to get this vehicle to Bolivia.

As Bill talked about this problem with Charles Christensen, another Adventist missionary, they decided to visit the minister of Indian affairs to get his response. When he heard their story, he immediately picked up the phone and called the president of Bolivia and made an appointment for them to talk with him. Once again, God provided the miracle needed.

The day came for Bill and Charles to keep their appointment with the president. They prayed before entering the president's office. There were many people sitting around waiting to see him. In only a few minutes the president's secretary came out and said, "The president will now see the Seventh-day Adventist missionaries."

Bill and Charles went through the open door, and there sat President Victor Paz Estensorro. He greeted them in a very friendly way and invited them to sit down. They promptly opened an envelope and showed him pictures of the 150 Seventh-day Adventist schools and told him of the work being done in his country.

The president smiled, thanked them, and said he knew about the Seventh-day Adventist work. He told them that he had lived near one of their hospitals and that he enjoyed reading the Spanish *Signs of the Times* magazine.

The president then asked Bill and Charles what he could do for them. They told him they needed several vehicles that could be transformed into clinics and educational vehicles. They requested the vehicles to come into the country duty-free. After hearing their request, the president quickly picked up his phone, which had a direct line to the minister of customs. A moment later permission was granted for them to bring the needed vehicles into the country absolutely duty-free. Praise God!

Bill and Charles were elated and thanked the president with sincere appreciation. Then the president shook hands with each of them and graciously said goodbye.

What a day of rejoicing that was, for they knew what a great blessing this would be to the poor Indians. Bill and the others could hardly wait for their vehicles to arrive. Until 1951 only the most primitive medical services had been available to the Indians. Now they could minister to thousands on the Altiplano and in the jungles just as the mission boat Luziero had ministered to those along the great Amazon River in Brazil. In Bill's heart he gave God all the glory for another miracle.

Chapter 38

Quime

"He gives strength to the weary and increases the power of the weak." Isaiah 40:29

Bill's rolling clinic had always been welcomed in Quime, Bolivia. Now, with his shiny new vehicle, all white with red crosses painted on the sides and Bolivia's red, yellow, and green flags painted on the doors, he wondered what would be in store for him and his helper.

Meetings were to be held in Quime to give the 5,000 Indian residents their chance to hear the wonderful message of Jesus' love and sacrifice. Bill was thrilled to be helping Ed Clifford. A lot of sickness was sweeping through that small town. Shortly after the meetings began, Bill found that most of his time was going to be spent helping the sick and not preparing the Indians for baptism.

Each night he made the rounds over the cobblestone streets. As he walked along the streets, he could not forget how wonderful it was to be a part of this great medical missionary program. Four years had passed since he had begun this work with his little red Jeep, carrying medicines in a Campbell's soup box. Now he had an up-to-date vehicle, dedicated fully to the medical work, and he praised God daily.

Sabbath dawned bright, and Bill arose a little earlier than usual to visit the Kolenberg daughters in their home. As soon as he entered their home, he immediately noticed that there was no fever left in the one who had been sick and that fourteen-year-old Lupi was apparently doing all right. However, when the parents informed Bill that Lupi had an attack about four o'clock that morning and could hardly get her breath, he promised to return later and check on her condition.

After the church service concluded, Bill returned to the Kolenberg home and found no change in Lupi, so he returned home. While he was eating dinner, several of Lupi's friends rushed in and said, "Come quick! Lupi is having another attack. You must come." Bill immediately left his dinner and hurried to the patient's home. Upon entering the house, he found the parents holding her in their arms as she fought to breathe. Her face was pale, her eyes closed, and it seemed that she was about to stop breathing.

Bill immediately began treating her with fomentations while praying that God would spare her life. In a little while they noticed she was beginning to improve. Without wasting time he decided to take her to a hospital in La Paz.

Bill will never forget that trip! The miles seemed much longer than they really were. He was tempted at times to step on the gas with all his might to get her there before she had another attack, but he knew speeding along those mountain roads was not the safe thing to do. They were about halfway there when Lupi had a third attack. Bill was afraid she was going to die trying to get her breath before he could get her to the hospital, but after a short time her breathing began to ease up a bit.

The rolling clinic was operating at its best as he traveled over those mountainous dirt roads. Bill was hoping and praying as they steadily climbed to higher altitudes that Lupi's condition would improve. All was quiet as they were going over the highest pass, The Three Crosses, at 13,000-feet elevation. Bill snapped on the dome light, and much to his relief, he saw that Lupi had fallen sound asleep.

As they neared the last town before reaching La Paz, Bill heard a groan come from the back. He immediately stopped the rolling clinic. As he gave Lupi an injection, he prayed with all his heart that this would hold her over until they arrived at the hospital. Almost immediately she was quiet again, and Bill thanked God for hearing his prayer.

Within a short time the Bolivian "Clinic of Mercy" reached the hospital and Bill thankfully left Lupi in the capable hands of Dr. Beck, the doctor who was in charge of the American Methodist Hospital. This amazing man had spent many years in Bolivia serving the people, and he immediately diagnosed the girl's illness and began treatment. He told Bill he had acted wisely in bringing her to the hospital as she probably would have died in Quime.

After three days in the hospital, Lupi was well and ready to return home. It was a happy occasion when she entered the rolling clinic for the return trip home. Along the way she sang "With Jesus in the Family" and other little songs she had learned as they drove over the mountainous roads. Her life had been spared by Jesus and the rolling clinic. Bill rejoiced and once again praised God for His blessings.

Chapter 39

Let's Eat Like the Locals

*"So whether you eat or drink or whatever you do,
do it all for the glory of God." 1 Corinthians 10:31*

    There were no McDonalds, Taco Bells, or Burger Kings in Bolivia during the time Bill was there, but he rarely took food with him on his trips into the mission field. If he did decide to take food with him, it was never very much, for he loved the Indians and did everything he could to make sure he did not insult the beautiful people who always cheerfully shared their food with him. Consequently, he ate what they ate, but many times there was very little of it. Besides that he always slept in the place they prepared for him, and this endeared him to them.
    Bill was in for a big surprise though when he and his helper arrived for a visit with the schools and churches at the Llanga Belen Mission Station in Bolivia. They were hungry, but neither the Indians nor the director offered them any food. As Bill and his helper grew hungrier, they soon began to feel that they were starving to death. What was wrong with these brothers and sisters in this field? The Indians loved missionaries. Not offering food to them when they came to visit was very unusual.
    When Bill gained the courage to ask the director what was going on, he was informed that the last missionaries to visit their mission had carried their food with them and would not eat the food the Indians offered. This had hurt their feelings deeply, and they vowed to never again feed missionaries.
    Bill understood then and told the director that he was not like those missionaries, that he always ate what the people ate and slept where they wished him to sleep. When the director told the Indians what Bill had said, they cheerfully brought them something to eat.
    Bill was soon handed a dozen boiled eggs. At an elevation of 12,000 feet, eggs can never be hard-boiled. They remain liquefied. So Bill asked, "How do I eat these?"
    The director said, "It is easy. Break the end of the eggshell, sprinkle some rock salt in it, and then suck out the insides." Bill soon learned that it was not as easy as it sounded, but the eggs did fully satisfy his hunger.
    Foods were different when Bill visited the villages in the Amazon jungle. There he usually found plenty of fish, monkey meat, and tropical fruits. To his delight, many times he was served avocados and bread. That was surely much tastier to him

than the "egg treat."

Another of the missions that Bill visited was the Rosario Mission Station. It was started by an American missionary and was the oldest one in Bolivia. Mario Piro was the director during Bill's time in Bolivia, and Bill soon discovered the food was always excellent. It was usually prepared by the wives of the Indian directors who had learned how to cook American food from the former American missionaries. When they knew Bill was coming to visit, they always planned ahead, and Bill thoroughly enjoyed every bite. The Ana Stahl Clinic was another place he enjoyed the food because it was also prepared American-style.

The food on the Altiplano generally consisted of Bolivian potatoes, mutton, and soup. If you were fortunate, eggs were available. Many times the Indians placed the food on a piece of "once white cloth" spread on the ground and expected everyone to help themselves. The mutton or potato soup the Indian women made was usually cooked over a little clay stove sitting on the ground in the center of their home.

The fuel used for the small stove was animal dung. Grains grown on the Altiplano were often included in the soup. Quinoa was one of those grains. It is a wonderful grain and similar to wheat, but healthier than any other grain. The seeds are red in color and must be washed until they are white before using them. Then they can be cooked like any other cereal, such as rice.

Bolivian woman and child stomping on potatoes to make chuños

While cooking, the Indian women would stir the soup with a wooden spoon in one hand and often grab a handful of animal dung with the other hand to throw into the fire when needed. This practice was not very sanitary, but that is the way they cooked in Bolivia and Peru. And it did not seem to harm them in any way.

Chuños (Bolivian potatoes) are a staple in the Indian diet. They are dug up and laid on a blanket in the sun and left to freeze at night. When the sun shines on them the next day, they begin to thaw and become soft. The Indian women then walk barefooted on them in order to remove the liquid. After several days of this procedure the potatoes become like dried pieces of wood and can be stored safely for the future.

When the missionaries would visit the Indians, one of the women would often fill her clay pot with water, then boil and serve *chuños*. They are very nutritious and quite tasty. Bill and some of the other missionaries sometimes call *chuños* "feetus" just for the fun of it. But Bill never failed to thank the Lord for the foods he received from the Indians.

Toward the end of Bill's service in Bolivia, he and Charles Christensen visited the mission station in Chama Arriba. They were both quite hungry. As they looked around the hut that was "home" during their visit, they noticed some "things" hanging from the ceiling. What were they? Of course they had to investigate. Bill, being so tall, reached up and removed one of the black "things."

They had never seen anything like it before. Now they were hoping these black things were something good to eat. Bill quickly cut one open and saw that it was all white underneath the black. He held it up to his nose and said, "It smells all right! Shall we try it?" Charles was so hungry he didn't hesitate to say yes.

The black part was soon cut off, and they cautiously tasted a piece of the white cake. A moment later Bill and Charles looked at each other in amazement and said, "This is cheese!" They wasted no time in eating more of the delicious white cheese.

Later they learned that when the Indians milk their sheep and get enough to make a small cheese, they hang the cake up high in the ceiling of their hut. Over time the smoke and soot from their fires blackens the cheese.

Bill and Charles were very thankful that they had discovered these black cakes, for their deep physical hunger was satisfied. As Bill was eating, his thoughts began to turn to something Jesus had said long ago, *Man does not live by bread alone, but by every word that comes from the mouth of God,* and he praised God for providing not only physical food but for giving them Jesus, the true Bread of Life that fully satisfies the soul for spiritual food.

Chapter 40

One-Year Furlough

"You will be my witnesses in Jerusalem, and in all Judea and Samaria, and to the ends of the earth." Acts 1:8

In 1955, after four and a half years in the mission field, Bill and June were able to return to the United States for a one-year furlough. Bill took advantage of this time to further his education at Potomac University in Takoma Park, Maryland.

During their furlough Bill accepted many speaking engagements at churches, civic clubs, Missionary Volunteer meetings, camp meetings, and Vacation Bible Schools to tell of their experiences in the South American mission fields. He even appeared several times on nationwide television news channels.

This was a very busy time for Bill, and he sometimes found it difficult to find time for his studies. But he was thrilled to tell of the many challenges missionaries face in their work to win souls for the Lord. He also enjoyed showing the items he had brought home with him. One of those fascinating items was an Indian devil dancer's costume, which he had received as a gift from one of the natives. This was the most colorful and spectacular of all the items he had brought home. It had seven heads and ten horns and was worn only during devil dances. Other items he showed included some of the idols the Indians used in their pagan worship and the homemade wooden lock and key the Indians used to protect their huts. He also displayed a few of the Indians' staple foods, including *chuños,* which are small dehydrated potatoes.

Hearing Bill's exciting stories about the Indians, seeing the colorful costumes and headdresses, and looking at the fourteen-foot boa constrictor snakeskin always delighted the boys and girls. Bill prayed that what he was telling and showing them would inspire them to want to be workers for Jesus just as it had inspired him when he was a boy.

At last Bill finished some of the requirements for his master's degree in practical theology. What a relief that was, and he thanked the Lord for that blessing.

June was about to receive another blessing when she awakened early the morning of September 4, 1956. She knew at once that this was the day she had been waiting for, and by 9:45 a.m. she checked in at the Washington Adventist Hospital in Takoma Park, Maryland, waiting for the birth of their third child.

She did not have long to wait, for her active little baby decided he wanted to see the world. At 11:12 that morning Bill and June became the proud parents of an eight-pound, seven-ounce baby boy. They had never doubted their child would be a boy, so they already had a name for him—Kevin Neil Jamerson. Coincidently, Gary had been born on Bill and June's second wedding anniversary. Dennis had been born exactly four years and fifty-one days after Gary's birth. And Kevin was born exactly four years and fifty-one days after Dennis' birth.

Kevin had been very active in June's womb before he was born, and that did not change after his birth. However, he did begin to sleep through the night by the time he was two months old. June and Bill liked that, but they were not too happy about Kevin's baby talk during church. One Sabbath June decided that his chattering in church had to be stopped. She took him outside the church and gave him a couple of swats on his diapered bottom and told him he had to be quiet in church.

It just happened that a man saw this. When June looked up at him, he shook his finger at her. June has never forgotten that embarrassing moment. Nor has she forgotten the way Kevin would get on his knees and shake his crib when he awakened during the night. Many times he would sing to the rhythm he had going. His parents did not mind, for it was far better than hearing him cry, and June thought it was cute.

Shortly after Kevin's birth, Bill received a call from Elder Ray Jacobs, president of the Inca Union, inviting him to be the director of Sabbath School, radio, and personal ministries of the Peru Mission. They left Takoma Park right away and went back to California to visit their parents one more time before entering another term of service in South America. This time they would work in Peru. It was hard for the grandparents of those three little boys to see them leave again, but Bill and June were excited and looked forward to working with the Peruvians and living in Lima, Peru.

Upon arriving in Lima, the Jamerson family quickly moved into the home prepared for them. Bill enjoyed his work under the leadership of Elder Ted Webster, president of the Inca Union at that time. For the next five years he was kept busy as the director of Sabbath School, radio, and personal ministries of the Peru Mission. Later he did the same work in the Inca Union Mission, which included Bolivia, Peru, and Ecuador. Many times he wondered what exciting things the next five years would bring.

Chapter 41

Floating Islands

"For false witnesses rise up against me, breathing out violence." Psalm 27:12

Wellesley Muir, president of the Lake Titicaca Mission of Seventh-day Adventists, made arrangements for Bill to help him and his wife, Evelyn, with their work among the Indians on the Floating Islands of Lake Titicaca. Carlos Velasquez was also invited to accompany them as their interpreter. When they arrived, Wellesley said, "Well, there they are—the Floating Islands. In just a few minutes the boat will be ready to take us to visit those unfortunate Uros Indians."

After they were underway, they soon saw flocks of large rose-colored flamingos enjoying their paradise. What a beautiful sight they were against the blue of the lake and the sky. Bill listened as Elder Muir quietly reminded him that Lake Titicaca is the highest navigable lake in the world and that the descendants of the Incas still sail the waters of Lake Titicaca. Of all the people who live near this lake, the strangest were the Uros Indians who had hidden themselves away on their famous floating islands for hundreds of years. He explained again that they make the islands from totora, a grass reed that grows in the lake where the water is only three to five feet deep. He said walking on these spongy islands gives one a strange feeling, like trying to walk on a waterbed.

These Indians also make their homes and the mats they sleep on out of the totora reeds. In addition, they use this versatile reed to build their *balsa* canoes. The roots of the reed are used in their salads. Fish (fresh, baked, or dried) are one of their staple foods, but the dehydrated potatoes, *chuños*, are their main staple food.

Elder Muir talked about the progress of the mission station that Elder F. A. Stahl had established in 1911 and about the floating schools and floating churches that were

A missionary visits the Uros Indians

functioning. It seemed to Bill that the one-hour trip flew by when suddenly the motor was shut off on their little boat. They drifted closer to the shore of the island. An Indian was fishing nearby but paid no attention to them.

Poles were being used to reach the beach when several Indians came out of their huts carrying poles. Carlos talked with them in the Aymara dialect from a little distance. No one knew what Carlos was saying to the people, but within five minutes the threatening poles were out of sight. Gifts of bread and soap were given to the Indians. They liked the bread but were not quite sure about the soap.

Uros Indians listening to Bill's record player

Bill donned his white jacket prior to setting up his clinic. Soon he had the old Indian queen lying on a reed mat enjoying a vigorous arm rub. After that treatment there were many more arm rubs.

What amazed Bill the most was how anyone living on one of these islands surrounded by crystal clear water could be so filthy. He managed to massage their hands and arms and rub off some of the dirt as well as take care of their other physical problems. He vaccinated the children for smallpox.

Taking care of the Indians' physical needs prepared the way for the missionaries to reach their main objective, which was teaching them the good news of Jesus. Bill quickly got out his little red and blue finger-operated record player. The Indians were fascinated and could hardly believe their ears when they heard a voice speaking in their own language about the creation of the world. That was the way the Aymara Indians learned that God was the Creator of the world, and not Inti, the sun god.

Because of Bill's love of children, he gravitated to teaching the young ones about Jesus. They could not understand his Spanish when he tried to tell them Bible stories, but they loved the pictures on his picture rolls. Bill also tried to teach them a Christian song in Spanish, but their singing ability turned out to be more like moaning. One of the little girls who clung to Bill's knee sang with all her heart, and her parents and grandparents were very proud of her singing. Others were just as proud of the singing "noises" coming from their youngsters.

Wellesley and Evelyn Muir told Bill an interesting story about Emilio and Ignacia Velasquez. The grandparents had already rejected the gospel of Christ. The parents were not the least bit interested in hearing about the baby born in Bethlehem who came to save His people from their sins and give them eternal life, for they were expecting a child at that time. Before the baby was born, Emilio knelt down and placed twelve coca leaves on a flat stone on the patio of their adobe hut and mumbled to himself, "Witch doctor! Witch doctor!" while he prayed to the spirits, "I dedicate my son and heir to

The children enjoyed learning about Jesus via picture rolls

become a witch doctor."

Their child was born early the next morning, and the parents were filled with joy. They wondered what they should name him. Emilio looked at the highest mountain in the distance and said, "His name will be Carlos Anu Anuni. The spirits will protect him, and he will become a famous *hechicero* (witch doctor)."

Two years later a witch doctor predicted that Carlos would die, but that did not happen because God had a different plan for him. The boy was healed, and several years later he heard about the Bible from a Catholic priest. Against his father's will, Carlos bought a Bible. It changed his life, and today he tells everyone how the Holy Spirit led him.

All too soon it was time for Bill and his companions to say goodbye to their new friends on this floating island. Their next stop would be Puno, Peru, where the mission headquarters for this section of the country was located. It was only a one-hour journey, but it seemed as far away as the east is from the west. When Bill and Elder Muir arrived, they felt their mission trip had been a great success. Their only regret was that there was no school in which the Indians could learn to read and write the language of their country.

A few years later there was another floating Seventh-day Adventist school in operation. However, because of their superstitions, it was seven years before the first Indian was baptized.

****

Floating Islands, Peru – Seventh-day Adventist School

Truly, we have a wonderful and patient God who loves all people with an everlasting love. Jesus tells us that the harvest is ready, then He asks where the workers are. May everyone who reads this story develop a hunger and thirst to share God's love with those who do not know Him.

Chapter 42

Let's Go Fishing

"Friends, haven't you any fish?" John 21:5

One of Bill's responsibilities in Peru was to visit the many mission stations. Some were quite remote in the mountains while others were in remote areas of the Amazon jungle. It had been quite some time since Bill had last visited the Campa Indians living near the Nevati Mission Station. He decided it was time to make the necessary arrangements for a visit.

John and Marge Elick had accepted the call to this very isolated mission station at the same time Bill and June had accepted the call to La Paz, Bolivia. Bill was looking forward to seeing them and knew they would be even more excited at seeing another American missionary when he arrived. (A few years later John and Marge were replaced by Dwight and Betty Taylor.)

Bill packed what was needed for the trip and placed the items in his car. After prayer it was time to say goodbye to his sweet wife and precious sons. He climbed into the car and waved another goodbye to his family as his vehicle slowly moved onto the street. In the next three and a half hours, he went from sea level to an elevation of 12,500 feet. It would have been nice if he had carried oxygen with him, but no such luck. The carburetor needed more oxygen, too, so he had to make adjustments on it from time to time.

Bill's head began to ache before he reached his destination, but he kept going in spite of it. After traveling a few more hours, he reached a little tropical hotel in the jungle. The weather was quite warm, and his headache had vanished. He registered for one night at a little hotel and enjoyed a good night's rest. The next morning he got up bright and early, went directly to the little airport, purchased a ticket, and boarded a small one-engine plane. The pilot wasted no time getting the plane into the air, and thirty minutes later the plane set down on a dirt airstrip in the little town of Puerto Bermudez.

John Elick and some of the Campa Indians were there to meet Bill. They watched as he got off the plane and picked up his belongings. After a warm welcome, they led Bill to the river where their dugout canoes were waiting. The Indians made their canoes from half a log, which they hacked or burned out the inside until it was the size they wanted. After smoothing the rough edges, the canoe was ready to go.

They traveled the rest of the way by canoe and arrived in good time at the Nevati Mission Station. A few of the Indians gathered barbasco roots and beat the roots until they were soft. Bill wondered why they were doing that, but he did not ask about it when he learned they were planning a fishing trip.

Because Bill loved to fish, he asked if he could join them. The Indians were happy he wanted to go, so they led him to one of their twelve dugout canoes and told him to climb in. Bill climbed in and sat down, and soon the motor on the back of the canoe was pushing them up the river.

Bill looked at the other canoes and realized there were no fishing poles on any of them. *How can you fish without a fishing pole?* he wondered. He also noticed there were no containers of bait. *What is going on?* Bill could not understand. As the motor continued to push them farther and farther up the river, Bill began to notice the alligators sunning themselves on the beaches. He hoped none of their canoes would capsize.

Jungle of Peru – Nevati Mission Station – Campia Indians in a typical dugout canoe

One and a half hours later the canoes began to slow down. Bill saw an inlet on his left. It was not very big, only about one and a half blocks long. Then he noticed a Campa Indian standing in the water. What was he doing? Bill watched as he pushed some kind of screens down in the water, anchoring them to the bottom. When he finished, only a small opening was left, and it was just wide enough for a canoe.

All twelve canoes entered the inlet. Instead of fishing poles in the Indians' hands, some of them had barbasco roots. It looked like they were washing the roots in the water. Bill was really puzzled by their actions. Just then he noticed others were holding drawn bows with arrows in place. *What in the world is going on?* he thought.

Much to Bill's surprise fish soon began floating to the top of the water, and the Indians were shooting their arrows into them and tossing the fish into their canoes. They were small fish, but what a catch they had that day.

Bill did not catch any fish on this fishing trip, but what a joy it was for him to be there and see the way the Campa Indians fish. Later he learned that washing the barbasco roots in the water depleted the oxygen in the water, which caused the fish to rise to the surface of the water.

When their canoes were filled with fish, it was time to return to the mission. That evening Bill and the other missionaries sat down and ate a wonderful dinner with the

Campa Indians. Besides the fish and all kinds of fruit, there was a dish made of yucca root. It was boiled like potatoes and tasted similar, but the texture was not as fine.

Everyone had a great time fellowshipping together that night, and Bill was impressed again with how important it was to eat with the Indians, which led him to think about Jesus' example. *That's why Jesus spent so much of His time eating with the people while He was here on earth. Somehow that drew people closer, and they became one with each other.* Bill then bowed his head and prayed, *Lord, with your help I promise I will follow in Your footprints forever. Amen!*

Chapter 43

Nevati, Peru

"Greater love has no one than this, that he lay down his life for his friends." John 15:13

The last time Bill had visited the Nevati Mission Station was when John and Marge Elick were the directors. They had done a wonderful work there, and Bill was almost sure the simple but large church had been built by them. Later, John became president of the union that oversaw Bolivia, Peru, and Ecuador.

Dwight and Betty Taylor were now living in the isolated Nevati Mission Station in the middle of the Peruvian jungle. Later Dwight became the director of Adventist Development and Relief Agency (ADRA), which operates to assist the poor. Dwight held this position longer than any of the missionaries preceding him.

Knowing how isolated the mission station was, Bill tried to visit there at least twice a year. The last time he had visited this mission he had preached a powerful sermon about Jesus and heaven.

That had been many months ago, so he decided it was time to visit the Taylors again. Once again he traveled in his international van from the coast of Lima, Peru, for about three hours before he arrived at El Ticleo. The trip up the mountain was slow as the altitude grew higher and higher until it reached approximately 15,000 feet. As the oxygen became thinner, it became necessary to adjust the carburetor in the car. Bill needed more oxygen too, but there was none for him.

Bill continued his trip down the other side of the mountain to a small town on the border of the Peruvian jungle. After a day of driving over the narrow curving dirt roads, it was a real joy to check in at the primitive hotel where he could rest in comfort. He soon realized he was very hungry, so he ate some of the delicious local fruits, such as pineapples and bananas. Then it was time to go to bed. Much to his sorrow he soon learned the bed was the hardest bed he ever laid on.

The next morning Bill was up early to board a small airplane that flew him to Puerto Bermudez. It was a very small airport, and only a few people lived nearby. When Bill arrived, he was very happy to see Dwight Taylor there to meet him. After a warm greeting, Dwight led Bill to his dugout canoe where two Campa Indians were waiting. Dwight had a Johnson outboard motor on the back of his dugout canoe, and soon they were on their way to the Nevati Mission Station.

Along the river's edge they could see alligators basking in the warm sunshine on the sandy beaches. Bill was not too happy to see them. However, he always enjoyed seeing the beautiful and very colorful birds of the jungles. Some were in the air overhead, but many more were perched on the trees lining the river.

An hour after leaving Puerto Bermudez, they arrived at the Nevati Mission Station. Dwight led the way up the trail to the mission home, which was elevated off the ground by about eight feet. It was all open underneath. This was to keep the house free from animals, insects, and especially snakes. It was a wonderful little home, and no one could ask more of a jungle home.

Betty had been patiently waiting for Bill's visit, for she treasured the sweet fellowship with a fellow American missionary. After warm greetings and hugs, she led Bill and Dwight to the table, which was laden with delicious things to eat. What a treat it was to eat Betty's jungle food. It was all so good!

As the two men conversed, Dwight asked, "Bill, do you remember how you preached to the Indians on your last visit?" Bill had forgotten, so Dwight reminded him he had preached about witnessing to each other and to the other Indians living in the Peruvian jungle. Dwight continued, "You must hear what happened."

He then proceeded to tell Bill the rest of the story. Some time after Bill's sermon one of the Campa Indians came to Dwight and said, "I must go up the river about three days journey to the Gran Pajanal and tell them about Jesus. No missionary has ever been there."

Dwight said he was amazed the Indian wanted to go and share the good news about Jesus with another village. He gave him a picture roll and cautioned him to be careful. They had prayer together, and Dwight said, "Go now and God be with you." The Indian smiled, took the picture roll, climbed into his canoe, secured the picture roll, and went up the river. With no Johnson motor to push him up the river, he had to use the pole in his hand to push upstream, which was much harder.

After some days the Indian arrived at the village. The local Campa Indians had spotted the stranger coming to their village and arrows soon began to fly. The Adventist Campa Indian got down on the ground and crawled toward their village. When he safely arrived at the village, the Indians could not believe he had managed to get through their barrage of flying arrows without being hit. They began to treat him as a friend. He stayed with them for many days, displaying his picture roll and telling them the wonderful story of Jesus and His love for all people. After several Indians gave their hearts to Jesus, it was time for the visiting stranger to leave them and return to the Nevati Mission Station.

Dwight and Betty were thrilled when he told them his missionary story about how God had used him to tell the story of Jesus to unreached people. Some time later this same Indian came to Dwight again, telling him he wanted to go back to Gran Pajanal. He asked for another picture roll to take with him, and Dwight gave him one. They prayed together, and the Indian was again reminded to be very careful. A moment later he joyfully climbed in his canoe, waved goodbye, and began poling up

Nevati Mission Station – Campa Indian family

the river, ready to instruct the Indians again.

After some time the missionary Indian returned to the Nevati Mission Station. Dwight told Bill that he had never seen such a happy and satisfied look on anyone's face as on that Indian. God had used him in a mighty way and richly blessed his ministry.

A few weeks later Dwight and Betty were called to the Indian's hut. He was very sick with a tropical fever. Dwight and Betty prayed for him. Betty nursed him and did all she could for him, but to no avail. He quietly fell asleep, awaiting Jesus' second coming, happy and satisfied that he had witnessed for Jesus to the glory of God.

Dwight's report of this Indian was thrilling to Bill. He thought of all the dangers, hard trials, and hunger he had endured and knew that it was worth it all just to hear reports like this. He thanked God for leading him to be a missionary to the Bolivian and Peruvian Indians.

Bill thought about how wonderful it would be if more people would be inspired to tell the good news of Jesus as done by Bill and this Campa Indian living in the isolated jungles of Peru.

Chapter 44

Another River Trip

"I will extend peace to her like a river." Isaiah 66:12

    Not all missionary trips worked out as well as others. Bill's home base was in Lima, Peru. While he was still working in the Inca Union in South America, the conference leaders there had voted for him to go to the Lake Titicaca Mission. This mission field extended from Arequipa to Cusco and Puno, which is located next to Lake Titicaca.

    As always, Bill was eager to spread the good news of Jesus and His saving grace, so he packed his gear and was soon waving goodbye to his precious family as he boarded a plane that flew him to Arequipa. From there he traveled by train to Puno. On the way, the train took him through Juliaca where the Seventh-day Adventist university was located. When the train arrived in Puno, Wellesley Muir, the president of Lake Titicaca Mission at that time, was at the station to greet him and take him to the mission office.

    Bill was curious about what Wellesley had in mind for him to do. It did not take long before Wellesley turned to him and said, "Bill, I heard there are about 10,000 Indians living in the jungles down river, and no missionary has ever visited them. They do not know Jesus, so our mission is going to be to introduce Him to them."

    Bill did not hesitate. "Let's go! I am packed and ready."

    Wellesley and Bill awoke early the next morning. After breakfast, Wellesley hired three Indian men to carry their food and supplies for the trip. Wellesley's car was soon loaded, and his wife, Evelyn, drove them out of town. When she stopped and parked the car, Bill soon realized there were no roads ahead, only jungle trails. The Indian men began removing all of the food and the other equipment. After prayer, Wellesley and Bill waved goodbye and headed down the trail.

    They followed the trail farther into the jungle, stopping occasionally to eat an orange or two. There were plenty of them, so Bill ate several. The acid in the citrus fruit made Bill's teeth hurt until he said, "Please do not give me any more oranges."

    The next day they arrived at a small village occupied mostly by Adventist Christians. They spent a very enjoyable day with them. Early the next morning they said goodbye and were soon on the jungle trail again.

    Bill felt sorry for the young Indian men carrying their heavy equipment up and down the green jungle hills, but they never complained. From time to time, beautiful parrots would fly out of the trees. A few monkeys were seen now and then, too, besides large lizards and other creeping things. Bill wondered if the Indians enjoyed seeing them as much as he and Wellesley.

Finally, there was the river before them, and it was a rushing one at that! To Bill, that meant it could have a lot of white rapids and strong whirlpools, and he was concerned. Wellesley did not seem to be worried. He immediately found their rubber boat, and as soon as it was inflated, everyone began loading it with their supplies.

Wellesley was an adventurous leader and, as soon as the boat was loaded, "Captain Wellesley" was ready to push off and head down the river to find some of those 10,000 heathen Indians. But Bill was not so sure he was all that adventurous.

As Bill stood beside the loaded boat, he said, "Wellesley, I know you have a wife and two daughters in Puno, but I have a wife and three sons in Lima. It is my thought that you and the supplies and one of the Indians should go ahead in the boat and see how it all goes. The three of us will walk alongside the river, and we will join you where you stop to wait for us."

Wellesley agreed and shoved off into the fast moving water. Bill and the two Indians with him walked along the jungle trail. Bill was happy he had no supplies to carry. He would be able to enjoy seeing the beautiful birds, colorful butterflies, and other jungle creatures along the trail.

As they reached the top of another hill, Bill could see the river below. Where was the boat with Wellesley and the Indian? Something must have gone wrong. Bill and the Indians kept walking along. When they came to another hilltop and glanced at the river again, there was still no boat in sight.

The jungle trail finally led them closer to the river. Then Bill saw Wellesley hobbling along the riverbank toward him. *Oh happy day!* he thought. *He's alive! But what about the Indian, the boat, and their supplies?*

When Bill joined Wellesley on the edge of the river, he could see that he had several injuries and was in pain. They decided that it would be best to make camp there while it was still daylight. That evening Bill finally asked what had happened.

Captain Wellesley took a long breath before sharing his story. They had been traveling beautifully down the river for about a mile. Suddenly they were sucked into a terrible whirlpool, and they could not control the boat. It turned over, and they went under the water. He said he thought he was a goner for sure and would never come up, but at last he did, and with God's help, he was able to make it to shore. He reported that he had seen his Indian helper farther down the river and hoped that he was able to find his way home. Wellesley and Bill prayed and thanked the Lord for His blessings and that the four of them were alive. Only time would tell the whole story about the other Indian's adventure.

After sleeping through the night, they were awakened early the next morning by their Indian helpers singing a Christian hymn. What a joy it was to be awakened that way. When Bill stood up ready to hit the jungle trail, Wellesley commented, "Bill, my leg hurts so bad it is killing me, and I know I can never make it back home."

Before he could say anything more, Bill said, "Wellesley, if I have to carry you on my back, you are going back to Evelyn and your two daughters and that is final." Wellesley stood up, and they headed for the jungle trail and home.

Many times Wellesley thought he could not continue but Bill kept encouraging him and half carried him all the way back to the village. Wellesley's injuries were soon treated. That night the two missionaries had a good rest.

****

Bill still remembers the joy he experienced as he and Wellesley went in search of the 10,000 heathen Indians to proclaim the good news of Jesus so they could be set free from sin. He has often hoped that another missionary's trip down the river was more successful than theirs.

Bill prays, too, that readers of his story will want to experience the same joy and happiness that he had by going into all the world and preaching the gospel. The good news is that all you have to do is say, "Here I am, Lord; send me," and God will do the rest.

Chapter 45

The Jamersons' Three Musketeers

*"The righteous man leads a blameless life;
blessed are his children after him." Proverbs 20:7*

The Jamersons enjoyed many adventures with their three sons as they grew from babies to young children to teenagers to adults. More than one chapter could be devoted to the stresses and joys of raising their three musketeers, but following are a few memorable events that happened with each of the boys. But at the end of the day, they love each one dearly and thank God for the happiness the boys have brought to their lives.

Gary

Bill had been busy all day getting ready to go on another mission trip. His bags were packed and the little red Jeep was almost loaded and ready to go. June reminded him dinner was almost ready. He replied, "I'm sorry, Honey, but I can't wait. I must get to the Transit Office before it is too late." With kisses and hugs he said goodbye to his precious family.

Bill hurried to the Transit Office located at a higher altitude on the outskirts of La Paz. It was necessary that he leave a slip of paper there before he departed telling the officer in charge who was driving the vehicle, to whom it belonged, the license number, and his destination. The transit officer needed this information in case there were any problems as there were no telephones or gas stations on the Altiplano where one could stop and make a call. Bill did not know then that his family would soon be needing him.

The house in which the Jamerson family lived was built on a hill. Their kitchen window faced the street, so June had a very nice view. Their garage was built below the house, and twelve or more concrete steps led up to the living area. Around the top step was an area for flowerbeds. June had cautioned seven-year-old Gary and three-year-old Dennis many times never to stand in that area as they might fall and land on the hard concrete below, but this was where the two boys had gone to wave another farewell to their daddy.

Dinner was ready to serve when June looked out the window and saw Dennis standing at the head of the concrete steps. As soon as she opened the back door,

Dennis said, "Mommy, Gary fell." June hurried to the steps and looked down. Her heart dropped, for Gary was lying in a heap on the concrete landing below. She ran down and picked him up. There was a cut over his left eye, and he had vomited through his nose. What was she to do? She had to take him to a doctor.

She went immediately to her neighbor Jane Haratani. She and her husband were close friends from Oakland. They immediately took June and Gary to the Inter-American Public Health Service in La Paz where Jane's husband worked. Dennis remained at home with the Jamersons' live-in maid. While June and Jane took Gary to the doctor's office, Jane's husband went to his office to phone the Transit Office. He asked the officer in charge if Bill had arrived and was told that he had not. He asked the officer to inform Bill that his son had been injured and to return home.

The doctor's receptionist informed the doctor that a child had fallen down a flight of stairs. He examined Gary right away, but as it was closing time for siesta, he told June to bring Gary back later for X-rays. June was not happy about that and thought he was not a very dedicated physician, but that is what happens at siesta time.

They left the building and returned to the Haratani's car. Gary's body began to convulse, his eyes rolled around, and he began to vomit. June was frantic, but Jane's husband calmly turned the car into the street and said, "We'll take him to the Methodist hospital to see Dr. Beck."

Dr. Beck examined Gary and said, "I don't believe any bones were broken, so you can take him home. He will probably have a headache, so keep him quiet, and do not let him go to sleep until later tonight."

On the way home from the hospital, they met Bill, so both cars arrived home at the same time. Bill picked up Gary and climbed the stairs into the house. Gary seemed fine for a while but later vomited several times. June and Bill stayed close by him, praying and watching carefully for any adverse signs while keeping him awake.

They still believe God was in control of Gary's fall, for although he had bumped his left eye hard on the concrete steps as he fell, his vision was not damaged. They praised God and thanked Him for that blessing. Gary's eye remained black and very swollen for about a week before it gradually began to turn various colors as it returned to normal.

Being alone so often with the boys was difficult for June, but being in a foreign land with no car was really scary for her. Had Gary been in a worse situation it would have been even more difficult. Fortunately, the Jamersons had good neighbors like the Haratanis, but it was times like these that June's faith was tested. Gary had no further emergencies as he was growing up, and his parents praised God for that.

****

As a young man Gary was still living at home and going to college the day he ran into a girl named Carlene. She was very interested in Gary and hoped to get better acquainted with him. It just happened that the University of Tennessee was playing football against UCLA that day, and she said, "Gary, if Tennessee wins, you take me to lunch, but if UCLA wins, I will take you to lunch." Who won? Tennessee!

Gary did not know at the time that Carlene had made the same offer with another fellow, but he was very happy he was the final winner because a year later Carlene became his sweet wife. They were both winners.

Dennis

Bill and Don Von Pohle, the Missionary Volunteer leader of the Inca Union, left La Paz on a mission trip to Chulumani where Bill planned to meet up with June. This trip would take them several weeks. June had been looking forward to this as she was anxious to get out of the cold La Paz weather. The Chulumani Hospital was a delightful place to stay for a little vacation, and the warm tropical weather there was beautiful. She sang a hymn as she happily packed the things that she and the boys would need while vacationing. Soon, she, with seven-week-old Dennis in her arms and four-year-old Gary beside her, climbed into the truck that would take them to Chulumani.

June enjoyed the beauty of the scenic mountains as they rode along the curvy dirt road to Chulumani. She was thankful the driver never failed to honk his horn at each curve. When he stopped at a quaint stone café along the way, she hoped he was not getting an alcoholic beverage. She decided this would be a good time to warm Dennis' bottle. She was shocked when the waitress refused her request, but she said nothing and quietly returned to the truck with the cold milk. Warm or cold, it seemed not to matter one bit to little Dennis.

June was enjoying her vacation and the warm Chulumani weather when Bill and Don arrived. She was very happy to see them. Now she and Bill could have a little vacation time together. Alf Johnson, who was a Canadian and the treasurer of the Bolivian Mission, arrived in Chulumani the same day. That evening they came for fellowship and a delicious dinner.

Don invited them and the hospital staff to watch his *1952 Paris Youth Conference* film the next night. The film would be shown at the hospital's Seventh-day Adventist church. That evening June left Dennis asleep in his crib and instructed the nurse on duty to leave the bedroom door open so she could hear him if he awakened.

Bill and June enjoyed the film, but as they were returning to their quarters, Octavio, the lab technician on loan from Lima, Peru, met them and said, "Come quickly. Dennis is crying. Donny, Alf Johnson's son, heard Dennis crying, went into the room, and tried to pick him up and dropped him."

Bill hurried into the bedroom and took Dennis in his arms. His lips were swollen from the fall, but June could tell by his crying that he was not seriously injured. As Bill comforted him, June gave him a bottle of milk, and he soon calmed down.

The next day, just to be safe, they took him to see a doctor who reassured them that he had no broken bones. Thus ended June's vacation, and she and the boys returned to the cold climate of La Paz. Fortunately, there were no further major events during Dennis' years growing from childhood to manhood.

****

Early in his life Dennis revealed a warm heart for people and animals. When he was about seven or eight years old, he picked a bouquet of fragrant sweet peas and took them to one of their neighbors. The surprised neighbor loved them, and she loved Dennis for being so thoughtful.

Around that time he had a pet turtle named Pete. When he went in the backyard to play with it one day, he discovered his pet was dead. June heard him crying and went to see if he was hurt. When she learned the turtle had died, she consoled him and prayed with him. The next day, much to Dennis's delight, he discovered Pete was alive again, and he told everyone it was a miracle and an answer to their prayer.

Another incident when he was a young man testifies to his service to others. Dennis was traveling somewhere when he saw three Spanish girls being followed. He realized that this was a serious situation, so he shouted to the girls in Spanish to run, assuring them that he would prevent the guys from catching up with them. For his rescue effort, he received a badly cut lip and had to go to the hospital for a couple of stitches. But he was thankful the girls had been saved from danger. The police department gave him a letter of commendation for his service, which made him proud.

Kevin

One day after June had bathed and dressed eighteen-month-old Kevin, she began to get herself ready for the day. While she was combing her hair, Kevin decided to go downstairs. He could only go down those stairs by sitting on each step as he climbed down. June always thought that was so cute.

When June went downstairs to find Kevin, she did not see him anywhere. She asked Dennis, "Where is Kevin?"

"I don't know," he replied. June began looking for him again, first downstairs, then upstairs. No Kevin. Where was he? Then she noticed the open door and knew at once Kevin had gone outside.

After calling him several times and receiving no answer, June went in search of the little rascal. She looked up and down the street. No Kevin. By this time she was becoming very frightened. She was still walking down the street calling for Kevin when a man driving a black car stopped at the curb and asked, "*Señora*, are you looking for a little boy?"

June quickly answered, "Yes." The man told her to get into the car and he would take her to the boy. Just a block and a half down the street June saw the man's maid standing on the sidewalk holding Kevin by his hand. What a relief. As June held Kevin in her arms, she thanked the man and his maid over and over again for their kindness. Then she joyfully returned home.

The street on which Kevin was found was named Santa Cruz. It was a very busy street, and June thought about how heartbroken she would have been if he had been kidnapped or hit by a car. She thanked God anew for watching over him.

****

Kevin had no trouble learning Spanish early in life. One Sabbath morning he began singing the doxology right along with the church congregation. He sang, *"Santo, Santo, Santo, Dios,"* He could not pronounce the other Spanish words, so he hummed the rest of the melody. Later he would sing, "Mommy, Mommy, Mommy…" June was very proud of her young son's singing ability.

When they moved back to the States, Kevin was able to use his talent for singing. It was Doug Neslund's deep love for music that led him to organize a choir for boys. He named the group the California Boys Choir. When Kevin grew older he had the privilege of singing in Mr. Neslund's choir, and he enjoyed the times they traveled to different places in California.

Chapter 46

Three Churches

*"Unless you change and become like little children,
you will never enter the kingdom of heaven." Matthew 18:3*

The Jamerson family returned to the United States in 1961. They moved to Michigan, and Bill enrolled at Andrews University. When he received his master's degree, he also received a call from Elder Carl Becker, president of the Northern California Conference, to be pastor of the Arcata, Orleans, and Trinidad Seventh-day Adventist churches. Elder Becker was the man who had encouraged Bill to accept the call to South America.

Bill's desire had always been to win souls for the Lord, but he was really hoping to get a call to work with the youth. Children held a special place in his heart—he loved the mental image he had of Jesus holding a child on his lap and telling the people, "Unless you change and become like little children, you will never enter the kingdom of heaven." But he thanked God that he had received this call. The family quickly packed and moved to northern California.

The locals welcomed Bill, June, and their little family with open arms and open hearts. One of those couples was Paul and Marguerite Flemming who became their lifelong friends. (You might be interested to learn that Marguerite's father, Elder Herbert Lacy, worked with Ellen G. White in Australia, and his sister, Mae, became the second wife of Willie White, Ellen G. White's youngest son.)

Paul and Bill's friendship extended into support of Bill's ministry. On one occasion, Bill called Paul before sunrise and asked him to meet him at the hospital for an anointing service. A young man had called Bill at 3:00 a.m. telling him that his pregnant wife had suffered a stroke and asking him to come anoint her at the hospital. As soon as they arrived at the hospital, the husband met Bill and Paul and immediately took them to his wife's room where they anointed her with oil. It was a miracle when she recovered fully and later delivered a healthy baby boy whom they named Adam.

****

Early in 1963 Bill decided it was time to hold an evangelistic series. He made arrangements with Elder Ralph Larson and Elder Maurice Bascom to lead out and then rented a large air bubble tent to set up in the plaza in the center of downtown McKinleyville. When the series ended, Bill was thrilled to see the many souls who had accepted the messages, given their hearts to the Lord, and were baptized. That was an exciting time for Bill, but more exciting times were just ahead for the Jamerson family.

In 1964 Bill received a call from Elder Walter Blehm inviting him to be the full-time youth pastor at Orangewood Academy, which is located in Orange County in the Southeastern California Conference. Bill quickly accepted the long-hoped-for-call. Again, the Jamerson family packed their belongings and were on their way to live in sunny Garden Grove, California. Yes, exciting things were ahead. Now his dream of working with young people was coming true, but in what ways would God inspire Bill to reach the hearts of those young people?

Chapter 47

Orangewood Academy Student Missionaries

"Speak, Lord, for your servant is listening." 1 Samuel 3:9

The staff and students welcomed Bill with open arms when he arrived on the campus of Orangewood Academy. The students liked him immediately and began calling him Elder J which pleased Bill. However, he was disappointed with his office. It was not what he expected, but he decided to make it work.

Bob Patchin and Jim Dean both had children attending the academy, and after hearing the glowing reports about Elder J, they decided to visit him. After visiting with him in his office, they felt he deserved a more suitable one somewhere else on campus. With God's inspiration and the help of others, a building project began. Soon Elder J moved into his new office. He really needed that large office of his own because God had big plans for his ministry in Orange County. He was thrilled and thankful for his new friends.

Elder J had always loved children and young people and done his best to inspire them to become workers for God. Now, as the youth pastor of Orange County, God inspired him with the idea to take student missionaries on a trip to a mission field. The more he thought of this, the more determined he was to make it a reality. He wrote a letter to Elder Robert Folkenberg, the president of the Central American Union, asking him what he thought of the idea.

Elder Folkenberg thought it was a great idea. He notified Elder J right away that he would clear the path for his mission and would get back to him as soon as possible. The next day Elder J talked to the junior class. He asked how many students would like to become student missionaries and go on real mission trips. Many hands were raised. He then told them about his talk with Elder Folkenberg and explained that each student would need to raise $250. When they returned from their mission trip, he would make arrangements for them to visit churches and schools to tell of their exciting adventure so others would be inspired to become future missionaries. The students were thrilled.

Sometime later Elder Folkenberg called Elder J and gave him the information he needed to make arrangements for the students to go to Guatemala and other cities in Central America. He was elated, and so were the students when he told them the good news. They were already so excited they could hardly wait for their adventure to begin.

The twelve students began at once to raise the funds needed for the trip. A few students came up short, so Elder J called some of the Adventist doctors and dentists in the area. When they heard about the mission trip and its financial needs, they willingly provided the necessary funds. Several even decided they would like to join the students and help minister to the sick.

On June 12, 1966, twelve Orangewood Academy student missionaries, along with Elder J and June and their sons, Gary, Dennis, and Kevin, were ready for their trip to Seventh-day Adventist mission posts in Guatemala, Honduras, and Nicaragua.

Bill, June, Gary, Kevin, and Dennis

The morning they were to leave was a jumble of loading, jabbering, and trying to get the students lined up for a photograph before the trip. About the time they thought all pictures had been taken, someone would call out, "Wait a minute! Wait a minute! Smile!" Then Linda Borem, one of the students going on the mission trip, dropped her camera. "What a way to begin life as a student missionary!" she declared, "I can tell this is going to be a bad day."

At last the excited students were in the vehicles, which consisted of one Volkswagen bus and one camper pulling a trailer loaded with their luggage. Prayers were offered, and at exactly 10:30 a.m. everyone cheered and waved their last goodbyes.

Their high spirits were short-lived though. Thirty miles down the road the caravan suddenly stopped. It turned out that Elder J had forgotten the medical records and the insurance papers. Without them no one could cross the Mexican border, so he and the students in the Volkswagen bus had to leave the students in the camper and return to Orangewood Academy to retrieve the missing documents.

Mrs. J, as June was called, supervised the students while the others were gone. Their high spirits returned as soon as they resumed their trip. When they reached the California-Arizona border, they stopped and waited for the Volkswagen bus to catch up with them. It was rather hot, but they passed the time playing *Password* in the only shade available, which was the sign on the side of the road that said, "Welcome to Arizona."

Two hours later the Volkswagen bus caught up with them. When Elder J asked if they were ready to go, no one reminded him that they had been ready to go hours ago. Cheers were raised when they began to move again.

The caravan finally arrived at the Mexican border at 9:20 that night. They were met by a little man who looked them over and then spoke to Elder J in Spanish. As Elder J smiled and gave him a box of chocolates, everyone hoped and prayed this would keep the officials from inspecting their luggage. The girls especially did not want that to happen because they did not know how they would get all their stuff packed again. What a relief when the papers were signed. God had graciously answered their prayers, and as they said, "Thank you, Jesus," the caravan was on the road again.

Satan must not have been happy that these young missionary students were ready to experience life in the mission field, for a few miles down the road the trailer had a flat tire. Groans went up! More time wasted. When the tire was repaired, Elder J decided they should travel all night in order to stay on schedule. Their plan had been to arrive in Hermosillo, Mexico, by 11:00 p.m. Wednesday. But they did not arrive there until 7:00 a.m. Thursday.

Satan had different plans. First, they had to repair another flat tire on the trailer. Later, they had a broken trailer hitch, which had to be wired together. By 9:30 that night they were still thirty miles north of Mazatlan. They were really tired, so the caravan pulled onto a dirt turnout by the side of the road, and everyone managed to get some sleep to the tune of passing trucks.

By Friday morning they were desperately wishing they could take a shower and change their clothes. But that was not going to happen until later that night when they reached the beautiful city of Guadalajara and rented a room in a hotel. Yes. Real beds, real showers, and clean clothes! They loved it and slept until noon Sabbath. After breakfast they all enjoyed Sabbath and church service on the hotel's beautiful lawn.

Later, Darryl Courser, an Adventist medical student at the University of Mexico in Guadalajara, came by and showed them around town. One of the places they visited was a beautiful cathedral. Inside, many people walked up the aisles carrying flowers and singing. That was nice. Sadly, superstitions led some to walk on their knees hoping to gain favor with God.

Another interesting place Darryl showed them was the statue *Ninos Heroes* (Child Heroes). Darryl told them about the Mexican revolution and the garrison that was comprised entirely of teenaged boys. The fighting was fierce, but the boys would not quit. The leaders of their enemy finally either fell on their swords or committed suicide by jumping off the cliff. The city fathers were so proud of those brave boys that they erected a huge monument in the center of the city to honor them.

As the students admired this monument, Elder J told them that there would come a time when young people and adults alike would have to bravely stand for the cause of Christ no matter what happened. He assured them that those who stand firm will have an eternal home in heaven.

All too soon their sightseeing in Guadalajara ended and the caravan was on the road again. When they reached Mexico City, the students had their first experience of tasting local foods. That was an eye-opener, for it was the first time they felt like true missionaries. They were excited about that, but not the food.

On June 20 they arrived at the Mexico-Guatemala border. Again they were praying that the officials would not insist on inspecting their luggage. Elder J quickly got out of the Volkswagen bus, smiled, and shook hands with the official as he said, *"Buenos dias, señor."* Elder J's knowledge of the Latin people and a box of chocolates saved the day. The trailer was not inspected. Praise God.

It was raining when they arrived in Guatemala City, and everyone breathed a sigh of relief. Rain does not stop Satan from stirring up problems. When the Volkswagen bus had to make a fast stop for a red light, their wet brakes failed, and it plowed into the back of the camper's trailer. Elder J had to have a stitch on a cut over his eye, but he was the only one injured in the accident. Praise God again. After that incident everyone could enjoy staying in real homes with real American missionaries and eating real Adventist food again. The students were even hungry for "wheat meat."

Elder and Mrs. Lynn Baerg, president of the Guatemala Mission; Mr. and Mrs. Eugene Remmers, treasurer of the Central American Union; and Elder and Mrs. I. M. Nation, education director and Missionary Volunteer secretary of the Central American Union, were the hosts. They graciously gave the visiting missionaries the royal treatment. Needless to say, everyone loved it.

They all enjoyed a trip to the market in Guatemala City. It was located in a large building where the vendors spread their wares in booths or on the floor. The students found it was great fun to barter. No one was ever expected to pay the first price because that was just the way it was throughout Latin America. What fun!

Sabbath in Guatemala City was a real mission experience for two of the girls, Rhonda Butler and Corla Crase. They went to the small Central church, which was not well lit and the divisions were a little cramped, but everyone was happy. The two girls were interviewed that morning in Spanish and in front of the church. They were expected to answer in Spanish. Since each girl had only studied Spanish for one year, their answers were brief. The people laughed but were happy the students were there. The congregation especially appreciated Corla's special music.

One of the boys, Jerry Hamm, went to the Flores church and preached the sermon. Elder Baerg was his translator, and Joyce Carpenter and Liz Bowes presented a special music. The student missionary choir went to the Zone Five (Barefoot) church where they sang a couple of hymns. At 5:00 p.m. everyone went to the Central church for vespers where the students presented the entire program. When the services ended, all the church members came outside to shake their hands and thank them. They were so appreciative, and this thrilled the students. All good things come to an end though, and early Sunday morning the happy student missionaries were on the road again.

Chapter 48

Student Missionaries Minister

"Serve one another in love." Galatians 5:13

The caravan arrived safely at *Clinica Vista Hermosa* in San Cristobal, Totonicapan, Guatemala, Sunday afternoon, June 23, at 3:30 p.m. Everyone was elated and gave thanks to the Lord. The clinic had not been used for three years and was quite dirty. The students were really astonished to see such a thick coating of grime covering everything. They felt good when they saw a fireplace in the living room until they learned it was the only source of heat in the whole house.

After taking a deep breath, everyone pitched in, and soon the living quarters in the clinic were transformed into a student-missionary dormitory. Bill, June, and Kevin had one bedroom, three girls had a second bedroom, and four girls had the third bedroom. A sheet draped over a rope provided some privacy for three of the boys to sleep behind. The other two boys were happy to sleep in the camper.

After the house was in order, everyone stood back and admired their accomplishments. Then some went off to take a quick shower, while others were so tired they decided to wait until the next morning. Bad decision. During the night the water pump broke. No more running water. No more showers. Worst of all, no more toilet facilities.

The student missionaries who had not taken a shower the previous night soon regretted their choice. Up until now no one realized the luxury of running water. When it came back on the following Thursday, they all gave a loud cheer.

The clinic officially opened Monday morning. Their first patient was a little four-month-old boy who looked more like a newborn. He was so undernourished that he looked like a bag of bones. The mother was fifteen years old and had been married for a year. The little family was so poor they could not afford to buy the milk their child needed. The worst thing for the student missionaries was that they could do nothing for their first patient. They all knew that the baby would be dead in just a few more days.

The next patient was an eight-year-old boy who was suffering from a huge boil the size of a golf ball. Elder J gave him a shot of Novocain and then lanced the boil. The little boy was brave, but the Novocain was not enough to deaden the pain, and he screamed until he was almost sick. Those that were with him were sick, too.

That was the sad news. The good news was that in one week they treated forty-eight medical patients and twenty dental patients. This was done without any advertising. Praise God.

Sabbath, June 29, was a very interesting day. Sabbath School was held in a semi-open-air church. Soft green pine needles covered the floor and gave off their pleasing fragrance. There was no piano or other musical instruments, so most of the service consisted of special music. You might say they "made a joyful noise unto the Lord." The children had a special part in the thirteenth Sabbath program. They sang "Jesus Loves the Little Ones Like Me" in Spanish, of course. They said their memory verses in Spanish, also, while looking at the English picture roll. That truly was a very special Sabbath for the student missionaries.

An evangelistic meeting was held Sunday night in the home of the first elder who lived in the city of San Cristobal. He had big amplifiers that broadcast the Voice of Prophecy Sabbath services and Elder J's sermon over the entire city. Thirty-five people attended the first night's meeting, and everyone was very happy for them. The evangelistic meetings continued to be held every Sunday, Wednesday, and Friday night. The last night seventy-six precious souls attended the meeting, and everyone praised the Lord.

Satan was not through trying to discourage the student missionaries. The water pump worked fine when one of the students turned it on at 1:00 in the afternoon, but by morning there was only a half-inch of water in the bottom of the tank. The well was dry. Once again water was a rationed luxury.

That was the day Dr. Armando Hernandez arrived from Santa Ana, California, to be the official doctor for one week. His arrival meant it was time to advertise that a real doctor had come to the clinic. Everyone knew their workload would soon be doubled, but having to ration water was going to make it even more difficult. Still, they were very happy to see the doctor arrive.

Chapter 49

Clinica Vista Hermosa

"It is not the healthy who need a doctor, but the sick." Matthew 9:12

The clinic was named *Clinica Vista Hermosa*, which means clinic of beautiful views. It was appropriately named. In the distance they could see the majestic volcano called Santa Maria. In the valley below they could see the town of San Cristobal with its old, quaint Catholic church in the foreground. And on the hills above the town they could see the farmlands where different crops made a picturesque patchwork quilt. At different times of the day and weather, the scene changed, and each time it was lovely. It was good for the soul that they stepped out once in a while in their busy schedules and paused to look at the beautiful view, thanking God for the things He had made in just six days.

At one end of the clinic was a small back room equipped with a dental chair, a small autoclave to sterilize instruments, a filing cabinet, and assorted dental equipment. This was where Elder J and his two assistants were kept busy pulling teeth. His record for pulling teeth there was fifty in eleven hours.

Beside that room was the medical room with the examining table, desk, and shelves for medicine. When a real doctor was not there, Bill Hall and Ken Nelson, both student missionaries, and two other students did their best to attend to the needs of the Indians.

Ken, along with student missionaries Linda Borem and Liz Bowes, had been assigned to the medical room pharmacy. They did an outstanding job of organizing, alphabetizing, and categorizing everything. Thanks to the generosity of several mission-minded doctors the Orange County Youth Association had been given about $5,000 worth of the newest medications for the clinic pharmacy. Many times they praised God for this blessing.

Of course, there was other work to be done. Mrs. J was in charge of the kitchen. Preparing meals was quite a chore because at that altitude it took beans seven hours to cook. She had only one helper, so she was kept very busy. The person who was June's helper was especially busy on market day because all the fruits and vegetables had to be washed in soapy water and iodine—a very tedious chore to say the least— but those helpers learned a lot about cooking healthy, delicious meals.

Other students were in charge of the rest of the house and clinic. They were kept busy sweeping the floors, keeping the fire burning in the fireplace, and generally cleaning the house and keeping things neat.

Two boys were in charge of maintaining and repairing the driveway leading up to the clinic. But it was almost a hopeless case. The dirt driveway was 200 feet long. It was full of holes, washes, and crevices. It came up the hill at a forty-five-degree angle, so it was commonly called the washboard. Since it rained frequently, the driver of the Volkswagen bus was constantly trying to keep it controlled as it slipped and slid from side to side. Scary? They sure could have used some good American asphalt!

Chapter 50

A Typical Day for Student Missionaries

"For we are God's fellow workers." 1 Corinthians 3:9

A typical day for the student missionaries began at 7:30 a.m. Sometimes Elder J would wake them up by calling out, "It's great to be alive!" At that time of morning the students thought the only thing great was sleep. Other times Elder J would wake them up by pounding on the door and calling out, "It's 7:30, and all is well."

The students' reply was not as cheerful. "Elder J! All was well until you woke us up."

At other times Elder J would stick his head into each room and loudly sing a children's Sabbath School song in Spanish. Elder J was not very musical and could hardly carry a tune in a bucket, so the students quickly arose. A short time later he would call out, "Time for worship." After worship they ate breakfast, checked their schedules, and separated to perform their various duties.

Last, but certainly not the least in the minds of the student missionaries, was their day off. In addition to Sabbath, everyone had one day off during the week. On this day they could relax, be lazy, write letters, etc., so they all looked forward to "their" day. Best of all, it was the time they could go into town and get away from it all. Just being able to see the town as it normally was, sometimes buying a sweet or something special to take home as a reminder of their mission trip, was a real treat.

Evenings for the students were full, too. Meetings were held every Sunday, Wednesday, and Friday night. "Involvement" was Elder J's favorite word, so he made sure there were plenty of opportunities for each one to get involved as often as possible. The evenings they were not involved were spent talking, goofing around, and getting to stay up as long as they wanted. Their favorite pastime was playing *Stilts, Creeps, and Bangs,* which was a simple game that only required a coin and a hand and could be played even in the most remote mission field.

On Thursday night, July 4, a few of the students went to the home of a radio operator. Elder J explained to him that the youth were student missionaries, telling him a little about the organization to which they belonged. They were then given the opportunity to put telephone patches through to their parents. It was pouring rain that night, but when they heard the voices of their loved ones at home, it was thrilling. The man who operated the radio in the United States said, "The Lord must really be on your side as the contact is really fuzzy, but when you get on the line, it is as clear as it can be." They agreed. Then Elder J took the opportunity to impress them with a good thought. "See! You never know when or where you can be a witness for God."

Sabbath, July 6, was another unique day, for they all went to Sabbath School and church in the city of Totonicapan. Joyce Carpenter and Liz Bowes sang a duet, and the nine-member student missionary choir sang *"Cuando Alla Se Pase Lista"* ("When the Roll is Called Up Yonder") for church. The people really enjoyed hearing the students sing in their own language.

Sabbath afternoon the whole group went to beautiful Lake Atitlan at the foot of a volcano. They stopped at a beautiful spot on the shore and quietly looked over the lake. All was so peaceful that everyone suddenly felt like pouring their hearts out in gratitude to God.

On their way back to the clinic, they stopped to look at a waterfall. Unfortunately, somehow Ken managed to drop his glasses in the pool at the foot of the falls. He climbed down and began searching for them in the water but could not find them, so he climbed back up, went to the camper, and put on his swimming trunks. When he came back to the pool, he plunged into the ice-cold water, determined to find his glasses, and with his determination and the prayers of the other members of the group, he found them. When he climbed out of the water, his blue lips were smiling as he triumphantly held his glasses in his hand.

It was near sundown by then, and the group could see the fog beginning to cover the volcano, then the lake, and finally the waterfall. They all thought, *What a beautiful way to end the Sabbath day.* Everyone agreed that the day had been a very special one. The places they had seen would be remembered and treasured for the rest of their lives.

When they returned to the clinic that night, they had to say goodbye to Dr. Hernandez. He was leaving to catch the bus that would take him to Guatemala City where he would fly back to the United States. Everyone was sorry to see him leave but excited that another doctor would soon be with them.

Sunday, July 7, was a day off for everyone—their first real vacation day. They all went to Antigua and Chichicastenango. Antigua is one of the oldest cities in Guatemala. It had once been the capital of the ancient Spanish Empire but had been destroyed by a flood. The people built another city in a different location, but it, too, was completely destroyed in 1773 by an earthquake. The city was never rebuilt, but the ruins had been partly restored as a tourist attraction. The students were able to see a partially restored Catholic church that was built in 1541.

Everyone thought the Catholic church in Chichicastenango was very strange as they had catered to the customs of the Indians by borrowing some of their pagan ways. The man standing at the door and waving a censer of incense, reminded them of a forest fire. Inside the church, blocks were placed in the center aisle for the people to lay their candles and flowers on, and many people were lighting candles and mumbling prayers.

This trip was very educational for the students, and they were happy to have a break from their duties. They enjoyed their day and had been inspired. But it felt good to return to their missionary duties.

Chapter 51

Missing People

"For the Son of Man came to seek and to save what was lost." Luke 19:10

God's plan to use Elder J to inspire young people to serve Him and others was working very well. Five students—Linda Borem, Corla Crase, Jerry Hamm, Ken and Alan Nelson—quickly volunteered to make up the crew who would paint the outside of the Totonicapan Seventh-day Adventist Church during the last week they were in Guatemala. Elder J was thrilled.

The church was an ugly washed-out green that looked like it had not had a coat of fresh paint for many years. The students were excited to start painting. As soon as they had their bucket of paint, they lathered their brush and began spreading on the paint.

It was not long before they had an audience watching them. Two students were leaning over the roof painting down the wall as far as they could reach, two were on the ground painting upwards, and one was on a very rickety Guatemalan ladder painting the in-between. By the end of each day their faces, arms, hands, hair, and clothes were speckled with paint. What a mess! But they were back at it early the next morning, very happy and proud that what they were doing was making a big difference in the appearance of the church.

It took only three days for them to give the church two coats of paint. They felt a great deal of satisfaction and joy when they went to the Totonicapan church the following Sabbath and saw their handiwork being admired by everyone. The members were so appreciative and thanked them over and over again. Each student felt that being a missionary was well worth all the effort they put into it.

Thursday was an exciting day, for several doctors and their wives were flying in to visit the clinic and minister to the needs of the local Indians. Elder J, his son Kevin, Liz Bowes, Diana Bauer, and Rhonda Butler left the clinic early that morning to greet the doctors at the Guatemala City airport.

The students were excited and began their chores early that morning so everything would be in shipshape order when Elder J returned with their guests. When all their assignments had been completed, each gave a sigh of relief and sat down to admire the results of their hard work. They waited and waited some more. As they continued waiting, they kept asking over and over again, "When are they coming? What is happening?" By 1:00 a.m. Friday they decided they were not coming. They said goodnight to each other, switched off the light, and went to bed.

Friday morning after worship and breakfast there was not much to do except sit around and wait some more. But what had happened? They should have been there long ago. The hours passed slowly, and soon it was time for the evangelistic meeting in San Cristobal to begin. What should they do? They decided the program had to go on, so they went to the meeting hoping Elder J and the others would arrive soon. But they did not.

The people were very disappointed. They had made special preparations to welcome Elwyn Platner, the public relation director for the Southeastern California Conference of Seventh-day Adventists. They had put crepe paper streamers on the ceiling and pine needles on the floor as Elder J told them that he would be taking a lot of pictures. Mrs. Alvarado, the wife of the head elder, had prepared a special hot drink for their guest. When he did not arrive, she served the drink to the student missionaries.

After the meeting ended, the students hurried back to the clinic hoping that Elder J and the guests had arrived. But they were very disappointed to learn they had not returned. Now their anxiety grew. They were tired of sitting around not knowing what was going on.

Ken Nelson decided to take the camper and see if he could find the missing people. Most of the students decided to go with him, and praise God, they soon found the missing people at the San Cristobal church. Even though it was late, Elder J held the meeting.

The few students who had stayed at the clinic were still worrying. A short time later Ken returned, followed by the Volkswagen bus full of their guests. In a moment, *Clinica Vista Hermosa* was a jumble of excited greetings.

When the guests were comfortably seated in front of the fireplace in the clinic living room, they explained their delay. The plane had to stop in Mexico City to get some legal papers. This meant going to the embassy, which was very time consuming. It was late when they finished with all the red tape, so they stayed at a motel for the night. That is why Elder J and those with him had to spend a night in a motel. The guests' and students' sleeping quarters had been prepared earlier for their guests. After listening to their story, it was time for everyone to get a good night's rest.

The next morning the paint crew and the student missionary choir went to the Totonicapan church for Sabbath School. Later they joined the others at the San Cristobal church for the church service. It was there that Elder J announced they would hold a free clinic that afternoon for only Adventists. But he forgot that his words were broadcast over the entire city. Was he in for a big surprise!

After dinner they all hurried to the Quezaltenango church for their afternoon program. When they returned to the clinic, there were more than forty Indians waiting for the "Adventist only" free clinic and more were streaming up the driveway. When it was all over, everyone felt like they had converted the whole city to Adventism.

Saturday night Elder J and some of the guests went to the meeting in San Cristobal, while Dr. and Mrs. Fisher and Dr. Herrick stayed behind. They were in for another surprise. Twelve spirited, fun-loving teenagers decided it was time to let off some steam. They had a shaving cream war. The screaming, laughing youth were a mess, and shaving cream was all over the house. They had not hurt anyone or anything, so it was just good, clean fun. Afterward came their penalty when they had to clean the house and make sure it was once again free of shaving cream.

The student missionaries requested to be awakened early Sunday morning, July 14, so they could say goodbye to Elder and Mrs. J, who had to leave early to go to Europe for an upcoming Youth Congress. But they were in for a big disappointment. Elder J, Mrs. J, and Kevin felt they could not face the sad faces and tears of goodbye. So they, along with the doctors and Mr. Platner, had quietly slipped away to fly back to the United States without awakening them.

Dr. Roy Bowes and his wife, Dena, and Ken Butler were left in charge of the students. They wondered how they would awaken them, but they had nothing to fear for Bill Hall took it upon himself to replace Elder J Each morning he would come around and shout, "It's GREAT to be alive." All the kids agreed. But soon it was time to think about packing up and heading home.

Thursday morning, July 18, the students arose early. They were eager to get home. Suddenly they were sad to be leaving. They thought that the five weeks they had been there were the most fun they had in their whole lives.

After all the hassle of packing and seeing that nothing was left behind, they were finally ready to hit the road. As the caravan slowly headed down the driveway at 6:30 that morning, the students all began singing "We are a Missionary Band." What memories they treasured.

Their return trip was uneventful until the Volkswagen bus blew its engine. The shop in Guadalajara wanted two times the price for a new engine compared to the price for one in the United States. The decision was made to empty their luggage out of the trailer, pile it into the Volkswagen bus, drop the trailer, and tow the Volkswagen bus behind the camper. After that, the only stops they made before reaching home were for gas.

As they rolled onto the campus of Orangewood Academy at 9:00 a.m. on July 25, they laughingly began singing their theme song, "We are a Missionary Band," for the last time. Their great adventure had ended. Or was it only just beginning? Only God knew, but their six-week adventure would be something they would never forget.

But their adventure was not over. Elder J had already made arrangements for the missionary students to visit churches, camp meetings, Vacation Bible Schools, and other places to share their exciting experiences in the mission field. They hoped that other students would be inspired with the desire to "go into all the world and teach the gospel." The students soon discovered that this was yet another inspiring and exciting adventure.

Elder J continued his work as Orange County Adventist Youth Coordinator after the Guatemala mission trip. Guatemala had been the very first student missionary trip, but it certainly was not the last one. On Sunday, June 8, 1969, Elder J led twelve students from the Orangewood Academy in Garden Grove, California, on another mission trip. This time to San Pedro Sula on the southern coast of Honduras.

The students who went on this mission adventure were Dennis Callendar, Brent Border, John Whirledge, Portia Shidler, Karen Reindel, Jeff Nash, Jackie Baker, Gwen Chueta, Donna Rogers, and Jeanette Hickman, along with Elder J, Mrs. J, Gary, Dennis, and Kevin. Alma Sturtz, the Orangewood Academy home economics teacher, two physicians, a dentist, four paramedical assistants, and a few people from the Northern and Central California Conferences made up the rest of the missionary group.

****

For several consecutive summers Elder J took other student missionaries on mission adventures. His idea to inspire students to become missionaries by taking them on student missionary trips turned out to be such a great idea that other schools soon followed his example. Now mission trips are planned every year to inspire youth to find their happiness in serving God. The world needs to praise God and thank Him for inspiring Elder J with this wonderful idea. Yes, the student missionaries had truly found joy in serving the Lord. You, too, will find that your cup of joy will soon be full and overflowing as you serve Him and others.

Chapter 52

Youth on the Beach

"Feed my lambs." John 21:15

The Southeastern California Conference had given Elder J a full load when they called him to be the youth pastor at Orangewood Academy and the full-time youth pastor for the Adventist youth of Orange County. This was the first time a youth pastor had ever been assigned to the county, but it was not the last.

The student missionaries kept Elder J quite busy his first year. But God knew there was more for him to accomplish because of his deep desire to inspire students to be workers for Him. After praying about this, he soon received his answer. God inspired two students, Doug Clark and Dennis Lee, to come to him with an idea. They said, "Elder J, what do you think about doing beach evangelism?"

When Elder J heard this, he was instantly inspired, for he was aware that these two students knew a lot about the drug culture that was so prevalent in the world. "This is a great idea! Let's do it!" he said.

Plans were made for the beach evangelism program to be conducted in the resort area of Newport Beach for the last four weeks of the summer. With divine guidance, Elder J petitioned the American Legion Post for the use of the scout building behind their hall. It was only a block from the beach and would be perfect for the beach ministry. The authorities were a little reluctant about giving their permission, but after Elder J assured them there would be no trouble, permission was granted.

On August 8, Elder J and a group of helpers descended on the hall armed with paint, brushes, sanders, mops, and other materials. By Sunday morning everything was ready for the grand opening of "The Eternal Bliss" ministry. That was the name the youth gave the beach ministry because it clearly epitomized what they knew the people desired.

A psychedelic sign was made to point the people to the little building where they could watch a film, have free refreshments, read, or hang out. The youth began coming right away to investigate the center. Jeanette Hickman, a junior at Loma Linda University, offered the guys and girls cookies and punch. Most of them were wearing surfer gear, swimsuits, or bikinis.

The first film shown was *The Parable*. Dennis Lee had chosen it. He encouraged the audience to watch it in silence to "catch the vibrations" of what they would see and, at the end, to meditate on what they had seen and felt. For those interested in discussing the film, he announced he would be willing to meet with them later. Other films were shown throughout the day—some were on the use of drugs, others on teen marriage and sex, and the problems youth were facing in the world's new morality.

Elder J was thrilled with the beach ministry program. It was a great success from the first day. Mrs. J, Paul and Marguerite Flemming, and the twenty student helpers who made up his staff were also thrilled. What a big help they had been to him. He appreciated each one so much, and especially seventy-year-old Shirley (Grandma) Cline who graciously prepared the refreshments and the noon meals for the staff. She was a wonderful lady, and everyone loved her.

All four of Elder J's core staff were juniors at Loma Linda University; there was Jeanette Hickman, Doug Clark, Terry Shaw (a theology student), and Dennis Lee (a premed student) who had knowledge of all types of drugs. Dennis had studied various religions looking for his "thing," and eighteen months prior he had made his decision to follow Christ.

It was mentioned in one of the staff meetings that many of the beach youth came from affluent homes and drove nice cars. Some came to "The Eternal Bliss" center fifteen or twenty times a week. Jeanette remarked that she felt the youth wearing beads and long hair had been prejudged and that their physical appearance had nothing to do with what they were inside or what they were seeking. This was an eye-opener for the staff, but they learned to wait for the young people to come to them. They also learned to discern whether they came to listen and talk seriously or simply to argue.

Many times Elder J asked the young people what the films meant to them. One San Diego State College engineering senior answered, "It makes real sense to me that there is happiness in serving others. I am certainly deeply impressed about all this."

Toward the end of the four-week project, four different musical ensembles came to perform on the beaches as well as at the center. They included The Paramount Trio, the Wayside Trio (both from La Sierra), The Message Unit (a ten-member group from Glendale), and The Pine Springs Ranch Quartet.

Elder J found that the question of life for most of the beach youth was, "Where is it?" He hoped and prayed that his pilot project would stimulate all of them to consider what Smoking Sam, a dummy used for stop-smoking demonstrations, had taught them. He also prayed that the films they had seen on the unselfish and loving lives of others would impress them with God's better way of living.

As the youth left "The Eternal Bliss" building for the very last time, each was given a copy of *This is the End* to take with them. At the last count Elder J felt the Lord had changed the outlook of at least 260 youth during their four-week beach ministry. He praised God for each and every one of them.

The expense for this first beach ministry had only been $1,000, and $119 of that had been contributed by two employees of the Legion Hall who were impressed with the aim and results of the program. Charles Hunt was one of those two employees, and he explained the reason for their gift. "All the members and neighbors appreciate what is being done to provide something for the youth to do. We hope that Preacher Bill will be back next year." No one knew then that Elder J was already planning the very next beach project.

That was not the end of their beach ministry. Elder J was inspired to organize a scuba diving club, which he named the Kelp Krawlers. Dave Johnson was the instructor, and eventually there were about fifty certified scuba divers. Usually about twenty divers went on their outings. Sometimes they traveled to Baja, California, or to Catalina Island to scuba dive. They were all very happy to camp out and sleep on the beaches.

But God was not done inspiring Bill with other projects!

Chapter 53

Platte Valley Academy Miracle

"Faith comes from hearing the message." Romans 10:17

God chose Elder Bill Jamerson to be the guest speaker for the Week of Prayer at the Seventh-day Adventist Platte Valley Academy in Shelton, Nebraska. The first day there he stood before the students holding a copy of *Good News for Modern Man*. The cover was very colorful and the designs were rather bizarre, so it immediately caught the students' attention. As he waved this little book before them, he said he would tell them about it later. He proceeded to share with the students about his work with youth and how important it was to have Christ in their lives. One thing he did not tell the students was that they had to do this or that. He merely pointed out the advantages of letting Christ lead in their lives.

At the right time the students separated for their prayer bands. At first they just stood around, self-conscious about their feelings. But during the next few days Elder J spent a lot of time talking with the students, and they began to relax. He listened carefully as each one did their best to tell him about their strange feelings and thoughts of Christ coming into their lives. Many did not know what to say or how to explain just why they wanted to talk with him. He counseled and prayed with each student, and as each one left, he felt as if their burdens had really been rolled away, and he praised God.

Elder J loved sports, so he joined the students in their games. This really surprised them, but it was his athletic abilities that truly amazed them. Revealing his special talents helped to endear him to all the students.

It soon became evident that some of the students had met Christ but, Elder J was very concerned about the others. Would some of those doubters be too hardened to believe they needed to be, or could be, changed by Christ? This was the crucial point of the Week of Prayer. But how would Christ reach those students?

As Elder J mingled among the students and heard the kind of music they were listening to, he realized that this was part of their problem. He patiently pointed out the danger of listening to the satanic beat of their music, the foul language, and bad story lines. Later that afternoon he arranged for a campfire to be held Thursday night.

Some students came early that evening to watch as he lit the fire. The flames blazed brighter and brighter, and as the sky darkened, more students arrived and gathered around the pile of burning wood. When the flames were blazing high in the night sky, Elder J watched in amazement as one by one the students brought their once treasured records and tapes and threw them into the flames. When the last one had been tossed into the fire, everyone cheered and praised God. What a victory celebration that night turned out to be. But the best was yet to come.

Shara Williams, a seventeen-year-old senior, was the instrument God used in the conversion of other students who had not yet been reached. Since December 1968, she could barely speak. She had a misplaced cartilage in her throat, which was often swollen and very painful. The doctors said that surgery would not help. They told her that if she had to speak she should do so only in a whisper, and if she was to sing, to do so with moderation. This was quite a burden to Shara, for she had been singing, as she put it, "since she was knee-high to a grasshopper."

In spite of the carefulness Shara exercised, her condition worsened. In August 1969, she was forbidden to sing. In September the doctors forbid her to even whisper for fear she would permanently damage her throat. So Shara remained silent.

Elder J remembers September 30 when Shara walked into his office the first time. She could not speak, but she had written everything she wanted to say to him in a letter. Elder J quietly read the letter, then tenderly took her hand, and said, "Shara, what this academy needs is a miracle, so I am asking you to sing in chapel tomorrow. Will you sing for me?"

Shara smiled her sweet smile, and although she felt a little doubtful, she nodded her head in agreement. Elder J suggested they kneel and pray that the Lord would bless her and make it possible for her to sing the next day. Tears were in Shara's eyes when the prayer ended. She stood up, smiled at Elder J, and mouthed a little, "Thank you."

The next day Elder J wondered, *Will Shara sing? Will God work a miracle?* A hush fell upon all those assembled in the PVA chapel as Elder J told them about Shara. He then invited her to come and sing for the students. She was smiling as she advanced to the chapel pulpit while the students were leaning and twisting in their seats to get a better view of her.

Shara began to sing. Her beautiful voice was heard ringing clear and strong throughout the chapel. A big smile suddenly appeared on Elder J's face, and he praised God. Yes! A true miracle! An honest to goodness true-life miracle had taken place at Platte Valley Academy! Elder J and the students were humbled and sat in awe as she sang. How could anyone ever doubt God's grace again?

A change had surely come to PVA. A certain peacefulness reigned on campus that was indescribable. Students rededicated themselves to God, and everyone witnessed a miraculous transformation in their lives. Several students began to prepare for the baptism planned for Sabbath, October 4. They prayed together and studied together as well as with other students who were interested in sharing the joy of knowing their Savior.

Before communion and the baptism were held that Friday evening, five young men were brought before the student body and ordained as junior deacons. Praise God! The communion service that night was a new way of experiencing the Lord's Supper for the students. This time they were served large cups of pure grape juice and large pieces of bread instead of the usual swallow of grape juice and morsel of bread. As they ate the bread and sipped the sweet grape juice in the candlelit cafeteria, they quietly meditated for at least a full five minutes.

Then someone began reading the words of Christ. His promises seemed to take on new meaning and new beauty as they fell on ears that were no longer deaf to the call of Jesus. Everyone there felt the presence of Christ that night. Words cannot describe the joy Elder J saw on the faces of those students. What a wonderful and awesome way for the Week of Prayer at PVA to end!

Chapter 54

Nebraska

"You heard my cry for mercy when I called to you for help." Psalm 31:22

It was early in the spring of 1969 that Bill received an invitation from Elder Sanders, the president of the Nebraska Conference, to be their youth director. *At last,* Bill thought, *God has worked out my goal to work with the youth.* He thanked the Lord for this blessing.

In the same breath, Bill was sad because he knew he would miss Orangewood Academy. The students were sad, too, when they learned he had accepted the call. But soon, with the help of the staff, plans were made for a big farewell party for Elder J and his family. That night there was music, speeches, laughter, tears, and plenty of delicious food. Before anyone realized it, school was out for the summer and the Jamerson family was on the road heading for Lincoln, Nebraska.

Much to Bill's surprise he learned that the union youth director was Jim Harris, his former classmate at Alhambra Union High School in California. They had taken shop class together when Jim was not an Adventist. Jim and Bill had met again at Pacific Union College in 1945, and now for the third time in Nebraska. Jim had survived the Bataan death march as a prisoner of war in the South Pacific, and Bill had survived the Battle of the Bulge in Europe. Now the two of them learned they would be working together for the youth. Amazing! What a wonderful way God had of leading these two friends together again.

Living in Lincoln, Nebraska, was not an easy adjustment for the Jamerson family after living in beautiful, sunny Orange County, California. It was especially difficult for June. She disliked the high humidity, chilling cold, and freezing winds blowing over the snowy field outside her kitchen window. She was not happy that Bill had to spend so much time away from home, either. She had all the responsibility of the three boys on her shoulders, and this was not easy.

Neither Kevin nor Dennis adjusted well to the move. Kevin missed his friends at Orangewood Academy, although he did love the snow and snow sports. Dennis had a difficult time as well. He, too, missed his friends at Orangewood Academy. He was not interested in any of his studies in Lincoln. He was not too happy about working part time in the broom factory at school either, but Bill and June thought that would be good for him.

Gary was living at home while attending Union College in Lincoln. Soon a cute little red-headed girl caught his attention. Their relationship moved quickly, and when school ended, the two of them left for California with plans of getting married. But plans do not always go as desired and before the summer was over they had broken up. Gary took their break up pretty hard because he had deep feelings for her. But Bill reminded him that God had better plans for him. The problems the boys were having adjusting to their new surroundings was a big concern for Bill and June.

Living in Nebraska was equally hard on Bill, but for different reasons. Bill had to travel the dangerous highways in all kinds of weather. He could handle the rain, but he had no experience driving in blowing snow or on icy streets. One time Bill and June were driving somewhere when their car hit a patch of black ice and spun around until they were facing oncoming traffic. That was one scary moment and an unforgettable experience!

Another scary trip for Bill was when he left home to go to Omaha to attend a youth committee meeting. That evening trucks and cars were driving far too fast in the blowing snow. The snow began to fall heavier until visibility was almost impossible. Bill wondered if he was going to make it to Omaha. He silently prayed, "Lord! Is this really where You want me?"

He was very tense the whole time he was fighting the blowing snow and traffic. He was also getting very tired and began thinking maybe it was time to cut his trip short. When he came to the next motel and saw the vacancy sign, he stopped and registered. After closing the motel door behind him, he fell on the bed utterly exhausted by his ordeal. He had made it to the outskirts of Omaha but would not make it to the meeting. A few minutes later he knelt and thanked the Lord for His many blessings before crawling into bed. The nice warm blankets gave him a wonderful feeling of safety, and a moment later he was sound asleep. The storm passed during the night, so he was able to return home the next day.

Their home in Lincoln was near Union College, and Bill's office was just across the street. Despite the difficulties adjusting to their new home. Bill still had a heart for serving the Lord, and he began to look for ways to engage the youth in service. One day he was impressed to start some music groups who could go to small churches and sing and play their instruments while giving their testimonies for Jesus. Several teams were organized, and soon they were going out nearly every week, which proved to be a wonderful blessing to the churches in the community.

Before school ended Bill began thinking of the scheduled junior camps. When he went to visit the camp, the first thing he noticed were canoes and a lake for skiing. He thought, *This is great! Children love canoeing and waterskiing!* But he noticed that more cabins were needed, so he got busy and built one. Many more cabins were needed, so he started a Million Penny Fund Drive, which turned out to be a great success and a blessing as it provided for more cabins.

Junior camp was a real challenge for Bill because he had never led one before.

He had faith that God would see him through, and He did. That summer's junior camp turned out to be a great success.

Unfortunately, there had been no success in solving the Jamerson family problems. What should they do? Bill felt he could not tolerate another snowy and icy winter. June did not enjoy the cold or the humidity, or being alone so much while Bill traveled. The boys were not doing well either. The whole family was miserable.

Bill decided they should get together and talk about their situation. After discussing their options, they knelt and prayed together. Each one asked God for wisdom to know what was best for them and what they should do. Then they thanked Him for hearing and answering their prayers.

Jim Harris, Bill's friend from high school, seemed to sense their difficulty in adjusting to Nebraska, and one day he came to Bill and said, "Bill, if this situation is too much for you and your family, I just want you to know that we will understand, and you can return to California at any time."

Bill was relieved to hear this, and he thanked Jim for his understanding and consideration. He told Jim he was sorry. This was the first time Bill had not completed his call, but he was sure God understood their situation and would prepare the way before them.

June and the boys were elated when they heard the news. Then Bill mentioned the fact that now he was out of work. So they knelt for prayer, and Bill said, "Lord, You know I need a job to go back to California. We are putting all our needs in Your hands, and we pray that You will do for me and my family what is best."

Chapter 55

What's Next?

"For the LORD watches over the way of the righteous." Psalm 1:6

At this time Ed Bryan was chaplain at Glendale Adventist Hospital. He and his wife, Dorothy, had been close friends of Bill and June during their years in Peru. When he heard that Bill needed a job, God inspired him to speak to John Robertson, the senior pastor of the Vallejo Drive Church.

Pastor Robertson showed great interest in having Bill join the church staff. A few days later Bill and June received a call from Elder Helmeth Retzer, president of the Southern California Conference, inviting him to be associate pastor at the Vallejo Drive Seventh-day Adventist Church in Glendale. He would be in charge of youth and church growth. Bill happily accepted the call, and the Jamerson family was soon on their way to sunny southern California. This ministry fit Bill perfectly, and he and his family praised God for arranging things. What a blessing. God had been in control all along the way.

Elder Leonard Webb was then treasurer of the Southern California Conference, and he advised Bill not to buy a home at that time because prices were much too high. He made arrangements for Bill and his family to move into a parish home on the hills above Glendale. The Jamersons lived in that house for three years.

During that time Bill and June began a walking health program. They began by walking ten minutes, fifteen, then thirty minutes until they worked up to a forty-five minute daily walk. (At age eighty-seven and eighty-four, they are still carrying on this physical fitness habit.)

They were happily settled in their home and community when, in 1971, Bill and June awoke around 6:00 a.m. to their house shaking. They knew instantly it was a California earthquake, but it was a bad one. Many people were killed—buildings, hospitals, and parts of some freeways were destroyed by what is now called the Sylmar earthquake. Bill and June suffered no injury and no loss, and they thanked God for His care over them.

Bill worked hand-in-hand with Elders Robertson and John Todorovich at the Vallejo Drive Church. He was really enjoying his work, but one morning God suddenly brought something to his attention. *What are you doing for the parents who work at the conference, Adventist Book Center, hospital, and Voice of Prophecy?*

Don't they need an outlet for their children during the summer?

The more Bill thought about this, the more determined he was to do something about it. He submitted plans to Elder Robertson for a children's day camp. It would be open from 6:30 a.m. to 6:30 p.m. for ten weeks each summer. Elders Robertson and Todorovich liked his idea very much and gave him their full approval.

Bill immediately began arranging trips to the beach, mountains, amusement parks, museums, gardens, and educational centers. Seventh-day Adventist college and academy students were hired as camp counselors. Zara Lemon, recently retired from Glendale Hospital, became the grandmother for the camp. Ted Miller was one of the day camp's bus drivers.

Jean Duke was one of the parents who needed help for the summer. She worked at the Adventist Book Center in Glendale. School was ending soon, and she was worried about what to do with her nine-year-old son, John, until school started. When she heard about the day camp, she felt it was an answer to her prayer. What a blessing it would be for him to be safely in "Uncle Bill's" care for the summer.

Camp attendance averaged about forty children per day. Counselors were given an average of five children to care for on each excursion, which was no easy task. On their trips to Disneyland, it was decided the castle would be home base. At certain hours each counselor was to check in with Uncle Bill to account for the children in his/her care.

On one of their trips to Disneyland, everything went well until the last hour when one counselor reported a boy had been lost on Tom Sawyer Island. This was Bill's most dreaded moment, and to make matters worse the boy was epileptic! "Please, God, help us find him," Bill prayed. At 5:30 p.m. the rest of the staff and children boarded the bus for the return trip to Glendale, leaving Bill to look for the lost boy.

Bill started walking the streets of Disneyland looking for the boy while his parents, who had been contacted and had arrived at the theme park, walked in another direction, praying constantly to find their lost son. This was a nightmare for them. Before long Bill saw the boy walking toward him—he felt as if he was in seventh heaven. The boy was happy to see Uncle Bill, also, and together they soon located his parents. With thankful hearts they all praised God and thanked Him for the boy's safety.

The children's day camp was a great success in spite of this upsetting situation. The parents loved Uncle Bill, his program, and leadership, and so did the children. George and Roberta Pierce especially appreciated this program and never failed to send their three children to day camp.

That first year's day camp inspired other churches to organize their own day camps. Many of which are still going strong.

****

When George and Roberta's youngest son, Richard, was grown and fell in love with Marcia, he asked Uncle Bill to perform their marriage ceremony. Bill was very happy he could do this for one of his "kids."

It is a joy for Bill to see his "kids" all grown up and ready to start a family of their own. Uncle Bill still sees the Pierce family from time to time and thanks God for them.

Chapter 56

Warned

"Warn a divisive person once, and then warn him a second time." Titus 3:10

On another day camp outing, the children were taken to a beach in southern California. They had a lot of fun on the bus singing and laughing, and they knew the bus was loaded with sweet corn and other good things to eat. Later in the day they built a nice bonfire. Everyone had a great time playing ball, swimming in the surf, and eating the roasted corn and marshmallows. All too soon it was time to get back on the bus for their return trip to Glendale.

As they were preparing to leave, one of the camp counselors invited Jim,* the lifeguard, to come to a special Bible class that evening in Glendale. Much to everyone's surprise and delight, he showed up and continued to come and fellowship with the day camp staff.

Jim soon became the day camp director. Later he and his girlfriend asked Uncle Bill to officiate at their wedding. This young couple were not Seventh-day Adventists. After the wedding ceremony, there was plenty of dancing and drinking. The young Adventist guests were not interested in that because they wanted to study the Bible. When someone discovered the basement, they all decided that would be a perfect place to study in peace and quiet until the reception was done.

School was about to start when Jim decided to attend college in northern California. When Bill heard about this, he asked his good friends Paul and Marguerite Flemming to take special care of Jim and his wife. The Flemmings were happy to do this and began Bible studies with them. Before long Jim and his wife were baptized.

Jim was attending Pacific Union College when he decided to become a minister. After his graduation he was invited to be an associate pastor of an Adventist church. Sadly, the pastor of that church was transferred not long after Jim accepted the position. This left Jim alone with no leadership to follow, and he became so discouraged that he just walked away.

Bill was shocked and worked diligently with him but he could not get him to stay with the church. He learned later that Jim became involved with an eastern religion, which saddened Bill. He felt strongly that Jim could have become a great youth leader in an Adventist church or even a future conference youth director.

This truly was a very sad thing to happen to a young man with such promise. But Bill thanks God for the other day camp attendees who were inspired to faithfully follow Jesus.

*a pseudonym

Chapter 57

How God Worked

"He who watches over Israel will neither slumber nor sleep." Psalm 121:4

During Bill and June's third year of living in the parish house, the state of California decided to build a freeway next to it. Bill heard that the state was selling adjoining lots next to the freeway only a half block from their parish house. The lot had a wonderful view so Bill told the conference treasurer they should buy it. He said they would not buy it, but he suggested that Bill should purchase it. Bill thought about it the next few days and put in a bid for not more than $3,000. God saw that this was a good investment for the Jamersons, and they bought the property.

Dave Johnson, the diving instructor for the students at Orangewood Academy, called Bill one day and told him the state was selling a lot only three blocks from the conference office in Glendale. Bill said he was not interested in buying and selling property but told Dave he would look at it. After seeing that the lot was such a beautiful piece of property, Bill decided to put a bid on it of up to $10,000. His bid was the only one made, so it was accepted. Putting these two pieces of property into the Jamerson's hands was the beginning of the way God was helping them to have a home fully paid for by the time they were ready to retire. What an awesome God we serve. He not only takes care of our daily needs, He provides for our future needs as well. Praise God.

In 1976 Bill received a call from Elder Phil Follett, president of the Northern California Conference, inviting him to be the associate pastor at Sacramento Central church. Bill thought it over for a moment and accepted the call. After getting settled in their new home, it was not long before Bill was organizing a day camp program and a sports program for that area. It, too, became a great success.

Two and a half years later Bill received another call from Glendale. This call was asking Bill to be the assistant Sabbath School director for the Southern California Conference under the leadership of Pastor Earlene Calkins. Bill gladly accepted the call because his goal was to inspire young people to follow Jesus. He was soon making plans to hold meetings for children during the adult evangelistic meetings. His Tots to Teens programs included crusades, which was the term for seminars at that time.

Bill sometimes asked Jean Duke, who was the kindergarten leader at her church, to teach children ages five through nine while he worked with those ten years of age and older. They worked together several times for groups holding meetings in various places, including Camp Cedar Falls located in the Angeles National Forest. Although Jean did not speak Spanish, they even did a Spanish crusade held by Pastor Isaac Lara at the White Memorial Church. This was the beginning of many crusades they did together over the years that followed.

Chapter 58

Who Needs Friends?

"A friend loves at all times." Proverbs 17:17

Bill wonders what he would have done without certain friends during his ministry at Vallejo Drive church in Glendale. He will remember some of them forever. Greg, Wes, and Shirley Chaison were members of the church. They were delighted when they heard Bill was organizing a strong sports program for children. God knew Bill needed these spiritually strong people behind him. What a blessing they were to Bill. His dream of Seventh-day Adventist organized baseball teams for Glendale became a reality with their help.

Greg was young and single. He worked for an ambulance company as an emergency medical technician, and he enjoyed baseball. From the very beginning he took over the program and scheduled fields where the teams could play. He suited each team with shirts and caps and made sure there were umpires for each game. You might say he was the spark plug that kept the six ball teams going during the baseball season. His parents loved baseball, too, and together they made a great team working behind the scene for the teams.

Bill also remembers Kenneth and Ruth Gaede and their two sons in a special way. They loved riding their motorcycles. One day they came to Bill and asked, "Why don't we organize a motorcycle club so we can spread the gospel to other motorcycle clubs?" The church was not too enthusiastic about this idea but finally decided to give it a short trial. Ken immediately began building a trailer that would hold six to eight bikes. When it was finished, it was loaded and taken for outings whenever possible. Other motorcyclists soon loaded their vehicles and joined them.

Bill never learned to ride a motorcycle, but Dennis and Kevin, his sons, did. They loved it and wanted their dad to buy one, but after Bill saw Kevin slide his uncontrolled cycle about twenty feet down a trail, there was no amount of pleading that could change his mind. Fortunately, Kevin only suffered scratches and no broken bones.

Bill always stayed in camp while the others took their cycles out on the mountain trials. On one outing he had been enjoying the peace and quiet of nature and reading a book when he happened to glance up to see twelve-year-old Kenny Dupper pushing his cycle across the field toward camp. He called out, "What's the matter?"

Kenny shouted back, "I hit a waterhole and now my cycle won't start."

This was a sad moment for Kenny. The day was young and now he was stuck in camp. Bill said, "Kenny, you know Uncle Bill knows nothing about motorcycles. But my friend Jesus does, so why don't we pray and ask Him to start your motorcycle?"

Kenny was not sure that would help, but he willingly knelt down with Bill for prayer. When they stood up, Bill said, "OK, Kenny. Now start your cycle."

Kenny went to his cycle, and much to his astonishment, the motor miraculously roared to life. He was overjoyed and smiled from ear to ear as he took off for the mountain trails. Bill was overjoyed, too, and he thanked God for answering their prayer. He knew Kenny would never forget that prayer can change things. What a beautiful lesson he had learned that morning.

Bill also has fond memories of Frank and Joanna Benna. They were two very short people, but every inch of them was filled with love for Jesus. They were such a happy couple and an inspiration to everyone. They were always smiling and so willing to help Uncle Bill wherever they could. Besides that, they cheerfully helped with whatever needed to be done around the church. Truly, they were a blessing to all who knew them.

Two other young men, Dennis Yoder and Clayton Jantzi, became fast friends with Bill while he ministered in Glendale. Dennis was twenty-one and Clayton was eighteen-years-old when they were drafted into the army. Due to their religious beliefs as Mennonites, they were conscientious objectors, which means they refused to take life. The army classified them as 1W so they received no military basic training, did not carry weapons, and received no service benefits or pay. Both were assigned to serve out their military duties at Glendale Adventist Hospital, where they were paid by the hospital.

Part of Bill's work in Glendale was to have worship for the nursing students and to find ways to entertain them. The gym next to the church was an ideal place to begin. Every Wednesday night was set aside for volleyball games. The students never failed to come, and one night the two young Mennonite men came. After that first night, Dennis and Clayton never missed a Wednesday night's game. It was such fun and very good exercise. After several months of playing volleyball, these two young men began attending church. After all, they were already religious, and the church was nearby, so why not. What they learned became a rich blessing to them later.

It was during these Wednesday night games that Dennis met and fell in love with Anna Mary Green, and a wedding soon followed. They soon became involved with another activity that Bill had inherited when he came to Glendale—waterskiing. The church provided a chuck wagon to carry the food needed on the two trips planned each year. Sometimes as many as 100 young people went on these weekend outings. They had great fun skiing on Lake Mojave, which is part of the Colorado River.

Then one day Anna Mary's father, Harvey Green, told Bill he was interested

The Yoder Family

in becoming a Seventh-day Adventist Christian. Not long after that Bill baptized him in the hospital swimming pool.

Around that time, Dennis Yoder and Bill's son Gary were working for Bob Jones in the hospital's Respiratory Department. Bill encouraged them many times to become respiratory therapists. But Gary moved east, while Dennis stayed in Glendale and became a therapist. Years later, Dennis Yoder and Bob Jones both moved their families to Paradise, California, where they were employed by the Feather River Hospital in the Pulmonary Department. Bob was the director, Dennis a therapist, and Anna Mary a nurse. Eventually Clayton and his wife, Barbara, moved to Paradise, and he became a member of the Feather River Hospital's Maintenance Department.

These friends had no way of knowing then that Bill would also move to Paradise when the right time came, or that Dennis would become Pathfinder leader for the church and that he would eventually become head of the Pulmonary Department. But God has a way of leading those who are willing to be led. Instead of the military, God placed them in Glendale Adventist Hospital where they could be trained to carry on a great work for Him.

Years later Bill had the privilege of baptizing Dennis and Anna Mary's two daughters, Denise and Deborah, and both became nurses. God is so good.

Another individual who Bill worked closely with was Jean Duke. She loved children and child evangelism and was dedicated to serving God. She happily held Sabbath School workshops every quarter for the Southern California Conference of Seventh-day Adventists. This led her to gradually begin working closely with Bill. When Bill asked her to be the kindergarten leader one year for the Vallejo Drive church Vacation Bible School, she quickly and happily accepted.

Bill was watching her lead one morning when she noticed a young boy, Tony Anobile, earnestly singing. She invited him to come up and lead the music for the children, which he did cheerfully. The children loved it. What a voice this six-year-old lad had. When he grew up, he became the assistant youth director of the Southern California Conference and eventually the president of the Arizona Seventh-day Adventist Conference. This shows that Vacation Bible Schools can play a major role in leading children to follow Jesus.

Chapter 59

God Works in Strange Ways

"Whether you turn to the right or to the left, your ears will hear a voice behind you, saying, 'This is the way; walk in it.'" Isaiah 30:21

Bill received a call from Elder John Howard informing him that Elder Herb Larson, president of the Alberta Seventh-day Adventist Conference, was planning to hold a series of evangelism meetings in Edmonton, Alberta, Canada. He asked Bill to come and hold the meetings for the youth during the adult meetings starting March 17. Bill was always excited about inspiring children to follow Jesus, and he quickly agreed.

He was thinking about those meetings one morning when he suddenly said to himself, *Why don't I ask Jean to go to Canada with me and do the meetings for the younger children?* He immediately called her to his office and explained what he had in mind.

Jean was surprised and said, "I am sorry, but there is no way I can do that. First of all, I do not have a planned program for a month of meetings. Besides that, we have to move. On top of that, I have to take care of my mother who cannot see to drive anymore."

Bill was touched, but he said, "Well, let's pray about it."

Jean and her husband, Dalco, wanted to get out of the city and had promised God they would go and do what He wanted. If He would open the door, they would follow. A few days later they learned that God surely works in strange ways, for Jean's mother suddenly passed away on Valentine's Day, the day after she had celebrated her seventy-fourth birthday.

The day after the funeral Jean went to work early. As she got out of her car, Bill opened the window of his office on the second floor of the building and called out to her to come up to his office. When she entered, Bill said, "I feel the Lord is telling me to ask you one more time to go to Canada with me."

Jean said, "Well, if this is what God wants me to do, He will have to help me move and gather the materials I will need. I surely cannot do it without Him." They quietly knelt and had prayer, depending completely on the Lord's guidance.

The next day Jean and her family moved into her mother's home. A few days later she began packing assorted visuals, music, pictures, old picture rolls, and stories—anything she felt she could use in her programs. Soon the car was packed, and they were on their way to Alberta. Three days later they arrived at the Seventh-day Adventist church in Edmonton.

Jean was in pain because she developed bursitis in her shoulder from leaning against the cold window of the car. She could barely lift her right arm. Prayer was offered for her, and she was healed that same day. Praise God.

Jean and Dalco were directed to the home of their hostess, a lady who had lost her husband in a traffic accident the same day Jean's mother had died. God surely works in strange ways, but they were a blessing to each other. They are still very close friends.

Jean and Dalco got up early the day the meetings began. After breakfast and morning worship, they went directly to the church. Dalco helped Bill with his program while Jean worked on the program she would be doing that night. This was to be their routine for the whole crusade.

The church was filled with adults and children the first evening. Jean usually had fifty children in her meeting, and she thanked God for each one. Bill's meeting also had good attendance. The adult attendance continued to grow, and several people were baptized. Everyone praised God. Then it was time to bid a sad farewell to their new Canadian friends and return to southern California.

During the summer Bill received a call to hold meetings for the youth in Anchorage, Alaska. As always, it did not take him long to accept. A few minutes later he called Jean and told her the exciting news. She was excited when he invited her to come with him. This time she had no problem, for her program was ready. By the first of November Bill, June, Jean, and Dalco were in Anchorage holding meetings for the youth while the adults attended the evangelistic meetings.

The pastor's ten-year-old son, Steve, was the first to enter Jean's room on the first night of the seminar. She could tell right away that coming to these meetings was the last thing he wanted to do. He was tired of going to meetings and thought they were boring. But Steve was in for a surprise. Jean always made sure the children had fun learning about Jesus and His love for them. In the end Steve was one of the most enthusiastic of all those attending the seminar.

Bill, June, Jean, and Dalco enjoyed seeing the sights in and around Anchorage. Majestic Mount McKinley seemed to be constantly covered in clouds. The clouds finally lifted one evening, and they could see the mountain bathed in its pink glory. This was truly a beautiful sight to see. They also looked for moose roaming around the city but saw none until they returned to the church one afternoon. There was a mother and her baby in the churchyard.

Bill and June had a scheduling conflict the day they were all invited to fly to Valdez in a little one-engine plane, but Dalco and Jean were delighted to go. It was very cold and a little foggy as they drove to the airport. Just as they turned onto the street leading to the airport parking lot, the sun began to shine. They seemed to be driving through what Jean called angel dust. It was a glorious sight! Something they had never seen before or even dreamed of seeing. After parking the car they just sat there for a few minutes gazing at the awesome and glorious sight. Later they learned the angel dust was frozen fog shimmering in the sunlight.

The pilot led Dalco and Jean to his plane. A moment later the motor roared, and they raced down the runway. A few minutes later they were flying over mountains and glaciers. The pilot gave each a name. Much to their amazement and delight they had the privilege of seeing a magnificent glacier calf as a large chunk of the glacier broke off and fell into the ocean. This was a rarity in those days, but not so much now.

After lunch in Valdez, the pilot told them they would return to Anchorage a different route because fog was rolling in. A moment after they were airborne they flew over lofty snow-clad mountains and huge icy glaciers. After a while the pilot said, "Oh, now I know where we are." He had been unable to receive an answer from anyone on his radio, but when he saw the highway from Anchorage to Fairbanks, he knew their exact location. Dalco and Jean had been completely unaware of his problem and thoroughly enjoyed the majestic sights. Their Valdez trip was very exciting. They praised God for the beauty they saw that day and for their safe return. It was one trip they will never forget.

Bill had an experience in Anchorage that he would never forget. It involved three young boys who regularly attended his meetings. They soon learned to love Jesus and to accept Him as their forever Friend. Toward the close of the meetings these three boys asked to be baptized. Their parents rejoiced on learning the good news and readily approved of the boys' decisions. All three families wanted the baptisms to take place in their home church, so arrangements were soon made for this happy occasion.

Bill drove the ten miles to their home church on that special Sabbath morning. The pastor greeted him and took him to the baptismal rooms. Bill checked the baptistery, and everything seemed to be in perfect order.

Bill was dressed in a suit, white shirt, and tie and was just ready to remove his suit pants to put on the baptismal gown when the pastor said, "Bill, why don't you leave your clothes on and put on these waders. They come up pretty high so that way you will still be dressed and can quickly get back to the other church."

Bill was not sure about this but accepted the pastor's advice and put on the waders. A moment later he stepped into the baptistery. The three boys were already lined up and waiting for their turn to be baptized. When the first boy stepped into the water, he suddenly let out a shout, "The water is too hot!" Bill had not felt how hot the water was through the waders, but the boy sure did. Cold water was quickly added, and soon he was back in the water ready to be baptized. Bill began in his usual way, baptizing him in the name of the Father, Son, and Holy Spirit. Everything proceeded as normal for the second boy's baptism.

The problem arose when Bill went to baptize the third boy. Bill is tall, and the third boy was short. As Bill leaned over and lowered him beneath the water, he suddenly felt warm water filling the waders. *Oh no!* he thought. But it was too late. His clothes were soaked.

Bill removed the waders as soon as he was out of the baptistery. Wearing his soaking wet clothes in zero-degree weather, he drove home as quickly as he could to change into dry clothing.

Jean made an altar call for the children in her class that day. Each child placed a little felt heart around the felt Jesus on the felt board to show they had given their hearts to Jesus. Jean still praises God for "her kids" and often wonders how many were baptized later.

All too soon the seminar ended and the Tots to Teens team had to say goodbye to their new Alaskan friends and board the plane for their trip home. They waved once again as the plane pulled away, and all praised God for the precious souls saved in Anchorage.

Chapter 60

Paradise

"Let the little children come to me, and do not hinder them, for the kingdom of heaven belongs to such as these." Matthew 19:14

In the fall of 1982 Bill began thinking about Ellen White's counsel to leave the cities and live in the country. As he drove on the congested Los Angeles freeway to work early one morning, he said, "June, I feel in my heart we will be leaving this city by the end of the year."

June replied, "What are you saying? I have the best job I ever had as a top administrative secretary. We cannot leave now." Bill reminded her again that the city was not the best place for God's people to live. This gave her a lot to think about, so they were quiet the rest of their trip to Glendale.

A few weeks later Bill received a call from Lonnie Melashenko, senior pastor of the Seventh-day Adventist church in Paradise, California. He had interned under Bill and had not forgotten him when the church board was looking for a church growth pastor. He said, "Bill, how would you like to be one of the associate pastors here in Paradise?" Before he could answer, Lonnie said, "Come on up for a visit and see what you think of the area before you give me your answer."

Bill enjoyed visiting with Lonnie and his wife, Jeanne. After seeing the church and the quaint little town of Paradise nestled among the pine trees in the foothills of the Sierras, he quickly accepted Lonnie's offer. He called June right away and told her she would love Paradise and to put their home in Duarte on the market. June was not too happy about this move since she thoroughly enjoyed her job as secretary for Relious Walden, treasurer of the Southern California Conference. But she reluctantly agreed to do what Bill asked of her.

True to his prediction, Bill was out of the city before the end of the year. June stayed to sell their house. Property was slow moving at that time, but God sent a buyer for their home. June soon followed Bill to Paradise. She often wondered if they had made the right decision when it seemed to rain every day in Paradise—it rained more than 100 inches that year. Lonnie was strong on evangelism and held one seminar each year. Shortly after Bill arrived in Paradise, Lonnie invited his father, Pastor Joe Melanshenko, to come to Paradise and hold a series of evangelistic meetings. (Joe had been the bass singer with the King's Heralds before going into full-time singing evangelism.)

Bill was thrilled and immediately thought, *We could hold a Crusade for Jesus program for the children. Maybe I could make arrangements for Dalco and Jean to come. They could do the meetings for the kindergarten and primary youth.*

When Bill called Jean, he learned that Dalco had recently retired and Jean was free. He became very excited about Joe Melashenko's seminar. Once again he was reminded that God was in control and had timed the meetings perfectly, and he thanked Him for His blessings.

Jean loved nothing more than teaching the children about Jesus, so she happily packed their bags and her program materials. Soon she and Dalco were on their way to Paradise. This time Bill and June were their host and hostess. It could not have worked out better for all concerned.

Attendance for the adult, children, and youth meetings was quite high from the beginning of the seminar to the end. It was during this time that Jean met two ladies who were deeply involved with Sabbath School. Louise Rozelle was the kindergarten leader and Sybil Mautz was the primary leader for the Paradise church. Each of these ladies inspired Jean to make several new visuals and upgrade her program. When the children loved the new visuals, she made each lady a set to thank them for their ideas.

Every night Jean had about fifty children. They were very attentive and enjoyed the programs immensely. She and Dalco praised God for those children and continued to pray for them after the meetings ended.

A few months later, on June 15, 1985, much to Jean's sorrow, Dalco died in his sleep. Shortly after that Jean was called to the Northern California Conference to work in the Child Evangelism Department of the Adventist Book Center.

Two years later, Ray Willard, the boy who had lived next door to Jean when they were children, came to Sacramento. Jean was visiting her daughter in Sacramento at the time. When the phone rang, her daughter answered. Much to Jean's surprise her daughter said, "Mom, it's a man asking for you."

Ray invited Jean to dinner, and she accepted his invitation. It was nice getting reacquainted after so many years. They comforted each other over the loss of their mates. Ray had been raised an Adventist, and they each felt that God had brought them together. A few weeks later they were married. They still marvel at the way God works in the lives of people while they are totally unaware of His leading.

Chapter 61

Mike Thomas*

"For we were all baptized by one Spirit into one body—whether Jews or Greeks, slave or free." 1 Corinthians 12:13

When Bill was associate pastor at the Sacramento Central Adventist Church, he met Mike Thomas. The Thomas family moved to the United States when Mike was quite young. They came from eastern Europe where his aunt had been brutally raped while a priest stood over her with a crucifix saying, "This is what you get for killing Christ." With this experience behind him, one can only imagine the feelings he had toward Christianity. Many more Jews had similar experiences in those days, so it is no wonder they lacked love for Christianity.

Mike had a beautiful tenor voice. At the young age of thirteen, he debuted at Carnegie Hall as a cantor. He was a devoted student as he grew to manhood and received advanced education and became a rabbi. Sometime later he became a member of Governor Ronald Reagan's staff in Sacramento as a researcher. If there were any questions about any subject, he was the one who did the research and found the answers.

Because of his family's history, Mike had a very negative attitude toward Christianity and would never touch the New Testament. However, he knew the Jewish Old Testament (Torah) extremely well, as would any highly educated rabbi. One day he became acquainted with *Patriarchs and Prophets* by Ellen White. He was astonished when he read it and wanted to know more about Ellen White. He went to the Weimar Institute near Auburn, California, in search of the answer, and in 1978 he met Elfred Lee for the first time, and they became friends.

Mike was amazed at Ellen White's knowledge and said that the information in *Patriarchs and Prophets* was "Mishnahic." The Mishnah is the collection of Hebrew laws and had only been translated into English around 1948. Only high-level rabbis had this information. Mike then said, "The Mishnah is the history of my people and it is very, very accurate. You have to know Hebrew to be able to write like she did." Then he explained that her sentence structure was not English, but Hebrew, and though the rhythm, meter, arrangement of words, and expressions were in English, it was as if she had written it in Hebrew and then translated it into English. Mike was utterly amazed!

Elfred and his family became very good friends with Mike and his family. Mike and Elfred spent many hours together studying the Bible and some of Ellen White's books. One day Mike said, "I am convinced that Ellen White was inspired by the same source that inspired the Hebrew prophets."

Even though the Old Testament Hebrew Bible is full of prophecies pointing to the Messiah, it took Ellen White's writings to prove to Mike that Jesus Christ was the fulfillment of all the Hebrew prophecies. Only then did he pick up the New Testament and read about his Jewish Messiah.

When Mike left Weimar, he met Ralph Sturgill, a member of the Meadow Vista Seventh-day Adventist Church. They began studying the Bible together.

Bill Jamerson was the associate pastor of the Sacramento Central Seventh-day Adventist Church at that time, and the church was preparing to hold an evangelistic series with Elder Bryon Spears. Bill knew Elder Spears would need a car while in Sacramento, so he contacted Ralph who owned a lease/rental business and arranged a car for him.

Sometime later Ralph called the church office and asked to speak to Bill. He told him he was studying the Bible with a Jewish rabbi and asked if he would be willing to have lunch with them as the rabbi had questions regarding the Seventh-day Adventist faith. Of course Bill was more than willing to go to lunch with them and assist Ralph in their studies.

After that meeting Bill and Ralph studied the Seventh-day Adventist doctrines with Mike. When the studies were completed, Mike accepted Jesus as the Messiah and requested to be baptized by Bill. What a privilege! Bill and Ralph were elated.

Mike chose the Bear River east of Sacramento for his baptism. He requested that it remain a secret so his wife and son would not know of his decision. If they knew he was accepting Christianity, he would be cut off from his family, his Jewish friends, and his race. He revealed later that he and his son David occasionally attended the Sacramento Seventh-day Adventist Church together.

December 22, 1979, was a bleak and cold Sabbath afternoon. But a small group—Ralph Sturgill and his wife, Bill, June, and a few others—were gathered to witness Mike's baptism. As he came up out of that cold Bear River, he was choking but praising God. Then he said, "I am now a completed Jew. I have accepted the Old and New Testaments and the Messiah that all the Jewish prophets told us about." That touched everyone's heart, and they all praised God for Mike as June draped a warm blanket around his shoulders.

A short time after Mike's baptism, Bill accepted a call from Glendale to be the associate Sabbath School director for the Southern California Conference. Sad to say, he never again was in contact with Mike or Ralph.

Years later after moving to Paradise Bill learned more about Mike's story through a copy of an e-mail he received from David Whitaker. Bill immediately phoned a friend, an elder in the Meadow Vista Seventh-day Adventist Church where Ralph attended. He was told that Ralph had passed away about four years before, but he gave Bill the phone number of Ralph's brother. Bill called him, and he verified that the Jewish rabbi who Bill had baptized was indeed Mike Thomas.

What a thrill it was for Bill to learn about Mike's connection to Elfred Lee and his commission to paint the large mural for the world headquarters of the Seventh-day Adventist Church in Washington, D.C. The painting was called "Christ, The Way of Life." It had originally been inspired by James and Ellen White who had commissioned an engraver to do a black-and-white drawing of the subject.

Mike was in Washington at the time of Elfred's commission, and soon became involved with the painting. He confirmed to Elfred that Ellen White's concept of the whole plan of salvation in both the Old and New Testament was accurate and said that the engraver had misrepresented her concepts. Mike helped Elfred in many details to make the painting historically accurate, especially regarding the sanctuary section, the Hebrew writing on the cross, and the Last Supper scene. He also told Elfred to paint Jesus and His disciples at an oriental style table, sitting on floor mats, not Roman couches as the medieval artists had painted. Further, he said their heads would have been covered. He made sure that the wine, the unleavened bread, and the bitter herbs and their symbolism were painted exactly as they would have been in olden times. Mike proudly gave his approval when the painting was completed.

Mike wrote a song to go with the painting for the unveiling ceremony, which was held at the Auburn Seventh-day Adventist Church in 1979. Elfred had seen Mike cry many times as he worked on this painting. At the unveiling ceremony he saw Mike weep again as he sat at the organ and sang the words of Jesus on the cross. Quoting Mark, he sang, *"Eloi, Eloi, lama sabachthani?"* (My God, My God, why have you forsaken me?), weeping the whole time, his whole body shaking. His voice was so beautiful! There was not a dry eye in the whole church. Later Elfred said he could never have completed the project without the inspiration of Ellen White and Rabbi Mike Thomas.

This painting now hangs in the new Seventh-day Adventist world headquarters in Silver Spring, Maryland, where posters of the painting are available. What a thrill for Bill, knowing he had a part in Mike's story. He has wished many times since then that Mike was still alive, but he is looking forward to seeing him in heaven.

*pseudonym

Chapter 62

Retired—Retread

"A city on a hill cannot be hidden.... In the same way, let your light shine before men, that they may see your good deeds and praise your Father in heaven."
Matthew 5:14-16

An article appeared in the *Paradise Post* newspaper dated Friday, November 25, 1988, with the exciting story of Bill's gala retirement celebration at the Paradise Seventh-day Adventist Church, although he did not officially retire until the next day.

Vera Gosev was a jewel and made all the arrangements for Bill's special night. The church's fellowship center was full. There was plenty of excitement as the congregation waited for Bill to tell his life story, especially his thirty-eight years of ministry. (You now know much more than that group learned that night.)

When Bill ended his exciting story, he added, "I am retiring officially, but I want you to know that I love young people, and I am not about to stop working for them. Satan is working hard to capture their minds, but my goal is to inspire them. A life with Jesus can be far more exciting than experimenting in drugs, smoking cigarettes, and drinking alcohol. I am still doing my best to perfect a complete spiritual program for children of all ages, so please keep me in your prayers." Everyone applauded.

The next day Mike and Connie Danilov asked Bill to work part time for them in their furniture store. Bill accepted their offer but continued working to perfect his Tots to Teens programs (sometimes called Crusade for Jesus programs) for junior age and older. He never did fully retire and certainly not from child evangelism.

The Paradise Adventist Church still continued to hold evangelism seminars, although not as often after Lonnie was called to be speaker for the *Voice of Prophecy*.

It was during this time that Pastor Kenneth Cox invited Bill and June to do a seminar with him in Portland, Oregon. Jean and Ray were also invited. The adult meetings were held in a huge tent on the campgrounds near Portland. The children were bused to the church not far away for their meetings.

Paul and Marguerite Flemming also joined Bill's team for this seminar. They held a pre-session time for the youth who came early to the meetings. Paul taught them leather craft and how to make nice belts or wallets. The children loved that pre-session time, but they were even more excited when it was time for Uncle Bill's meeting to begin. Uncle Bill really appreciated Paul and Marguerite's help and their witnessing.

Uncle Bill had recently started collecting a few rebuses as a teaching tool. One evening he told the youth he would give them Crusader dollars if they would make one of their own on their computer at home. It was not long before they were bringing their creations to every meeting. One was: O + picture of a bed = Obed. Others were: A + picture of a bell = Abel. And E + fist knocking on a door = Enoch. Uncle Bill passed out a lot of Crusader dollars during that seminar, and the children loved it. He was always surprised at how good they became at making their rebuses.

During that series a funny thing happened one night in Auntie Jean's class. When Pastor Cox heard the story, it tickled his funny bone, too, and that night he related it to his congregation. When a father came to pick up his son at the end of the meeting, the boy was not there. They began looking all over the church for the lad but did not find him. Finally the mother came and asked, "What's keeping you?" The father replied, "We cannot find Stephen." The mother said, "We did not bring him." Jean and Ray were much relieved. Ken's congregation thought this story was very funny, and everyone had a good laugh.

It rains a lot in Portland, so Bill, June, Jean, and Ray did not do much sightseeing on their days off. When the seminar ended, it was a great thrill for them to see souls buried in the water of baptism. Many of them were youth from Uncle Bill's class, and he thanked the Lord for each of them.

A few months later Pastor Ken Cox contacted Bill and June again and invited them to join him at a seminar in Hawaii. Bill was delighted to say yes, then he contacted Jean and Ray. They were delighted to go as well, and who wouldn't be? The thrill of being welcomed by a Hawaiian welcoming committee with beautiful plumeria and pikake leis was wonderful. One they have never forgotten. Then they were taken to their hosts' homes.

Most adult women in Hawaii are called auntie as a term of respect. Uncle Bill had been called uncle for a long time and now June was called Auntie June. From then on the child evangelism team was uncle and auntie to the 175 to 200 children registered. More children were registered in that campaign than ever before, and they were a handful.

The meetings were held in the Central Seventh-day Adventist Church in Honolulu. Uncle Bill soon learned that there was a big difference between the Hawaiian and Samoan cultures. The Samoans always came to church prepared to spend the entire Sabbath.

Uncle Bill was also in for another surprise. The Samoan children in his class were not as quiet and attentive as the other cultures. Their custom was to speak right out no matter what was happening. These interruptions occurred quite frequently and really frustrated Uncle Bill. He finally decided to ask the Samoan fathers to come and help control the noisy children. To his frustration, this scheme did not change a thing. What was he to do?

He was told that the aunties in the Samoan culture rule the roost. Uncle Bill then told the fathers that the aunties would be helping him in the future and they could attend the seminar again. To Uncle Bill's relief, the Samoan children never failed to obey the aunties. At last he was teaching the beautiful lessons of Jesus' love and sacrifice to children who could hear what he was teaching. He was so thankful for the aunties' help.

Pastor Cox's meetings went longer than expected many times. One Sabbath afternoon the meeting went so long overtime that the children got hungry. Jean finally sent Ray and her helpers to the kitchen to find something for them to eat. After they had satisfied the children's hunger, they needed to find something to occupy the time before their parents came to get them. Jean was thankful that two of her helpers were academy teachers and knew several games the children enjoyed playing. They had a good time while waiting for their parents to get them.

Many times after the nightly meetings Bill, June, Jean, and Ray would stop at a frozen yogurt shop. While enjoying a frozen yogurt cone, they would chat about their meetings and plan what to do as tourists on their next day off. On one of those days they made a sad visit to the battleship Arizona, the ship that was sunk when the Japanese bombed Pearl Harbor on December 7, 1941. They also visited the pineapple fields and several other tourist attractions. They had a wonderful and exciting time in Hawaii, but the most excitement they had was when they were leading children to Jesus.

Chapter 63

Trade Winds Blow

"And he will send his angels ... and they will gather his elect from the four winds."
Matthew 24:31

A car had been loaned to Bill to drive while doing Pastor Cox's Hawaiian seminar. One day while they were driving around enjoying the scenery, they happened to see a young Hawaiian man docking his small fishing boat. Bill and Ray loved to fish, so Bill parked the car and everyone got out to see if he had caught any fish. When the fisherman proudly showed off his catch, Bill asked if he would be willing to take him and Ray fishing the next time he went out. The fisherman's father had taught his sons to be courteous and kind to the mainlanders, so he said he would be glad to take them and would call when everything was arranged.

Bill and Ray were very excited about their prospective fishing trip. When Bill told his host about it, he got excited and wanted to join them. When the young Hawaiian fisherman called, Bill asked if his host could come too. The fisherman agreed to include the host, but he would have to make some changes in the plans and would call later.

The happy day finally arrived when Bill, his host, and Ray met the young fisherman. They were in for a surprise because the fisherman was not in his little boat but in his brother's much larger boat. The three men thought that was great and promptly boarded the larger craft.

It was a beautiful day as the boat slowly moved into the gentle waters of the blue Pacific Ocean. When they were beyond the breakers and farther offshore, the two brothers began throwing out the fishing lines which trailed about fifty feet behind the boat. Suddenly a fish was hooked on a line. Ray was there at the right time and the right place, and he landed a beautifully colored mahi-mahi. Boy was he proud and happy.

Some time passed, but the fish were not finding those trolling lines. The brother operating the boat decided to move on, then sit in one place and still fish. At last, lines were let down and soon fish began to hook on. They caught yellowtail, some weighing seven pounds and more. A great catch.

Just then they noticed the wind had increased and a very dark cloud was quickly coming toward them. One of the brothers said it did not look good and they should head for shore as quickly as possible.

Much to Bill's sorrow the heavy waves began to make him seasick, so he went below deck and laid on the floor. It seemed to him like the heavy waves were beating the boat into pieces. As he lay there, he heard the radio crackle with a call for help. Another boat was sinking. The fishermen brothers immediately turned the boat to answer that call.

The storm seemed to be getting worse. Ocean spray and plastic window pieces from all directions began falling on Bill below deck. Other things were falling too, including fishing poles. Bill soon found that some of the hooks had secured themselves to his pant legs, and he was all tied up. The storm was very severe by this time. Bill felt for sure that Satan was after him and the boat was going to sink. Then he thought of all the children he had been teaching about Jesus. He recalled how many of them had memorized all sixty-six books of the Bible and that some had even learned to say them backwards. So he prayed earnestly, "Oh God, please save us. The boys and girls have so much more to learn about You."

In the meantime, up on deck a huge waterspout was seen through the pouring rain. When the radio crackled again, the brothers learned it was too late to answer the call for help. The boat had sunk but another boat had rescued the fishermen. So they quickly turned their boat and headed for shore.

After they were docked, Ray and the others helped untangle Bill. When he stepped out on firm ground, he said, "Thank you, Lord, for answering my prayer. You are the best Friend anyone could ever have."

It was still raining hard when they returned home. There they found their wives huddled before the television, waiting for news of the fishing expedition. Their wives were thrilled to have their husbands home safe and sound. That was one unforgettable fishing trip. The next day Bill, June, Jean, and Ray's thoughts were focused on child evangelism again, and they were in their rooms waiting for the children to arrive.

Besides the leather craft class, Uncle Bill always showed the boys and girls a religious film and then quizzed them. He gave them Crusader dollars when they answered his questions correctly, so they really enjoyed that learning experience. Uncle Bill always looked forward to see how many of his young people would sign the decision card for baptism. This was a very important step for them.

The Kenneth Cox seminar in Hawaii was a huge success. The Tots to Teens team and the parents came together to watch as their island young people followed Jesus' example and were buried under the cleansing water of baptism. What a day of rejoicing!

It was never easy for Uncle Bill, Auntie June, Auntie Jean, and Uncle Ray to say goodbye at the end of twenty-four meetings. This time the children and their parents came, placing beautiful flower leis around their necks. Some even brought gifts of colorful Hawaiian shirts. This was a tough moment, and tears flowed down their cheeks. Uncle Bill assured them that the greatest day was coming when everyone would be reunited at the second coming of Jesus.

Auntie Jean reminded her children again, "Don't forget! Be sure to meet me under the tree of life when we get there." Then they waved goodbye and boarded the plane. Soon they were flying over the blue Pacific Ocean toward home, very happy with another successful seminar.

Chapter 64

Can't Stop Now

"Praise be to the God and Father of our Lord Jesus Christ ... who comforts us in all our troubles, so that we can comfort those in any trouble with the comfort we ourselves have received from God." 2 Corinthians 1:3, 4

Bill received an unexpected phone call one day from Ralph Wyman, pastor of the Beaverton Seventh-day Adventist Church in Beaverton, Oregon, asking if he and June would be interested in doing the meetings for the juniors during the upcoming Amazing Facts seminar with Pastor Brian McMahon. Bill was delighted and quickly accepted. After informing Pastor Wyman that his ministry included another couple working with the younger children, Pastor Wyman said that was great. He then explained that he had accepted a call to another church and would be replaced by Pastor Terry Zull before the seminar began. In the meantime, Roger Dandino and his wife, Donna, would be in charge of all the preparations and would find lodging for both teams.

Bill did not waste any time telling Jean and Ray about the invitation to do the seminar with Amazing Facts. Jean was just as delighted as Bill had been and quickly started organizing her program materials. Before long, both child evangelism teams were caravanning their way to Beaverton, Oregon.

Brian had a full house when the seminar began and Bill, June, Jean, and Ray were delighted to see so many parents bringing their children. It was a wonderful seminar, and when it concluded, several adults were baptized.

It was during those meetings that Bill especially remembers a grandmother who attended the children's program. She came with her granddaughter, always sat behind her, rarely missing a meeting. He was curious as to why she did not attend the adult meetings. When he asked the grandmother, she told him that she was learning so much about the Bible in his class that she wanted to stay, which delighted Bill and June. At the end of the meetings, the grandmother and her granddaughter both made their decision to follow Jesus all the way.

It was during this seminar that Auntie Jean was teaching the children in her class to sing a song about Philippians 4:8. The words of the song were not arranged as in the Bible. During the potluck lunch one Sabbath, a little boy came up to her with his Bible in his hand and informed her she was wrong about Philippians 4:8. Jean then had to explain to him that the words in the song fit the music and were meant to teach what the verse said. That satisfied him. Auntie Jean was happy he was a "Berean" and had checked it out for himself to make sure she was telling the truth.

It was also during this seminar that Bill and June were reunited with Carol and Steven Sherman and their two children, Holly Ann and John. What a happy surprise that was to find these dear friends from their former years in Glendale now living in Beaverton. Carol and Steven were just as happy and immediately joined Bill's team of helpers. When Bill made his altar call at the end of another seminar in the Portland area, Holly Ann and John gave their hearts to Jesus, along with several others. All were baptized into Jesus at the end of the meetings. What a day of rejoicing that was for their parents!

The Beaverton seminar was the first time the Jamersons and the Willards had worked with Amazing Facts, but it was far from being the last. Evangelist Brian McMahon and his sweet wife, Heidi, were delighted with Bill and Jean's programs and asked them to come along with them to their Vancouver, British Columbia, seminar. Their invitation was quickly accepted, for the Jamersons and the Willards loved leading children to Jesus.

Shortly before the Vancouver seminar began, the McMahons welcomed a new addition to their little family. Their three-year-old daughter, Kara, now had an adorable little sister named Kelly.

Kara thought she was much too old for the baby class. Even though she was only three years old, Heidi asked Auntie Jean if she could attend her class. Kara blended in quite well with the older children and loved taking part in all the activities and singing the songs. She sang beautifully, too, and sang special music for the adult seminar one night. Ray asked for permission to video record her performance, and much to the delight of her proud parents, he presented them with the tape.

****

After being reunited with the Shermans, Bill and June stayed in touch with the family, and they were glad they did. Shortly after reconnecting with the family, hardship fell upon them.

Holly Ann was in college, but she did not want to settle down with her studies and soon dropped out. This was hard for Carol and Steven. Sadly, a little later Steven became very ill and died. Uncle Bill and June were so thankful they could support and comfort Carol and the children during this sad time.

Then, while living in the Portland area, Holly Ann met and fell in love with Richard (Richy), the son of Dr. Ronald and Kay White who lived in Paradise. When Richy returned to California, Holly Ann followed him. One day she found him very ill, just as her mother had found her father. After the doctor examined him, he said there was no hope for his recovery. Uncle Bill was quickly called. He and the elders anointed Richy, but God chose not to work a miracle and restore the young man's health. However, he and Holly Ann asked to be re-baptized. Carol was so happy when she saw them enter the baptistery. Pastor Ben Maxson and Bill were also very happy to be baptizing these two young people.

A short time later Bill officiated at the young couple's garden wedding in Ron and Kay White's beautiful country garden. Sadly, they were not married very long when Richy died. Bill and June were again so thankful they were there to comfort and support both families. The White family dearly loved their new daughter-in-law, and she lived with them for some time to help fill the void left by the loss of their only son.

Later, Holly Ann went back to college to study nursing. She then began to attend the Upper Ridge Seventh-day Adventist Church in Magalia, California, where there were young people her age. While taking part in the youth group's activities, she met and fell in love with Mike Vrbeta, a fine young Christian man. After a while the two were married. Holly then went back to school to study nursing. She graduated with a bachelor's degree in nursing in 2011.

John has not yet chosen to go back to college, but he has a loving mother who prays daily for God to bless and guide each of her children, and she has no doubt that God has a plan for him.

Life is not always easy for young people as they find their way. That is why Bill and Jean feel it is so important to have rich spiritual programs for children and that an evangelist should always hold these important meetings for children of all ages.

Chapter 65

Treasured Memories

"The LORD is far from the wicked but he hears the prayer of the righteous."
Proverbs 15:29

After the Vancouver seminar, Bill, June, Jean, and Ray followed wherever Brian's Amazing Facts seminars led them during the next several years. They went to several cities in California including San Jose (twice), Auburn, Santa Barbara, Sonora, Grass Valley, Pleasant Hill, Clovis, and Cerres. They also went to Peoria, Illinois; Las Vegas, Nevada (twice); Portland, Oregon; Amarillo, Texas; Vancouver, Washington; Auburn, Washington; Spokane, Washington; and Milwaukee, Wisconsin. Each was a wonderful seminar, and they praised God for each and every one!

Ray could not go with Jean when Amazing Facts held the seminar in Peoria, Illinois, so her friend, Fran Quattlebaum, went along as her helper. Fran quickly fell in love with one cute little boy in their class by the name of Cody. Of all the children attending, he was the most enthusiastic about the program.

Later in the seminar, when Jean began teaching the importance of putting on the Christian armor, Cody was even more enthusiastic. He loved the shield, helmet, and of course the sword of the Spirit, and he loved singing "I'm in the Lord's Army."

He was so fascinated with the Christian soldier's armor that the first thing he did when he went to his public school on Monday morning was tell his teacher and classmates that they needed to put on the Christian soldier's armor. Then they would be protected from Satan and his temptations. This did not go over well with his teacher, so he was sent to the principal's office. His mother was called right away and told that Cody could not speak about such things at school, but his mother stood up for her son's right of freedom of speech, and she was thankful that her precious son had sown important seeds of truth. Everyone hoped and prayed that the Holy Spirit would touch the hearts of his teacher and fellow classmates and that they would learn to put on the wonderful armor of God and be ready to meet the Lord when He comes again.

In August 2007 Fran was given a little doggie named Lollipop by a young handicapped girl who could no longer care for her. Fran thoroughly enjoyed Lollipop's antics and her companionship. Two days before Christmas Fran accepted an invitation to have lunch with her girlfriends, so she left her little doggie alone at home. When she returned home, she discovered Lollipop had gotten into mischief while she was gone. She had chewed on the cord of the Christmas lights, and it seemed as if she was paralyzed.

Fran rushed her to the veterinarian who told her that Lollipop had not been electrocuted but had a herniated disc that would keep her from ever using her hindquarters again. Not wanting to put her down, Fran kept her in a laundry basket and carried her around. She faithfully massaged her legs every day hoping that would help. Then one day she thought of having her harnessed to a cart with little wheels so she could get around on her own. Her friend liked the idea and made a cart for her. It did not take Lollipop long to get used to her wheels, and she loved the freedom they gave her.

One day Fran was talking with Bill on the phone, telling him about Lollipop's accident and how she had harnessed her to a cart with two little wheels. But Fran expressed her wish that Lollipop could be made well. Bill said, "Well, I never prayed for an animal, but Jesus is her Creator too, so why don't I come by and pray for her."

Fran was thrilled and said, "Oh, will you?" So Bill drove over to Fran's home, put his hands on Lollipop, and offered a simple prayer.

Two days later Fran saw Lollipop greet her with a weak wag of her little tail. She was thrilled, for she realized then that Lollipop had some feeling in her hindquarters. After Lollipop was fastened to her wheels, Fran saw her legs move, not much, but a little. Then she watched her take a few steps on her little wobbly legs. Fran was elated. She knew that Jesus had heard Bill's prayer and healed her little Lollipop. She praised God. Today her nine-year-old Lollipop runs and walks with her funny little gait. Fran is thankful for the devotion, love, and companionship Lollipop gives her.

Uncle Bill often wishes he had kept a diary of all his Crusade for Jesus and Amazing Facts seminars so he could instantly recall the children. These were wonderful times when they learned to know and love their Lord and Savior, Jesus Christ. Now, at the age of eighty-seven, he has a hard time remembering all "his kids" and that makes him sad. But he cherishes the ones he does remember, and now they are being recorded in this book. If he could remember all the children, another book would have to be written.

Chapter 66

More Treasured Memories

"A righteous man will be remembered forever." Psalm 112:6

Keith Mulligan pastored the Ceres Seventh-day Adventist Church when Amazing Facts held a seminar there. Bill fondly remembers he had three children from an unchurched family attending those meetings, and they always arrived quite early. The two boys in his class were a handful, so Bill did his best to become their special friend. This helped to make them more manageable. After a while, the boys revealed to Bill that they lived fifty miles away and that their parents were coming to the meetings because they wanted to find the true church. Bill was very impressed with their faithfulness, and by the time the meetings were coming to a close, the parents and the two boys asked to be baptized. What a joy it was for Bill when he saw the four family members standing together in the water of baptism! It was worth everything to him, and he praised God for them.

It was during the Ceres meetings that Jean and the church secretary developed a beautiful graduation certificate to present to the children. Jean's problem was correctly spelling the names of the twenty or more Spanish children, but she still remembers how proud the parents were when their children were called up to receive their certificate.

Bill remembers quite well the Amazing Facts seminar held in Sonora, California, at the Seventh-day Adventist church. Their host and hostess were Floyd and Doris Surprise. It truly was a surprise, for they had been very good friends while Bill was pastoring the Arcata and McKinleyville churches. They made a great team of helpers along with another lady.

It was during this time that Bill began handing out cards with Bible texts on them as a pre-session device. He explained to the children that if they memorized the texts he would reward them with 200 Crusade for Jesus dollars. Needless to say, the children did all they could to memorize those texts. It was a wonderfully fun way for them to hide God's written word in their heart.

In addition to those memories, Bill especially remembers the Amazing Facts seminar at the Grass Valley Seventh-day Adventist Church. It was there that the children made a big card for him at the close of the meetings. The white card was truly very big, about twenty-two inches by twenty-eight inches. A picture was in the middle, and around it the children had written some things for Uncle Bill. The following are some of their writings:

"Thank you so much for teaching us about Jesus," signed Halle Anderson.

"You are a very good teacher," signed "King."

"I had a lot of fun in your class," signed Peggy H.

"Thank you for teaching me the Holy Bible," wrote Sierra.

"Thank you for teaching me wonderful things so we can learn more about Jesus," signed Esther.

"Thank you for your hard work for us. THANK YOU!" signed Zech Stanton.

"Thank you for everything and for the money because it was the only Christmas money I got this year. I am glad. Thanks!" signed Tiffany Spiva.

"Thank you so much. You two shine the love of Jesus like few do and have taught our children gems of Scripture," signed Dave.

"Hey, Uncle Bill, I hope you will have a wonderful day. Remember me!!" wrote Anne Marie.

"Thank you for teaching us the Holy Bible," signed Kara McMahon.

"Elder and Mrs. J: This has been a very special time for Ivan and me ... it's been such a blessing. We love you," signed Kathy G.

"We love you guys. God bless. See you in Paradise!" signed G.M.C.

It's things like these that make up the beautiful treasured memories for Uncle Bill and Auntie June.

****

Jean was more fortunate than Bill, for she had written down some of her child evangelism experiences to tell at a teaching seminar. The following are just a few of her treasured memories:

She was still working at the Adventist Book Center in Pleasant Hill, California, when Doug Batchelor asked her to do the children's meeting during his seminar in Sacramento. (This was long before he became head pastor of the Sacramento Central Church.)

Fifty or so miles was too far to drive during the weekly meetings, so she was only able to lead those meetings on the weekends. She remembers clearly the night a mother came to pick up her son at the end of the meeting. He was so glad to see her and excitedly said, "Mom, I learned so much more about Jesus tonight than I ever did in Sunday School, and my heart tells me we just have to come back." Unfortunately, they never returned to any of the meetings. Jean often wonders if the adult meetings mentioned jewelry that night, for that mother had been wearing a lot of jewelry.

Jim and Dorothy Harris were Jean's host and hostess during the Amazing Facts Sonora seminar. Jim had been a prisoner of war in the Philippines during World War II and had never fully regained his health from that ordeal. He became a pastor and worked with Uncle Bill when he accepted the call to work with the youth in the Nebraska Seventh-day Adventist Conference. Jim collapsed at home one day, and Dorothy insists that Jean saved his life when she quickly did what she could to help him start breathing normally again.

Jean especially remembers the grandmother who faithfully brought her eight-year-old grandson to her class every night during that seminar. Jean prayed earnestly for her and her family. A few months after the seminar ended she received a phone call from Dorothy Harris telling her that the grandmother had been baptized that Sabbath morning and had declared from the baptistery that she had chosen to follow Jesus while attending Auntie Jean's program for children during the Amazing Facts seminar. Needless to say, Jean praised God for her decision, and she still remembers her in prayer from time to time, as she does for all of "her kids."

Jean also remembers a not-quite-three-year-old foster child who was in her class because she would not leave her two sisters. She had been teaching the boys and girls about the meaning of the colors in the sanctuary. As she reviewed each color, she would ask what it revealed about Jesus, and the children would give the answer. One night when she asked what the color "gold" teaches about Jesus, the not-quite-three-year-old piped up and said, "He's precious!" Jean was expecting to hear, "He's the same yesterday, today, and forever," for she had never used the word "precious," but she was thrilled with the little girl's answer. It was so right! This taught Jean that young children, while quietly playing alone, can and do learn and understand much more from what the adults around them say or do than one realizes.

The room for Jean's meetings at the Pleasant Hill Seventh-day Adventist Church had two doors that opened to the outside and the parking lot. A grandmother had been bringing her grandson nightly to the meetings but was not attending the adult meetings. She came to pick him up early one evening. The meeting had not ended, and the boy did not want to leave, so he left with her through one door and returned to the class through the other door. This happened several times before the grandmother decided to give in and let him stay. After that she let him stay until each meeting ended.

Jean was beginning a seminar in an area several miles from the Pleasant Hill church. The first night of the seminar a nine-year-old girl came to her and asked, "Did you do a seminar in Pleasant Hill?" When Jean said yes, she said, "Now I remember you."

Jean then asked, "What do you remember about the seminar?"

She replied, "The sanctuary!" Jean was thrilled with her answer for it had been several years since the Pleasant Hill seminar, and she praises God for inspiring her to teach the beautiful sanctuary lessons.

The saddest experience Jean ever had was when a little girl, about five-years-old, told her that her mother had just committed suicide. Hugs and words of comfort were not enough. Jean knew that with prayer God could do what she could not—He could bring healing to her little broken heart.

A boy in another seminar was so hyper and troublesome that a sitter was hired to sit with him and hold him on his/her lap when necessary to keep him under control. That worked out fine, and the good news is that Uncle Bill baptized him a few years later at another Amazing Facts seminar. It is true that all things work together for those who love God.

At another seminar Jean learned a good lesson. This was the first time she had used the felt fruit set she had made with the words of the fruits of the Spirit printed on them. After the children had placed all the fruits on the felt board, one little boy said to her, "I like all those fruits, but I am allergic to some of them." Jean realized she had to make sure the children understood that the words on the beautiful fruits were to teach them about Jesus' beautiful character, not the delicious fruits people eat.

Jean always had an altar call near the end of each seminar. All the children would place their little white felt hearts on a large red felt heart on the felt board. Jean was delighted when a little seven-year-old boy came to her and asked to be baptized. The pastor of the church said he was much too young. Evangelist Lyle Pollett was not sure, so he questioned him and learned that Jean's programs had actually prepared him to give his heart to Jesus. What a thrill it was for Jean to see him baptized along with his parents the following Sabbath!

Then there came the night a little girl cried like her heart would break because it was the last night of the meetings. Jean could sympathize with her, but she is looking forward to meeting "her kids" under the tree of life one of these days soon.

Bill and Jean can still see the beautiful faces of many of "their kids" in their mind's eye. There are so many wonderful stories that could be written if only they could be brought to remembrance. Both feel God has His book of remembrance so He can enjoy once again all the good things that have been done since Creation. He must treasure them even more than people do here on earth.

Chapter 67

God Worked Behind The Scene Again

"Never will I leave you; never will I forsake you." Hebrews 13:5

The Jamersons were living in Glendale when God began helping them prepare for their retirement by investing in property. Pastor Erling Calkins, the Sabbath School secretary of the Southern California Conference, was nearing retirement age when he thought a place around Grass Valley, California, would be a good place to retire. When he mentioned this area to Bill, Bill instantly agreed with him because he had lived there when he was a teenager and loved that area.

Bill and Erling knew God's plan was not for them to stay in big cities but to live in the country when they retired, so both felt the Grass Valley area would be perfect. The two soon made a trip to Grass Valley and contacted a realtor. When she learned what they were looking for, she found two ten-acre parcels next to each other near Rough 'n Ready with an irrigation ditch above to water their future gardens. They were delighted with what they saw and felt God had led them to these parcels. After talking it over with their wives and describing the property, they each purchased their future retirement property.

Bill was very satisfied with his future plans to leave the city of Los Angeles in eight years when he could retire. But God was in control and had called Bill to Paradise, where they rented a house not far from the church. One day some time later Bill was asked to call on someone who was interested in becoming a Seventh-day Adventist Christian. When he went to the home, he found that the woman, Mary Davis, was very interested, but her husband, Ken, was not interested in Bible studies at that time. After many prayers and a few studies, Ken became just as interested as his wife. Before long their son, Craig, and daughter, Shannan, were studying along with them. Soon all four members of the family were baptized and joined the church, and Bill praised God.

One day as Bill and June were on their usual morning walk they saw a "For Sale" sign on a vacant lot just around the corner from where they lived. They thought it would be a perfect place for them to build their own home. They had the money from selling their two lots in Glendale and their home in Duarte, so after much prayer they decided to purchase the lot. They immediately put their Grass Valley property on the market and thanked God that it quickly sold. They then contacted the Paradise seller and were able to buy his lot at a good price.

Next, they contacted an Adventist architect by the name of Wiggo Wake to draw up plans for their new home. When that was completed, they began looking for a builder. As always God was with the Jamersons. Bill remembered Ken Davis was a contractor and builder, so he called Ken and told him about their plans. Ken soon accepted the job. They went to the bank together. With the funds they had saved from southern California and a loan, their new house began to take form. When it was finished, Bill and June moved into their mortgage-free home. This would be their home for several years.

But that was not the end of their real estate transactions. Bill was beginning to feel that he had too much garden and orchard to maintain, and they needed a home on a much smaller lot. They listed their house with Doyle McFarland. It had not sold by the time the listing expired, so Bill listed it again, but for only one week. A man looked at the house and made an offer during that week, which Bill rejected. A little later a realtor brought a man and wife from Washington, D.C. to see the house. The realtor showed little interest in showing the property, so Bill was impressed to give the folks a tour. He showed them the fifty blooming rose bushes and the lovely fruit trees. After they had walked all over the half-acre corner property, the realtor said he had one more piece of property to show them. But the wife said, "No thank you. This is the house that will be our home." Because of the first offer, Doyle was able to get $2,500 more than the listing price. God had been at work.

Doyle quickly found another home for Bill and June on a much smaller lot. Praise God, they had cash to pay for it. However, after they moved in June soon began to feel it was too large a house and too much work to keep up at her age so that house was put on the market. The market was slow, and it did not sell right away.

When Pastor Doug Batchelor called and asked Bill to go with him to his Washington, D.C. Amazing Facts seminar, he accepted the call.

Uncle Bill always gave Crusade for Jesus dollars as a reward for children who answered his questions correctly. Doug's son, Steven, was a whiz at collecting these dollars, and Bill was very proud of him. He thinks Steven must have earned more than 10,000. No doubt "Daddy Doug" was proud of him, too. All the Amazing Facts team said it was a wonderful seminar, and they were thrilled with the many souls who were added to God's church family.

When Bill and June returned from the Washington, D.C. seminar they waited for their home to sell. They began looking at a gated community for senior citizens called The Plantation, which they had liked very much from the time it began to be built. Ray and Jean enjoyed living there, but after eight years they felt the time had come to move closer to family, so they had moved to Indio in southern California. Bill and June missed their child evangelism companions.

Doyle had not sold their home after three months. That is when their friends, Joe and Mary Pleso, advised them to get in touch with Barbara, another realtor. They felt that she would be the one to sell their house. Bill remembered she had shown their house several times, and he thought maybe she could sell their house, so he gave her a one-day listing.

The next morning Barbara brought a couple from San Jose, California, to see the house. They fell in love with it and said they would buy it. They asked for thirty days to sell their home. God was in control, and their house quickly sold.

It was at this time that another friend and resident of The Plantation, Fred Spruell, called and told Bill that a lady who owned the same floor plan they liked had just died and her son was at the house. Bill quickly told June to drop everything so that they could go meet the son. When they saw the house, they loved the location and the lovely backyard. Bill and June purchased the home in The Plantation, which had the floor plan they preferred.

Yes, God had been with the Jamersons all along, guiding and opening the way time after time for them to be able to own a home for their retirement years. He blessed Ray and Jean also, for their home is fully paid in Indio. Again, they praised and thanked God as they remembered, "Submit your ways to the Lord and He will direct your path."

Chapter 68

The Smiling Wheelchair Lady

"He sent forth his word and healed them." Psalm 107:20

Bill often saw a lady in a wheelchair as he traveled around the town of Paradise. The wheelchair had a green roof to shade her head and a large pole reaching up in the air. The most interesting thing Bill noticed about this lady was her beautiful smile. Bill had no inkling that the Lord had made a divine appointment for the two of them to meet.

Bill and June had recently joined the crew of the Community Service Center at the Paradise Seventh-day Adventist Church. They went there every Tuesday morning. June helped wherever she could, mostly bagging food for the poor. Bill was put in charge of all the books that had been dropped off overnight. One morning, much to his surprise, there was the smiling lady in her wheelchair. He noticed she had some kind of metal strips around her fingers and wondered what the reason was for them. She seemed to feel very much at home, and he quietly watched as she wheeled herself over to the bookshelves.

The lady could not quite reach a book on the upper shelf, so Bill went to her. He pointed to a certain book and asked, "Is that the book you want?" She smiled her lovely smile and thanked him. Bill found her to be very friendly and helped her fill the basket on her wheelchair with more books.

As she wheeled herself out of the center, Bill could hardly wait to ask Beverly Neuman and Joan Borges about this sweet smiling lady in the wheelchair. They said they knew her quite well, and they could not help but love her. Bill's heart went out to her, also. They told him her name was Elaine Stevens.* She had been crippled for many years, and doctors had never been able to help her find relief for the mistake of taking a certain medicine too long. It had really messed up her body, but she always seemed happy even in spite of her pain and grief.

One day while Elaine was looking at books in the Community Service Center, she heard someone mention that Bill was a minister who visited sick people and put oil on their forehead, and oftentimes they were healed. Hope suddenly filled her heart. She told her girlfriends that she had heard the Bible said something about the sick calling on the elders and they would put oil on the forehead of the sick and be healed. Her friends were excited and told her to go for it.

The following Tuesday Elaine was at the Community Service Center when it opened. When Bill arrived, she greeted him with her sweet smile and told him she had heard about the anointing service and asked if he would be willing to anoint her. To Bill's surprise, she then added, "And I would like you to baptize me."

Bill was thrilled with her decision, but then he thought, *There is no way she can get up those many steps and into the baptistery with her wheelchair; she will have to be carried.* Then he smiled and said, "I will be very happy to anoint you, and I will look forward to your baptism."

Elaine chose Laurene Cleveland to help her prepare for baptism. Laurene had previously taught Elaine how to live and eat healthfully. Laurene spent many hours studying with Elaine, and finally she was ready for the anointing service and her baptism into the Seventh-day Adventist Church.

Elaine had chosen seven other people she had faith in to be with her for the anointing service. One morning they met and assembled in front of the church. Bill opened his Bible and read from James 5:14, 15: "Is any one of you sick? He should call the elders of the church to pray over him and anoint him with oil in the name of the Lord. And the prayer offered in faith will make the sick person well."

When Bill asked if everyone believed this and they all answered with a firm yes, they knelt down. Bill then anointed Elaine's forehead with olive oil and prayed. When they got to their feet, tears were streaming down Elaine's cheeks. She said, "I want to get on my feet also." As Elaine slowly began to stand up, everyone was overjoyed to see that God had blessed her with a miracle.

A few Sabbaths later Elaine was ready for baptism. She climbed the steps into the baptistery and stepped into the cleansing water, ready to die to self and live for Jesus. Only God could have done this for her. What an awesome miracle had taken place! The whole church rejoiced and praised God.

Elaine was more than happy to give up her wheelchair and obtain a driver's license. When the Coronary Health Improvement Program (CHIP) began at the church, Elaine was always on time and attended every meeting. At the end she was determined to live a healthy, clean lifestyle for the rest of her life.

As she became friends with people at church, Elaine became acquainted with George Marley,* a nice looking man who was losing his eyesight. They found happiness together and were married. What a wonderful Lord and Savior we serve! He still works miracles, even in our day, just as he did in the days of the New Testament. Praise God!

*pseudonym

Chapter 69

Dangerous Ground! Beware!

"Surely I am with you always." Matthew 28:20

Bob Patchin had been Bill's close friend since his Orangewood Academy days. One day he came to Bill and said, "Bill, I don't like telling you this, but you had better be careful. I know you, and I know you won't be to blame, but you are too close to children and youth, and parents could sue you."

Bill laughed at the suggestion and replied, "Not me, Bob, that could never happen to me."

It was true that there were dangers being so closely involved in overnight campouts and other activities such as day camps, sports programs, and travel programs for children and youth. But after more than thirty years of ministry and trusting in God, Uncle Bill had never heard anyone say that he could not be trusted with children, so he was not worried.

Before retiring, Uncle Bill had planned a one-day trip for the youth at the Water Works in Chico, California. The children were excited and laughing as they climbed aboard the bus in Paradise. Uncle Bill waved goodbye to the happy boys and girls as soon as the bus was loaded, and then he got into his car. The bus had barely turned the corner when a mother and her two daughters arrived. They were late and the girls were downhearted. Uncle Bill, always compassionate, said, "It isn't too late. Get in my car, and I will catch up with the bus so you can have your fun-filled day after all!"

Uncle Bill drove down the highway until he was able to get the bus driver's attention to pull over so the two girls could board the bus. As the bus pulled away, the girls happily waved goodbye to Uncle Bill. He smiled and waved back, happy he could help.

All returned safely late that afternoon, tired, but still happy. The next day they climbed onto the bus and waved goodbye to Uncle Bill for another day of fun. They were barely out of sight when a police car drove up to the Day Camp Center. Bill asked, "What can I do for you, officer?"

The officer replied, "Is there a Bill Jamerson here?" Bill was surprised, but said he was Bill Jamerson. The officer then informed him he was being charged with child molestation.

It turned out that the two girls Bill had taken in his car to catch up with the bus yesterday had told their mother that Uncle Bill had molested them. This was a terrible shock to Bill! He had not driven more than five miles with those two girls in his car when he caught up with the bus! How could they say such a thing?

The police questioned some of the youth attending Uncle Bill's programs, but all were very supportive of him, and none believed the awful accusations made against him. The next few days were a nightmare for Bill and June. Bill called his best friend, Steve Trenholme, an attorney, who came to his rescue. Of course, he had to ask, "Is this charge true?"

Bill answered, "No, it is not true! I would never do such a thing."

Steve then asked if he would be willing to take a lie detector test, and Bill assured him he was more than willing. So Steve took Bill for the lie detector test that very day. Bill answered all the questions with a yes or no, then Steve took him home. The results of the test were given to the police department the next day. After reading the results, they declared the case was closed! How happy Bill was to be relieved of the false charges against him.

A couple of years later Tom Adams, the associate pastor, received a call from a day camp mother asking if Bill Jamerson was still alive. When Tom said yes, she asked him to arrange a time when she could meet with Bill, and he agreed to do so.

The day came for the meeting, and to Bill's surprise, it was with the mother and the two daughters who had made the disgraceful charge against him. After sitting down, the two girls admitted to Uncle Bill that they had lied about him. They told him they were sorry. Uncle Bill felt their sorrow and forgave them. Then the two girls wrote a letter to the Police Department admitting they had lied about Uncle Bill.

Bob had given Bill a warning, and sure enough it happened. But God was with Bill and saw that he was cleared of all charges, and Bill praised Him for His loving care. What a wonderful ending to the "case."

Bill learned some time later that the mother had a hair styling salon. Hoping to win her to Jesus, he began having her cut his hair. Sad to say, she still shows no interest in knowing Jesus. Her oldest daughter has turned away from all religious gatherings, and the youngest daughter is living in New York City studying to be an opera singer. Uncle Bill feels the seeds of truth have been sown and prays the Holy Spirit will one day draw the family to Jesus and lead them into all truth.

Chapter 70

Miracles Still Happen*

"There is a time for everything." Ecclesiastes 3:1

Steve Trenholme became Bill's good friend after Bill and June moved to Paradise. Steve grew up without a father in his home, and it did not take long until Bill was a trusted father figure and mentor for Steve.

Steve met his wife, Amy, when they were still in high school. They were married after Steve had earned a law degree and Amy had completed her college education and started working as an occupational therapist. After Steve and Amy married, they moved to Paradise, where they initially rented a small house. About a year later they had their first child whom they named Lyle after Steve's grandfather. The arrival of their first son made their tiny rented house too small, and they purchased a home in Magalia, which is very near Paradise. Two years later another son arrived, whom they named Matthew. Four years after that a baby girl arrived, and they named her Sarah. The arrival of their third child prompted the move to an even larger home, and Steve and Amy purchased a large, beautiful home in Paradise.

Soon after arriving in Paradise, Steve embarked on his legal career working as a public defender representing people in trouble with the law. In time he began working in a specialized court called "Drug Court" in which people who were convicted of crimes and who were addicted to drugs were given the opportunity to get involved in drug treatment programs and get their lives in order. Steve represented literally thousands of defendants, and he would frequently pray with his clients and seek to give them spiritual encouragement and instruction.

Steve and Amy were dedicated to serving Jesus. Shortly before they were married, they had been baptized into the Seventh-day Adventist Church in Sacramento by Pastor Bob Boney.

Bill met Steve and Amy soon after they moved to Paradise. Bill saw the potential Steve had to be a Bible teacher. In a very short time this led to Steve becoming a Sabbath School teacher. Eventually, at Bill's suggestion, Steve began preaching sermons at small churches in northern California. Steve also served as an elder in the church.

Amy was a great cook and enjoyed inviting people to their home after church on Sabbath for a delicious meal and good fellowship. She also became involved in the children's division of the Sabbath School program. She was always willing to help anyone she could in any way possible.

Over the years Bill became great friends with Steve and Amy. As their children arrived, Bill loved each one of them and enjoyed watching them grow. Bill was "Uncle Bill" to each of Steve and Amy's children. As they grew, Bill coached each of them in basketball skills, and each became an excellent player. Bill also organized a weekly baseball game for parents and children during the summers. Steve and his children enjoyed participating in that.

On Sunday, December 20, 2009, Steve decided the time had come to clean the pine needles out of the rain gutters and off the garage roof of his home. The garage roof at Steve's home is exceptionally high, and a twenty-foot extension ladder was needed to do the work. Steve admitted later that one of his character defects is being tight with money and that he did not want to pay someone to clean the rain gutters for him. Thus, Steve climbed the ladder and began cleaning the gutters. Unfortunately, the ladder slipped, and he fell approximately twenty feet, crushing his skull on a cement sidewalk. He did not know it at the time, but parts of his skull had shattered into pieces the size of pebbles, and he had suffered a traumatic brain injury. He also had compression fractures in his back and neck. A brain surgeon later said that the fall should have killed him.

Steve does not remember the fall. Based on things he found out later, he believes he laid on the cement approximately fifteen minutes when God gave him the strength and power he needed to get up and walk approximately forty yards to the back door of his home. Given his injuries, it is nothing short of a miracle that he was able to get up and walk. Nineteen-year-old Matthew had been in bed when the accident occurred and vaguely registered hearing a noise outside that woke him up. He did not know that his dad had fallen but decided to get up. A few minutes later he went into the kitchen to make himself breakfast. It was then that he saw his dad at the back door of their house covered in blood.

Matthew helped his dad into the house and then immediately called 9-1-1 for an ambulance. Steve's wife, Amy, was at work when the accident happened, but no one knew where she was working that day. She was not able to be contacted until nearly three hours after the accident had occurred. That left Matthew in charge of taking care of his dad. When the ambulance arrived, the driver wanted to take Steve to the closest local hospital. However, Amy, being an occupational therapist who frequently worked with people with head injuries, had taught her children that if anyone ever had a head injury they should immediately be taken to a trauma center. In light of what his mother had taught him, Matthew insisted that the ambulance driver take his dad to a trauma center in nearby Chico. The driver reluctantly agreed to Matthew's demand. However, Steve belonged to God, and He saw that Steve was taken to a place where he could receive appropriate medical treatment for his traumatic brain injury.

Once at the hospital the doctors rapidly discovered that Steve's skull had been crushed and that he had significant bleeding in his brain. However, Amy's consent was needed before they could perform surgery. The brain surgeon later stated that the part of Steve's brain that was injured was a part that he "didn't even like to touch" as it was so delicate. Three hours went by before Amy could be located and was able to give the required consent. Prior to the surgery, Steve's family was informed that the fall itself should have killed him, that there was little chance he would survive the brain surgery, and that if he did survive there was no telling what he would be like. He might lose his memory. He might lose his ability to talk. He might lose his personality. He might be a vegetable.

Amy did not give up hope. Amy, Matthew, and Sarah prayed constantly for Steve's recovery. Amy contacted the head pastor of their church, Ben Maxson, and arranged for an anointing service. After the surgery was performed, pastors, elders, friends, and family members gathered around Steve's bedside for the anointing service. Steve's head was so heavily bandaged that the elders decided his upper arm would be the best place to anoint him.

A year or two prior to the accident, Steve had created a durable power of attorney for healthcare. In it he had instructed that, if he should ever be in a state such that he could not make medical decisions for himself, he wanted an anointing service to be performed for his healing, and he had named Amy as the one to make decisions as to what medical treatment he should receive. Later, Steve thanked Amy for calling for the anointing service and was grateful to all those who had participated in it. Steve is alive and well today because God performed a miracle and restored him to good health.

Steve did not know it at the time, but the whole church was praying for his life and his recovery. Bill and June were visiting their son in Orlando, Florida, at the time of Steve's accident. When they received word of what had happened, they fell to their knees, and Bill prayed, "Oh Lord, our church is in need of an awesome miracle. Steve is Your faithful servant, so please bless him in a special way and restore him to full health and strength."

Others were also praying. Steve's friends and relatives contacted other friends and relatives all around the world asking them to pray for his recovery. People all over the world were praying for him. A group of about ninety people that included some of the drug addicted defendants he had represented as a public defender along with the local district attorney and other professional colleagues of Steve came together at a church in Oroville, California, to pray for his recovery. Steve was deeply touched when he found out that both his clients and professional colleagues had all come together to pray for his recovery.

When Steve awoke after the surgery, he was able to talk but was not very rational, and he suffered from double vision. His one desire was to leave the hospital immediately, and he did all he could to convince his wife and others to take him home right away. In his confused, irrational state he even made more than one attempt to leave the hospital on his own even though at that time he could barely walk a few steps. But during this time God was quietly working a miracle and restoring him to full health.

As Steve lay in his hospital bed, he listened to music. He listened to one song in particular over and over. It was called "I Came to Believe" by Johnny Cash. It was a spiritual song about a man who came to believe in the power of God and who surrendered his life to God. The truth and power of the lyrics of that song really registered with Steve.

Steve loved to read books but could hardly read anything at all while in the hospital due to the double vision. The inability to read was very frustrating to him. However, he read what little he could. One thing he read over and over were these verses from James 1:2, 3: "Consider it pure joy, my brothers, whenever you face trials of many kinds, because you know that the testing of your faith develops perseverance." He read and re-read James 1:4-8 as well. The truth and wisdom of these verses spoke to him.

The initial days after Steve's fall and surgery were rough, but God heard the prayers that went up before Him on Steve's behalf. While he was in the hospital, he enjoyed daily visits from many friends, including many members of the Paradise Seventh-day Adventist Church who sat with him for hours on end. After nearly six weeks in the hospital, the doctors decided Steve could go home. After he returned home, the church members continued to be faithful. Shortly after he returned home, a group of approximately twenty people came and performed many needed and helpful practical labors at Steve's home. Among other things, his front porch was completely rebuilt and handrails were built to assist him in navigating stairs at the entrances of various doors in his house. These handrails were needed as he was having problems maintaining his balance at that point. His friends from church also completely cleaned his yard of all the pesky pine needles that had led to this problem in the first place. What a wonderful way to obey Jesus' command to "Love one another ... and to do to others what you would have them do to you" (John 13:34; Matthew 7:12).

People now call Steve the "miracle man." Approximately three months after his injury, Steve was back in the courtroom defending his clients. He resumed teaching the Sabbath School class that he had taught nearly every week for more than twenty years prior to the accident. His class was elated to have him back, and they praised God for answering their prayers. In April 2010, approximately four months after the accident, Steve preached a sermon at the Paradise Seventh-day Adventist Church titled "Miracles Still Happen." He told the story of what happened to him and gave God the glory for his recovery. Steve has since preached that sermon at several other churches.

One more miraculous part of this story is that the compression fractures in Steve's back and neck all healed without the necessity of surgery. Steve has enjoyed running since he was a teenager, and he is now running again on a regular basis.

In mind and in body, God has restored Steve's life. Bill and Steve are thankful that God heard and answered the many prayers that ascended to His throne and that, even in this modern age, He still works miracles in the lives of His people.

* This chapter was written by Steve Trenholme.

Chapter 71

Looking Back and Looking Forward

"But in keeping with His promise we are looking forward to a new heaven and a new earth, the home of righteousness." 2 Peter 3:13

When Uncle Bill thinks of the last Crusade for Jesus he held for youth at the Paradise Seventh-day Adventist Church, he remembers three children in one particular family—Jonathan, Heidi, and Julie. They attended his earlier seminars when they were younger, and he involved them in baseball during the summers, so they were very special to him.

Toward the end of the seminar, Uncle Bill gave all the boys and girls who surrendered their lives to Jesus "Decision for Baptism" cards to take home for the parents to sign. He knows that some parents think twelve-year-old children are too young for baptism. But they are mistaken. Twelve years of age is just the right age for baptism. If children wait too long, some never take the step to be baptized.

He hoped with all his heart that when those "Decision for Baptism" cards were returned, all the parents would have signed them and given their permission for their children to be baptized, the next step in their spiritual journey to God's kingdom.

Uncle Bill knew Julie was much too young for baptism, and possibly Heidi was, too. Jonathan was at the perfect age to be baptized. But Jonathan's parents did not sign the card and that saddened Uncle Bill. They were good parents and wonderful Christians. They continued to pray that their children would make the decision to follow Jesus when they grew older.

One day when Julie was older she told the youth pastor of the Paradise Seventh-day Adventist Church that she would like to be baptized. Her family and Uncle Bill rejoiced with her decision and joyfully watched as she emerged from the baptistery. Uncle Bill wondered when Heidi and Jonathan's decision would come.

Months passed and all three youth went away to Christian colleges. The parents had done their best to teach them to follow Jesus. These three young people became fine Christians.

Heidi was in her junior year of college when she came to Uncle Bill and said, "Uncle Bill, will you baptize me now?" This was sweet music to Uncle Bill who was now eighty years of age. He visited her home several times during the following weeks and prepared her for baptism. The parents rejoiced as they watched Uncle Bill baptize their second daughter. Their prayers had been answered, and they held a great celebration to mark Heidi's special baptismal day.

These good Christian parents understood that Jesus came not to be served, but to serve. Jesus helped the two daughters to serve others over the years. They served the helpless and homeless people after hurricane Katrina in New Orleans. Heidi graduated from college and recently traveled to Haiti to help those in need after the terrible earthquake. Julie is in Guatemala serving in that mission field.

Uncle Bill praises God for all the Christian young people who grow up to follow Jesus' example to serve others. Because of them, many others will look forward to being in the kingdom of heaven. Praise the Lord.

Chapter 72

60th Alumni Reunion

"My purpose is that they may be encouraged in heart and united in love."
Colossians 2:2

The telephone rang, and on the other end of the line that day was Bill's friend Nick Paulos. He said, "Bill, I am calling from St. Helena to be sure you and June will attend the sixty year reunion at Pacific Union College on April 17, 2010. Sophia and I want you both to come and stay at our home."

Bill could not say no to that invitation. It would be wonderful to be with their old neighbors again and reminisce about all the good times they had shared. These two friends were the ones who had invited Bill and June to the social event at the Oakland Seventh-day Adventist Church so long ago. It was that invitation that had enabled Bill to receive his first call in the ministry. He happily assured Nick that he and June would attend the reunion.

Nick and Bill had graduated from Pacific Union College at the same time. They both studied for the ministry, so it was great to be together again. On Bill and June's first night with their friends, Nick and Sophia told them about the eight years they had worked as a team directing the Adventist work in Greece. After returning home, Nick had gone back to Pacific Union College and studied pre-med. He finished his medical studies in Mexico where he obtained his degree. He and Sophia had then moved to West Virginia where he established a private practice. They served in the city of Wheeling as missionaries, combining medicine and ministry work.

Nick and Sophia had led a very interesting life. Bill kept telling Nick he should write a book. Bill hopes with all his heart that Nick will do this one day. It would be a blessing and an inspiration to many who would read it.

The four friends talked for many hours over the weekend, catching up on the past years. During one of those hours, Nick was reminded of an experience he had while living in Angwin where they lived next door to Bill and June in Veteran Heights.

Being with Nick reminded Bill of an experience he had there in Angwin also, and he said, "I can still see this girl clearly in my mind's eye. She was in the prune orchard all alone near the Newton Observatory. I wondered if something was wrong. Was she sick? The Lord impressed me to pull my car over to the side of the road, get out, and walk toward her. When she looked up and saw me, I asked, 'Is there something wrong?' 'No' she said, 'I am here asking God to send someone to me so

I will know if I should accept Walter's marriage proposal, and you are the answer to my prayer.'"

When Bill finished telling of this experience, Nick laughed and said that he had seen the same girl, had gone out to see if anything was wrong, and had been told the same story. Nick and Bill were both surprised that God had used the two of them as a sign to give confirmation that she should marry Walter. The young woman did get married, and she and her husband became workers for God at La Sierra College, now a university, for many years.

This story reminded Bill that he, too, had asked God for a sign if he should marry June. It had been confirmed, and they celebrated sixty-five years of marriage on May 25, 2011. How wonderful and wise are the ways of our Lord. What a blessing it was to Nick, Sophia, Bill, and June as they heard how God had used them. Then, all too soon, the reunion was over and they had to say goodbye to their two dear friends.

Chapter 73

Sowing the Seeds of Truth

"Thus the saying 'One sows and another reaps' is true." John 4:37

Uncle Bill and Auntie Jean often think of the many children who attended their seminars. Each one will always have a special place in their hearts. Uncle Bill is especially proud that God inspired him to develop programs that would lead the youth to Christ. The good news is that they are still being used successfully today. It always thrills him when he hears or reads of the Story Hours being held, student missionary activities, beach evangelism, Christian Scuba Diving Clubs, Christian Motorcycle Clubs, day camps, baseball and basketball programs, and of course, the Tots to Teens evangelism rallies. He thanks the Lord for those many blessings and for the boys and girls who have given their hearts to Jesus over the years as a result of these ministries.

For Auntie Jean, two children stand out in her memories in a special way. One is a little girl named Tori Hirata. She attended the evangelism seminar held at the Vallejo Central Seventh-day Adventist Church. Tori was very enthusiastic and loved sharing the songs and Bible stories she learned at the meeting with the children in her private non-Christian school during recess.

On show-and-tell day she proudly took her new Bible to school and told her classmates they needed a Bible so they could learn about Jesus. Some of the children went home and told their parents they needed a Bible. The next day a grandmother came to Tori's school and thanked her personally for sharing her Bible with her granddaughter.

Another mother came to the school to ask Tori what church she attended since she and her family had been looking for a church for several months that ministered to the whole family. As a result of Tori's witness, they became Seventh-day Adventists. Kenly Hall, the pastor of the Vallejo Central Seventh-day Adventist Church, was amazed and thrilled when he heard her story and said, "What an example Tori has been to all of us about being unashamed to share the gospel. It is amazing to think of how many lives have been touched by this one little girl who was inspired with a love for Jesus through Jean Willard's program. I cannot imagine running another evangelistic series without a children's Bible Crusade."

Tori was too young to be baptized at the end of Auntie Jean's seminar, but she was not too young to give her heart to Jesus. She was baptized when she was eleven years of age. Now, at twenty-two years of age, she is in college majoring in history.

Tori's mother, Tamie, became very active in children's ministry after that Vallejo seminar. She is still leading out in the kindergarten division at her church and is actively involved with Pathfinders. Tori's younger brother, Alex, nineteen years old, is now a student missionary teacher on Yak Island in Micronesia. Praise God for this family's love for Jesus and their personal witness!

The other child Auntie Jean often thinks of is a boy named Tad Caviness. He was about five years old when he began attending the Tots to Teens evangelism seminars. Sadly, he was already showing early signs of an inherited brain disease. Jean was given a copy of the picture Tad drew when his kindergarten teacher asked her class to draw a picture of what they wanted to be when they grew up. The picture had a church, a cross, a Bible, and a stick figure. Tad wrote across the top, "I will be a preacher." His parents, Pastor Larry and Linda Caviness, were so proud of Tad's artwork that they had it framed and hung in a special place of honor in their home.

Tad attended every seminar that Auntie Jean held in the Bay area. Although he had problems with coordination, he loved the songs and participated in all the seminar activities. He also loved hearing stories about Jesus, especially the stories of His healing power. One evening he asked his dad, "Why doesn't Jesus heal me?"

Larry said he thought for a moment, then replied, "Tad, war broke out in heaven. All of us who love Jesus are Christian soldiers. We are still fighting that war, and as in all wars, sometimes soldiers get killed or wounded. We won't always understand everything now, but we will someday. The important thing is that we are faithful Christian soldiers while we wait for Jesus to come again." Tad liked that answer.

Sadly, Tad died at sixteen years of age. When his parents were trying to decide what to have written on his grave marker, Larry remembered the evening Tad noticed the sad expression on his face after they had prayed and how he had tenderly said, "It's OK, Dad. Jesus will fix it some day."

Tad's dream of being a preacher when he grew up did not turn out the way he expected. However, today he is a "preacher," for the words he spoke to his dad that evening are what hurting people read as they walk by his grave in the Lodi, California, cemetery—"It's OK; Jesus will fix it some day." Praise God for boys like Tad and girls like Tori.

Memories like these, and others, warm the hearts of Uncle Bill, Auntie June, Auntie Jean, and Uncle Ray. They are so thankful that the Lord used them to sow the seeds of truth and for the children who gave their heart to Jesus and were baptized.

The saying "one sows, another reaps" is true, and they realize that many of the children attending their Tots to Teens meetings will give their heart to Jesus later in life and will be baptized. Their prayer is that God will continue to bless the sown seeds until another evangelist comes along to reap the harvest.

The Tots to Teens team are looking forward to the joy they will have when they meet "their" children under the tree of life in heaven. What an awesome day of rejoicing that will be. "Come soon, Lord Jesus! Come soon! Amen!"

Chapter 74

Who Directs Your Life?

"And what more shall I say?" Hebrews 11:32

Bill and June continue serving the Lord where He has placed them. Their life of Christian service and devotion to meeting the needs of others and sharing the good news of Jesus' love for His children is an example to the hundreds and thousands of people that they have come in contact with throughout their lives. And God is not done with them yet.

Bill, June, Jean, and Ray continue to do all they can to prepare young and old alike for that great day when everyone will see Jesus coming in the clouds of glory. Until then, Bill is still faithfully following up with people who have expressed an interest in the Paradise Seventh-day Adventist Church and giving them Bible studies. And Jean is primary director for Sabbath School at the Palm Desert Oasis Seventh-day Adventist Church in Palm Desert, California.

As the life story of Bill Jamerson comes to a close, Bill would like to personally address his readers:

> "It has been my dream to have the many wonderful experiences I enjoyed over the years recorded in a book so my three sons—Gary, Dennis, and Kevin—and their families could read about my life journey. In addition, I hope that my story will inspire young people to lead other young people to follow Jesus. There truly is no joy like the joy you experience when winning souls for the kingdom of heaven.

> "My book is now a reality. I thank Jean Willard from the bottom of my heart for saying yes when I asked if she would be willing to write it for me. Over the years I wrote many of my experiences for this book in long hand. I also saved newspaper articles, plus several editions of *Review and Herald* and *Youth Instructor* magazines that contained reports of my mission activities. These were all given to Jean to review. She would then write a chapter, send it to me, and I would make any adjustments necessary and return it to her. When she returned the corrected material, I gave it to Joan Pleso to review for punctuation errors, grammar, etc. That is the way each chapter was finalized.

> "June and I have many more memories we could add to this book. I am

sure Jean and Ray do, too. But now it is time to say goodbye to the stories of my great journey. God has been so good. He took me from Michigan to California, Hawaii, Alaska, Wisconsin, Ohio, Nebraska, Texas, Arizona, Nevada, Washington, Oregon, Washington, D.C., Scotland, England, France, Utah Beach, Germany, Italy, Switzerland, Austria, Czechoslovakia, Argentina, Bolivia, Chile, Colombia, Ecuador, Peru, Uruguay, Mexico, Guatemala, Honduras, Panama, Salvador, and Canada. What a journey it has been!

"There was a time when I thought I should leave the ministry and go into medicine, but my good friend Walter Stiles encouraged me to stay in the ministry. Today, if I had the chance to live my life over again, I would not change a thing, for I still dearly love my wife, my sons, my church, and the ministry God blessed me with.

"So thank you, Jesus, for turning fishermen into disciples to fish for people. You did it for them, and You did it for me. We were humble men, ready and willing for You to change us. We obeyed Your word to go into the world and preach the good news. We baptized many souls in the name of the Father, the Son, and the Holy Spirit.

"It is really hard for me to put into words just how thankful I am for the way Jesus has guided me along His way. I treasure His promise that 'I can do all things through Jesus who strengthens me.' So I thank God for taking away my youthful lack of interest in education and inspiring me to try sports, which assisted me in gaining self-confidence. For taking me from under the wheels of an army Jeep, from the Utah beachhead landing in World War II, and through the Battle of the Bulge and bringing me safely home. God then led me to June, the wife He had chosen for me, then took me through Pacific Union College and Andrews University and on to South America where we labored to win souls for Him for ten years. God has led me through thirty-eight years as a minister, then through twenty-one years of service after retirement.

"Jesus is the greatest, and I'm ever so grateful for the way He has blessed and guided me. I give Him all the praise, honor, and glory now and forevermore. Paul tells us in Philippians 4:19: 'And my God will meet all your needs according to His glorious riches in Christ Jesus.' What glorious promises God has given us.

"My prayer now is that you will be blessed with the joy of knowing that God is ready and waiting to do great things for you, regardless of your background.

"The next stop in our journey will be to the New Jerusalem. So, remember what Jesus said, 'In my Father's house are many mansions: if it were not so,

I would have told you. I go to prepare a place for you. And if I go and prepare a place for you, I will come again, and receive you unto myself; that where I am, there ye may be also' (John 14:2, 3, KJV). We must be ready for that journey when Jesus returns.

"Thank you for reading my book. I look forward to hearing from you. My hope is to see you in the kingdom of heaven. I know you will be there if you will let Him direct your life, so please don't disappoint me, or God. Amen!"

Pastor William E. Jamerson

We invite you to view the complete
selection of titles we publish at:

www.TEACHServices.com

Scan with your mobile
device to go directly
to our website.

or write or email us your praises, reactions,
or thoughts about this or any other book we publish at:

TEACH Services, Inc.
P U B L I S H I N G

www.TEACHServices.com

P.O. Box 954
Ringgold, GA 30736

info@TEACHServices.com

TEACH Services, Inc., titles may be purchased in bulk for
educational, business, fund-raising, or sales promotional use.
For information, please e-mail

BulkSales@TEACHServices.com

Finally, if you are interested in seeing
your own book in print, please contact us at

publishing@teachservices.com

We would be happy to review your manuscript for free.

www.ingramcontent.com/pod-product-compliance
Lightning Source LLC
Chambersburg PA
CBHW070550160426
43199CB00014B/2446